Lessons 61-120

Formatting & Document Processing Essentials

MICROSOFT® WORD 2002 / MICROSOFT® WORD 2003

COLLEGE KEYBOARDING

Susie H. VanHuss, Ph.D.
University of South Carolina

Connie M. Forde, Ph.D.
Mississippi State University

Donna L. Woo
Cypress College, California

THOMSON
★
SOUTH-WESTERN

Australia · Canada · Mexico · Singapore · Spain · United Kingdom · United States

THOMSON
SOUTH-WESTERN

Formatting & Document Processing Essentials, Microsoft® Word 2002 / Microsoft® Word 2003, Lessons 61-120
Susie H. VanHuss, Connie M. Forde, Donna Woo

VP/Editorial Director:
Jack W. Calhoun

VP/Editor-in-Chief:
Dave Shaut

Senior Publisher:
Karen Schmohe

Acquisitions Editor:
Jane Phelan

Project Manager:
Dave Lafferty

Consulting Editor:
Mary Todd
Todd Publishing Services

Director Educational Marketing:
Carol Volz

Marketing Manager:
Lori Pegg

Production Editors:
Carol Spencer
Kim Kusnerak

Production Manager:
Tricia Boies

Manufacturing Coordinator:
Charlene Taylor

Media Production Editor:
Mike Jackson

Design Project Manager:
Stacy Jenkins Shirley

Permissions Editor:
Linda Ellis

Copyeditor:
Gary Morris

Production House:
D&G Limited, LLC

Cover Designer:
Craig LaGesse Ramsdell
www.ramsdelldesign.com

Cover Images:
© PhotoDisc, Inc.

Internal Designer:
Craig LaGesse Ramsdell
www.ramsdelldesign.com

Printer:
Quebecor World, Dubuque
Dubuque, Iowa

TABLE OF CONTENTS

Summary of Functions iv
About This Book v
Welcome to CheckPro ix
Software Training Manual ....TM 1

LEVEL 3

Mastering Document Design

Module 10 Skillbuilding and Editing Review
61   Skillbuilding and Editing Review..............................238
62   Skillbuilding and Editing Review..............................241
63   Skillbuilding and Editing Review..............................243

Module 11 Letter and Memo Mastery
64   Block Letter Format 246
65   Block Letter with Special Letter Parts............................251
66   Modified Block Letter Format ...255
67   Letters with Special Features......259
68   Two-Page Letters 263
69   Review Memo Format 266
70   Memo from Template 270
71   Review E-Mail.............................272
72   Assessment...................................274
     Checkpoint 11 277

Module 12 Report Mastery
73   Skillbuilding and Word Processing Basics............................278
74   Unbound Report with Title Page and References Page 285
75   Unbound Report with Table of Contents..................................289
76   Unbound Report with Styles......292
77   Unbound Report with Footnotes...................................294

78   Leftbound Report with Endnotes..................................299
79   Report with Sections...................305
80   Assessment...................................311
     Checkpoint 12 315

Module 13 Table Mastery
81   Table Review 316
82   Reviewing Editing and Formatting Tables.......................319
83   Calculations in Tables 322
84   Changing Page and Text Orientation..................................327
85   Assessment...................................330
     Checkpoint 13 333

Module 14 Forms and Financial Documents
86   Skillbuilding and Forms..............334
87   Fill-In and Online Forms 342
88   Custom Forms...............................346
89   Financial Documents 350
90   Budget...354
91   Assessment...................................357
     Checkpoint 14 360

LEVEL 4

Designing Specialized Documents

Module 15 Graphic Enhancements
92   Skillbuilding and Graphics 362
93   Columns and Newsletters............368
94   Announcements and Letterheads with Graphics 372
95   Newsletter with Columns 375
96   Newsletter with Graphics 378
97   News Releases 380
98   Assessment...................................383
     Checkpoint 15 387

Module 16 Mass Mailings
99   Skillbuilding and Mail Merge.....388
100   Practice Mail Merge....................395
101   Edit the Data Source..................397
102   Merge with Envelopes and Labels...401
103   Assessment...................................405
      Checkpoint 16 408

Module 17 Meeting Management
104   Skillbuilding and Agendas...........410
105   Minutes...414
106   Itineraries.....................................417
107   Name Badges and Labels............420
108   Assessment...................................424
      Checkpoint 17 428

Module 18 Legal, Medical, & Employment Applications
109   Legal Pleadings 429
110   Legal Forms 432
111   SOAP Notes and Medical Letterhead....................................435
112   Medical Forms..............................438
113   Resume 442
114–115 Application and Follow-Up Letters 444
116   Assessment...................................446
      Checkpoint 18 448

Module 19 Pommery Air Service, Inc.
117–119 Business Plan 449
120   Assessment...................................457
      Skill Builders 5 462

Reference Guide REF1
Function Summary REF10
Index...REF12

SUMMARY OF FUNCTIONS

NEW FUNCTIONS

Module 12 Report Mastery
73   Line and Page Breaks
Leader Tabs
Apply Styles (Review)
Change Number Format

78   Endnotes

79   Section Breaks

Module 13 Table Mastery
82   Decimal Tabs

83   Formulas
Calculate
Paste Function

84   Landscape
Rotate

Module 14 Forms and Financial Documents
86   Underline Tabs
Paragraph Borders and Shading
Forms
Form Fields
Test Form
Protect Document
Distribute and Use Forms

Module 15 Promotional Document Formats
92   Insert Picture
Drawing Tools
Word Art

93   Columns (Review)

Module 16 Mass Mailings with Merge
99   Merge

101   Edit Data Source
Sort Data Records
Filter Records

102   Labels and Envelopes with Merge

Module 17 Meeting Management
104   Save as Web Page

FUNCTIONS REVIEWED

Software Training Manual and Lessons

Getting Started

TM1   Document Screen
TM2   Menu Bar Commands
TM3   Toolbar Commands
TM4   Print
TM5   Print Preview, Close, Exit
TM6   Open, New Document

Basic Editing Commands

TM7   Select, Show Hide
TM8   Formatting Toolbar
TM9   Undo/Redo
          Paragraph Formats
TM10   Cut, Copy, and Paste
TM11   Office Clipboard
TM12   Center Page
TM13   Date and Time
TM14   Increase/Decrease Indent
TM16   Spelling and Grammar
          Find and Replace

Other Functions Reviewed

TM11   Bullets and Numbering
TM15   Tables
256   Envelopes
279   Page Numbers
295   Footnotes
363   ClipArt (insert, size, move)
365   Wrap Text Around Graphics
369   Columns

THE LATEST WORD IN KEYBOARDING

Focus on the Essentials

Building a skill takes practice, and that's what you'll get with the *Keyboarding Essentials* series. More timed writings, five supplemental keyboarding lessons using the keyboarding software, and technique drills throughout.

Keyboarding Pro—**Now with Web Reporting, especially designed for distance education**

Keyboarding Pro 4 Now with Web reporting and Spanish instruction!

Spice up your practice! *Keyboarding Pro 4* software uses graphics, games, progress graphs, videos, 3-D models for viewing proper posture and hand positions, sound effects, and a full-featured word processor to keep learning fun and meaningful. Students also have the option of e-mail or the Web for transferring their assignments to you. Instruction available in Spanish.

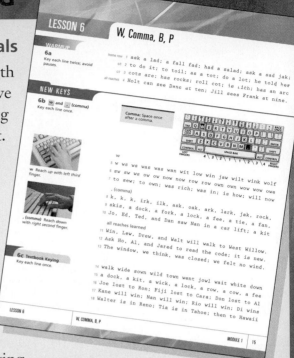

Extra skillbuilding lessons using *Keyboarding Pro*

The Latest Word
Microsoft® Word 2003 and Microsoft® Word 2002

The *Keyboarding Essentials* series teaches document formatting using the functions of Microsoft Word 2003 and 2002. Word processing commands are taught in the first lesson or two of each module and applied with simple drills. The remaining lessons provide extensive opportunities to apply the commands and reinforce new learning while extending keyboarding skills.

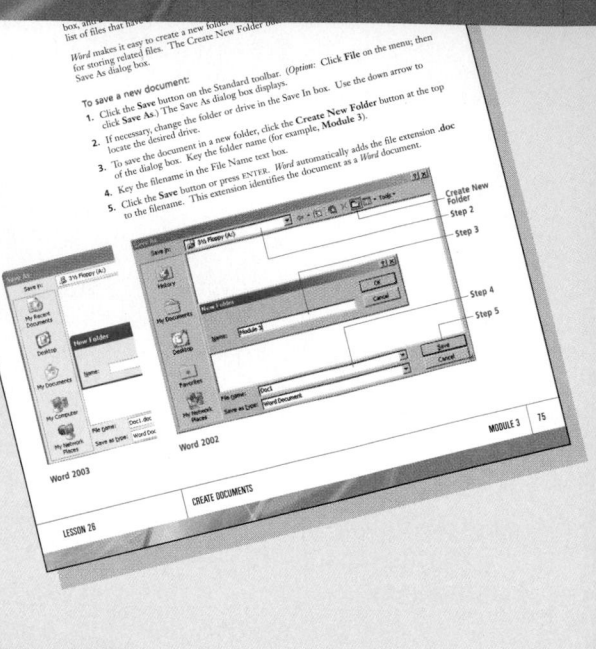

Up-to-Date Formats

New formats are explained and illustrated with callouts for proper placement.

The Software Training Manual reviews functions learned in Lessons 1–60.

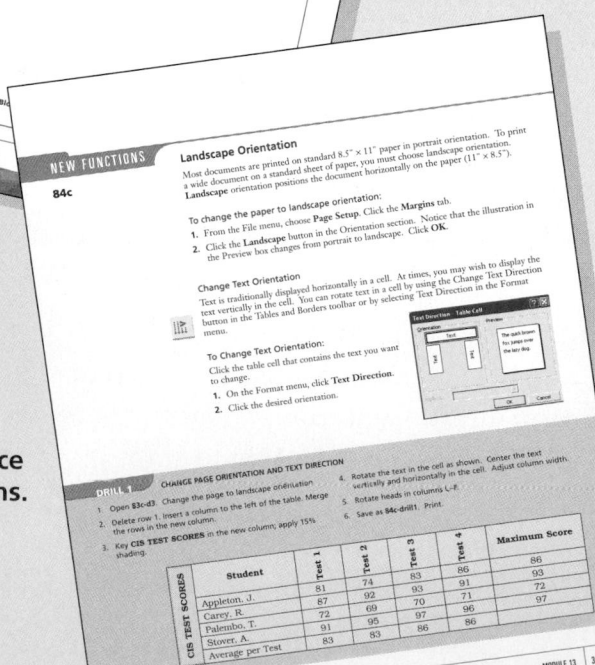

Drills reinforce new functions.

CLEARLY FOCUSED ON YOUR NEEDS

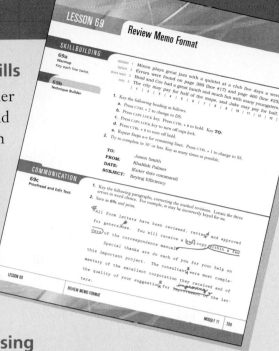

Communication Skills

Proofreading, composition, and other language arts skills are integrated and reinforced. Supplemental Communication Skills pages provide extra practice in Lessons 1–60.

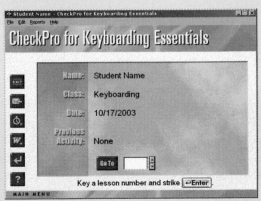

Document Processing

That's the focus of Lessons 61-120. Three new modules—18 lessons—address today's needs: Forms and Financial Documents, Graphic Enhancements, and Meeting Management.

Reference Manual

provides easy access to model documents.

CheckPro for Keyboarding Essentials
Now with Web reporting for distance education!

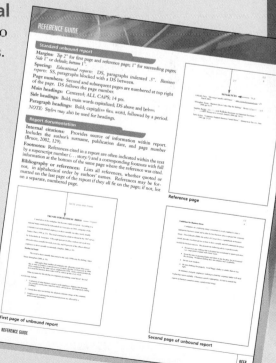

Transferring student data between students and instructors just gets easier. *CheckPro for Keyboarding Essentials* is enhanced to check most *Word* documents.

Product Family

Keyboarding & Formatting Essentials, Lessons 1-60
0-538-72757-8
Introductory text that teaches the foundation skills of keyboarding, document formatting, and basic Microsoft Word skills.

Keyboarding & Formatting Essentials, Lessons 1-120
0-538-72796-9

Instructor's Manual & Key, Lessons 61-120 (0-538-72776-4) and *Instructor's Resource CD, Lessons 61-120* (0-538-72775-6)
Solutions, data files, teaching tips, and tests—all in an easy-to-use format.

Technology Solutions

Keyboarding Pro 4
0-538-72802-7, Individual License. With Web reporting and Spanish.

CheckPro for Keyboarding Essentials
0-538-72798-5, Individual License. Now with Web reporting for your distance education needs.

MicroPace Pro, 2.0
0-538-72778-0, Individual License. Program software that correlates to *Keyboarding Essentials* and provides additional skillbuilding practice to increase technique and accuracy. Comprehensive error diagnostics.

KeyChamp, 2E
0-538-43390-6
Textbook and program software that builds speed by analyzing student's two-stroke key combinations and provides drills for building speed.

Visit us as www.collegekeyboarding.com

Instructor Approved

Lillie Begay
*San Juan College
Farmington, New Mexico*

Shirley Bennings
*Augusta Technical College
Augusta, Georgia*

Jane Clausen
*Western Iowa Technical College
Sioux City, Iowa*

Lucille Cusano
*Tunix Community College
Farmington, Connecticut*

Claudia Fortney
*Ramussen College
Mankato, Minnesota*

Lucille Graham
*San Antonio College
San Antonio, Texas*

Cindy Moss
*Appalachian Technical College
Jasper, Georgia*

Janice Salles
*Merced Community College
Merced, California*

A Word from the Authors

Thank you for your support of our keyboarding texts over the past many years. We have designed this text especially for those who need a traditional keyboarding and document formatting approach. We hope our new series meets your needs.

*Susie VanHuss
Connie Forde
Donna Woo*

CheckPro verifies the accuracy of the keystrokes in drills, timed writings, and documents that you key beginning in Module 4. The drill practice and timed writings features are built into the *CheckPro* program. For the document exercises, *CheckPro* works in conjunction with *Microsoft Word*. You will key documents using *Word* and then *CheckPro* error-checks your work.

CheckPro for Keyboarding Essentials has been greatly enhanced. It is now capable of checking documents that contain images, WordArt, columns, envelopes, embedded spreadsheets, comments, headers and footers, and more. Additionally, *CheckPro* can now check documents created from wizards or from templates.

Getting Started with *CheckPro*

To launch the program, click the **Start** button and then select **Programs**. Select the South-Western Keyboarding program group and click **CheckPro for Keyboarding Essentials**. Once the splash screen is removed, the Student Registration dialog box appears.

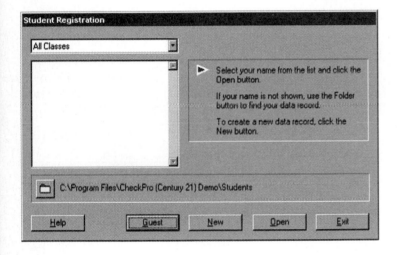

When you first use the *CheckPro* software, you must enter your user information and indicate where you will store your data. This process creates a student record. You will create a student record only once.

1. From the Student Registration dialog box, click **New**. This launches the New Student dialog box.

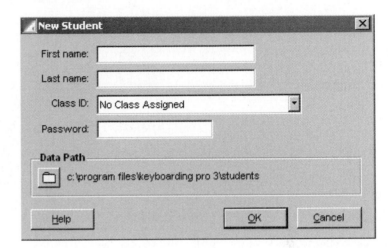

2. Enter your name and password and select your class if it is available on the drop-down list.

3. Specify the data location. The default storage path is **c:\Program Files\CheckProKE\Students**. If you will be storing on Drive A or if you have a student subdirectory on the network, set the path accordingly.

Each time you enter *CheckPro* after the first time, the Student Registration dialog box displays. Click your name and enter your password. If you do not see your name, click the folder icon and browse either Drive A or the folder on the network where your data is being saved to locate your data record.

Main Screen

After you start the program and log in, the program displays the *CheckPro* main screen. The main screen is the central navigation point for the entire program. From here you can select a lesson, e-mail a data file, or access the supplemental timings/documents. Supplemental timings refer to timed writings that are not located in a numbered lesson (for example, Skill Builders 2, 3, etc.). Supplemental documents include documents that cannot be accessed from numbered lessons (CheckPoints, projects, tests, and documents created by your instructor).

Choose a lesson by keying the lesson number or clicking on the arrows to the right of the Go To field. Then click on the **Go To** button or strike ENTER. You are now at a lesson screen, which will look *similar* to the example below.

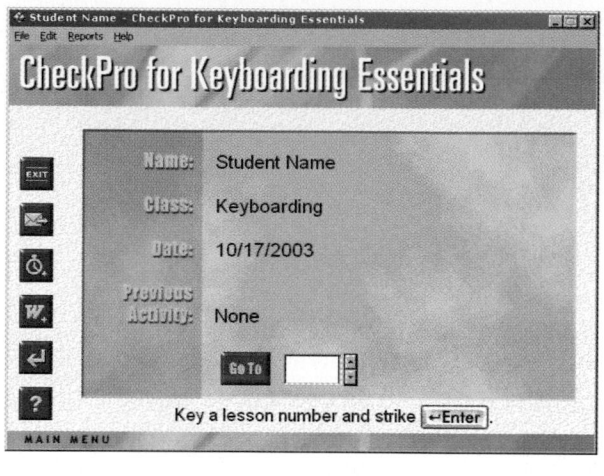

Lesson Screen

The lesson screen contains more activity options. Each activity corresponds directly with the activities for that lesson in your textbook. Click on the button next to an activity title to complete that activity. Drills and timed writings will be completed within the *CheckPro* software. *CheckPro* will launch *Word 2002* or *Word 2003* for you to complete documents or production tests.

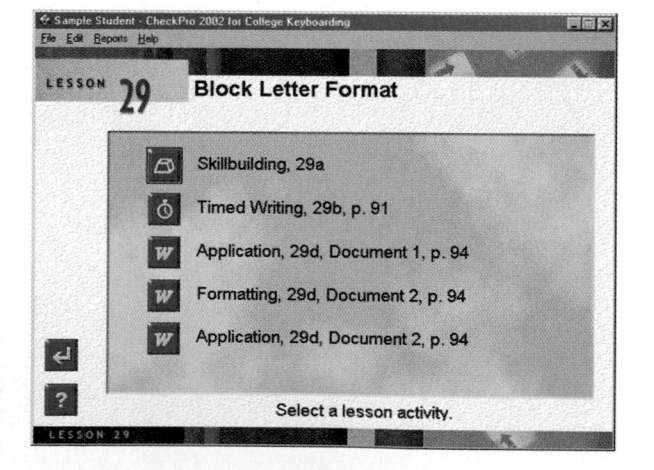

Drill Practice: For a drill practice activity, key each drill line as it appears on the screen. You can choose to repeat the activity when you finish the drill practice. A check mark appears next to the menu option on the lesson screen when you complete it.

Timed Writings: Click a **Timed Writing** button to take a timed writing. Then select the timing length and source. Key the timed writing from your textbook. The program shows the *gwam*, error rate, and actual errors when you finish the writing. You can print the timed writing report or save it to disk.

Documents and Production Tests: Select a document or assessment activity and choose **Begin new document**. You'll get a dialog box with important information, and then your word processor will be launched. *CheckPro* creates a document for you with the correct filename. The *CheckPro* toolbar will appear on top of the *Word 2002* document window. When you are finished proofreading the document, do not save the file. Instead, click on the check mark on the *CheckPro* toolbar. *CheckPro* will then save your document and open a checked version of it back in *CheckPro* for you to review your errors. To finish an exercise or revise a checked document, select the activity and choose **Open existing document**.

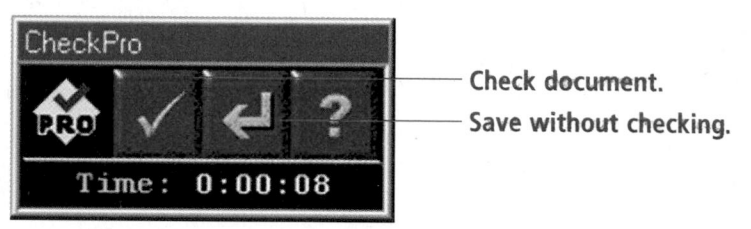

Reports

There are a number of reports available in *CheckPro*. Click on the **Reports** menu to see the selection. The Lesson Report provides a snapshot of your results for a specific lesson. Click on the **Activity Checklist** to see an overview of which activities have been completed. This report indicates the date each activity was completed, but provides no further information. Choose the **Reports** menu, **Summary Report** to view Drill, Timed Writing, Document, and Production Test summaries. All of the information for creating these reports is saved in your record file.

Special Features

CheckPro for Keyboarding Essentials makes it extremely easy to send your completed documents or student record to your instructor for evaluation. To learn more about using *CheckPro* for distance education, go to the website www.collegekeyboarding.com. A complete explanation is provided here.

The Supplemental Timed Writings button provides a way to check a timing located somewhere other than a numbered lesson (e.g. a timing located in a Skill Builder).

Select the Supplemental Documents button to complete any document exercise found in an unnumbered lesson (for example, an exercise from a project, a Communication Skill, or a document created by your instructor).

Software Training Manual

Start Word

When you first start *Word*, the screen appears with two windows. The left area is a blank document screen where you can enter text. The right area is called the **Task Pane**.

Follow the steps in Drill 1 to start *Microsoft Word*; then study the illustration of the opening *Word* screen to learn the various parts of the screen.

DRILL 1   START WORD

1. Turn on the computer and the monitor. When the *Windows* Log On screen displays, key your password and click **OK** to display the *Windows* desktop.

2. Click the **Start** button at the bottom of the screen. Point to **Programs** to display the Programs menu; then click **Microsoft Word 2002** to display the *Microsoft Word* document screen.

3. If the program does not fill the entire screen, you will need to maximize the window. You will learn about the Maximize button in the next section.

Microsoft Word 2003 Opening Screen

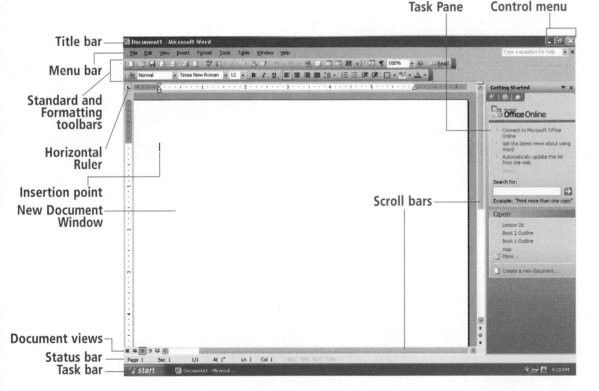

Microsoft Word 2002 Task Pane

The opening screens of *Word 2002* and *2003* are very similar; the Task Panes have some minor differences.

Enter Text

When you key text, it is entered at the insertion point (the blinking vertical bar). When a line is full, the text automatically moves to the next line. This feature is called **wordwrap.** To begin a new paragraph, press ENTER. To indent the first line of a paragraph to the first default tab, press the TAB key.

To change or edit text, you must move the insertion point around within the document. You can move to different parts of the document by using the mouse or the keyboard. To use the mouse, move the I-beam pointer to the desired position and click the left mouse button. You can also use the arrow keys on the keyboard to move the insertion point to a different position.

DRILL 2   ENTER TEXT

1. If the opening *Word* screen does not fill your entire screen, click the **Maximize** button.

2. Key the text that follows using wordwrap. Press ENTER twice only at the ends of paragraphs to DS between paragraphs. Ignore any red and green wavy lines that may appear under text as you key.

3. Using the mouse, move the insertion point immediately before the *S* at the beginning of the document.

4. Key your name. Press ENTER four times. Notice that ¶ 1 moves down 4 lines.

5. Use the right arrow key to move the insertion point to the left of the *h* in *homework.* Key the word **new** followed by a space. Notice that text moves to the right.

6. Keep the document on the screen for the next drill.

Serendipity, a homework research tool from Information Technology Company, is available to subscribers of the major online services via the World Wide Web. **(Press ENTER two times.)**

Offered as a subscription service aimed at college students, Serendipity is a collection of tens of thousands of articles from major encyclopedias, reference books, magazines, pamphlets, and Internet sources combined into a single searchable database.

Serendipity puts an electronic library right at students' fingertips. The program offers two browse-and-search capabilities. Users can find articles by entering questions in simple question format or browse the database by pointing and clicking on key words that identify related articles. For more information, call 800-555-0174 or address e-mail to lab@serendipity.com.

Menu Bar Commands

The commands available in *Word* are listed in menus located on the menu bar at the top of your screen. The names of the menus indicate the type of commands they contain. You can execute all commands using the proper menu. When you click an item on the menu bar, a menu cascades or pulls down and displays the available commands. Note that common shortcuts including toolbar buttons and keyboard commands are provided when appropriate. The File menu that follows illustrates the main characteristics of pull-down menus.

Toolbar button: indicates button to click to activate a command.

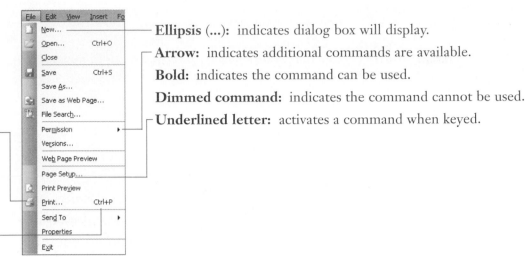

Ellipsis (...): indicates dialog box will display.

Arrow: indicates additional commands are available.

Bold: indicates the command can be used.

Dimmed command: indicates the command cannot be used.

Underlined letter: activates a command when keyed.

Keyboard shortcut: activates a command when keys are pressed.

Toolbar Commands

Frequently-used commands also can be accessed using the buttons on the Standard and Formatting toolbars. Whenever you use *Word*, make sure that both toolbars are displayed, with the Standard toolbar on top of the Formatting toolbar (**Tools** menu, **Customize Options** tab; add a checkmark next to Show Standard and Formatting toolbars on two rows). If either toolbar is missing or other toolbars display, change the display following these steps.

To display or hide a toolbar:

1. Position the mouse pointer over any toolbar and click the right mouse button; a shortcut menu appears listing all of the toolbars that are available. (*Option:* Click **View** on the menu bar; then click **Toolbars.**)

2. Click to the left of **Standard** or **Formatting**, placing a check mark next to its name. The toolbar displays. If toolbars other than the Standard or Formatting toolbars are displayed, click the toolbar name to remove the check mark and hide the toolbar.

3. If **Task Pane** is checked, click to the left of it to close the window. You can also close the Task Pane by clicking the **Close** button at the upper right of the Task Pane.

DRILL 3   **COMMANDS**

1. Check that the Standard and Formatting toolbars are the only ones that are displayed and that they each display on a separate row.

2. Point to several buttons on the Standard and Formatting toolbars. Notice the name of each button as it displays.

3. Click **File** on the menu bar. Point to the arrow at the bottom of the File menu, and click the left mouse button to display additional commands. If there is no arrow at the bottom of the File menu, then your entire menu is already displayed.

4. Click **Edit** on the menu bar. Note that *Cut* is dimmed. A dimmed command is not available; making it available requires another action.

5. Click **File** on the menu bar again. Note that the Save As command is followed by an ellipsis (...). Click **Save As** to display the Save As dialog box. Click **Cancel** to close the Save As dialog box.

6. Click each of the different View buttons on the status bar. Notice that a button is highlighted when that view is active. Return to Normal view.

Save/Save As

Use **Save** to preserve a document so that it can be used again. If a document is not saved, it will be lost when the computer is turned off. Use **Save As** to save and name a new document or to rename an existing document.

To save a document with its original name:

1. Click the **Save** button on the Standard toolbar.

2. The Save As dialog box does not display, and the document is saved with its original name.

To save a new document or to save a document with a different name:

1. On the File menu, click **Save As**.

2. Select the drive and folder in the Save in box. To save the document in a new folder, click the **Create New Folder** button and key the folder name.

3. Key the name of the file in the File name box.

4. Click **Save**.

DRILL 4

1. Save the document that is open on your screen as **tm-drill4**.

2. Add today's date on the first line just before your name; press the ENTER key.

3. Resave the document.

Print

The **Print** button on the Standard toolbar allows you to print an entire document by clicking the button. Other print options, such as printing multiple copies or specific pages, can be accessed from the Print dialog box.

To print a document:

1. Choose **Print** from the File menu.

2. Select options such as number of copies or pages to print.

3. Click **OK**.

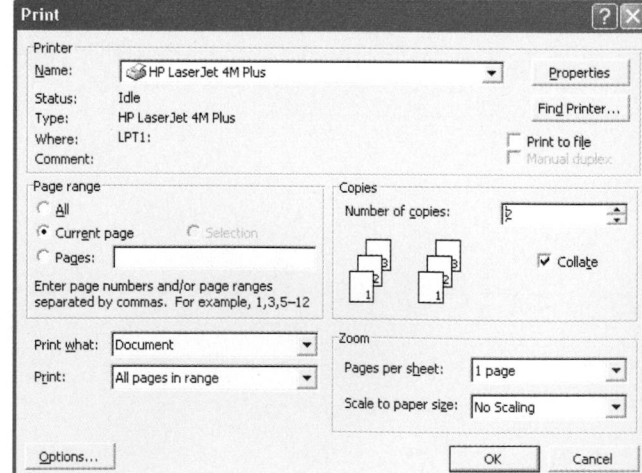

DRILL 5

1. With **tm-drill4** still open, add **Drill 5** on the line below your name.

2. Click the **Print** button to print the document.

3. Display the Print dialog box; select **Current page** and increase the number of copies to **2**.

4. Save the document as **tm-drill5**.

Print Preview

Print Preview displays a document exactly as it will be printed. Use Print Preview to check the layout of your document.

To preview a document:
1. Click the **Print Preview** button on the Standard toolbar or choose **Print Preview** from the File menu.
2. Select options from the Print Preview toolbar as desired; then click **Close**.

DRILL 6

1. With **tm-drill5** still open, change *Drill 5* to *Drill 6*.

2. Click the **Print Preview** button and check the layout of the document.

3. Save the document as **tm-drill6** and print.

Close and Exit

The **Close** command clears the screen. You will be prompted to save the document if you have not already done so. The Close command can also be accessed from the File menu. The red Exit button closes the *Word* software as well as the file.

To close a document:
1. Click the **Close** button or select **Close** on the File menu.
2. Save the document if prompted to do so.

To close a document and exit the software:
1. Click the **Exit** button.
2. Save the document if prompted to do so.

DRILL 7

1. With **tm-drill6** still open, change the drill number to 7.

2. Close the document.

3. When prompted to save the document, save it as **tm-drill7**.

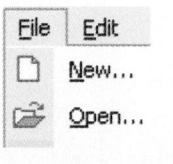

File   Edit

☐   New...

☞   Open...

Open Document

Documents previously stored may be displayed on the screen by clicking the **Open** button or by clicking **Open** on the File menu. The Open dialog box displays.

To open a document:

1. Select the drive and folder from the Look in box.

2. Select the file you wish to open by double-clicking its icon or its name in the list of files shown. You may also key the filename in the File name box and click **Open**.

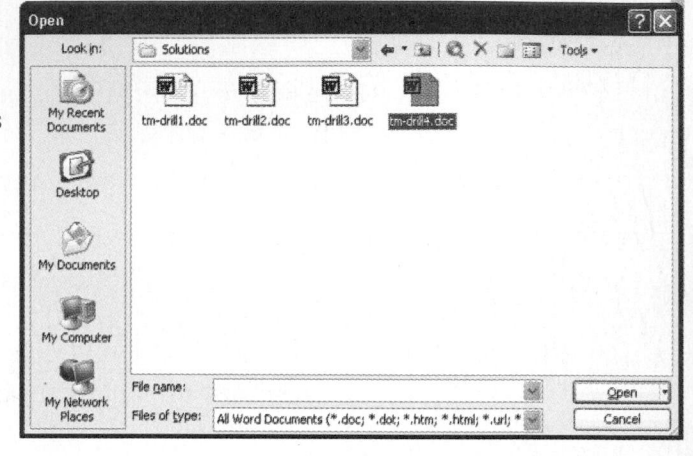

New Document

To create a new document, click the **New Blank Document** button or select **New** on the File menu. Use **Save As** to name the new document.

File   Edit

☐   New...

☞   Open...

DRILL 8

1. Open **tm-drill7**.

2. Change the drill number to 8.

3. Save as **tm-drill8** and close the document.

DRILL 9

1. Create a new document.

2. Key your name on the first line and **Drill 9** a double space below it.

3. Save as **tm-drill9** and close the document.

Insert/Delete

Insert and **Delete** features are used to correct errors or revise documents.

Insert: To insert text, position the insertion point at the location where the new text is to appear and key the text. Existing text moves to the right.

Delete: The DELETE key erases text that is no longer needed.

To delete a character: Position the insertion point to the left of the character to delete and press DELETE, or position the insertion point to the right of the character to delete and press BACKSPACE. Be careful not to hold down the DELETE or BACKSPACE keys since they will continue to erase characters.

To delete a word: Double-click the word to be deleted and press DELETE.

Select

Select identifies text that has been keyed so that it can be modified. Selected text appears black on the screen. Select text using the mouse.

To select text	Position the insertion point on the first character to be selected. Click the left mouse button and drag the mouse over the text to be selected. To cancel select, click the mouse again.
To select a word	Double-click the word.
To select a paragraph	Triple-click in the paragraph.
To select multiple lines	Click the left mouse button and drag in the area left of the lines.

DRILL 10

1. Open **Drill 10** from the data files.

2. Select the text and make the deletions shown. (Your document will be single-spaced.)

3. Make the insertions shown.

4. Save as **tm-drill10**.

Serendipity, a ~~homework~~ research tool from Information Technology Company, is available to subscribers of ~~the major~~ on-line services via the World Wide Web.

Offered as a subscription service aimed at ~~college~~ students, Serendipity is a collection of tens of thousands of articles from ~~major~~ encyclopedias, reference books, magazines, pamphlets, and Internet sources combined into a single searchable database.

Serendipity puts an electronic library right at students' fingertips. The program offers two browse-and-search capabilities. Users can find articles ⌃*on just about any subject* by entering questions in simple question format or browse the database by pointing and clicking on key words that identify related articles. For more information, call ⌃*1-*800-555-4374 or address e-mail to <<lab@serendipity.com>>. *with just a computer and a modem.*

Show/Hide

Click the **Show/Hide** button on the Standard toolbar to display all nonprinting characters such as paragraph (¶), tab (→), and space (·) markers. The Show/Hide button appears highlighted when it is active. To turn nonprinting characters off, click the Show/Hide button again.

Formatting Toolbar

The **Formatting toolbar** provides an efficient way to apply character formats, such as bold, italic, underline, fonts, and font sizes and to apply other commands such as align text, change line spacing, and indent. Position the mouse pointer over each button to display the function it applies.

To apply character formats as you key text:

1. Click the appropriate format button (button appears highlighted) and then key the text.

2. Click the format button again after the text has been keyed to turn off the feature.

To apply character formats after you key text:

1. Select the text.

2. Click the appropriate format button.

To change font:

1. Select the text.

2. Click the Font button down arrow.

3. Scroll through the list of available styles, and click the desired style.

To change font size:

1. Select the text.

2. Click the Font Size button down arrow.

3. Scroll through the list of available sizes, and click the desired size.

DRILL 11

1. Open a new blank document.

2. Apply the formats shown to Sentences 1 and 2 as you key them.

3. Key Sentences 3 and 4 and then apply formats shown.

4. Save as **tm-drill11**.

1. This sentence is keyed with words shown in **bold**, *italic*, and <u>underlined</u>.

2. This sentence is keyed in 11-point Times New Roman.

3. This sentence has words formatted in **bold**, *italic*, and <u>underlined</u>.

4. This sentence is formatted using 12-point Arial.

Undo/Redo

To undo the most recent action you have taken (such as inserting or deleting text, formatting characters, or changing spacing) click the **Undo** button. To reverse several actions, click the Undo button down arrow to display a list of recent actions. Then click the action you wish to reverse. All actions you performed prior to the action you select also will be reversed. Save and Print commands cannot be reversed. To redo the last undo, click the **Redo** button. Click the down arrow beside the Redo button to view all actions that can be redone.

DRILL 12

1. Open **Drill 12** from the data files.

2. Remove the Bold and Italic format from the last sentence.

3. Redo the Bold and Italic format in the last sentence.

4. Select and delete the third ¶.

5. Use Undo to restore the ¶.

6. Save as **tm-drill12**.

Paragraph Formats

Paragraph formats, such as alignment and spacing, apply to an entire paragraph and can be applied before or after a paragraph has been keyed. *Word* defines a paragraph as any text that ends with a hard return. Use Show/Hide to see where paragraphs begin and end.

To apply a paragraph format before you key the paragraph, click the appropriate format button and key the paragraph.

To apply a paragraph format to existing text, turn Show/Hide on; click in the paragraph to apply a format; and click the appropriate format button. (If you wish to apply the format to more than one paragraph, select the paragraphs and then click the appropriate format button.)

Alignment

Alignment refers to the way text lines up. Text can be aligned at the left, center, right, or justified (aligned at both margins). The following four paragraphs illustrate alignment:

This first paragraph is aligned at the left side. To key a left-aligned paragraph, click the **Align Left** button; then key the text. If the text exists, select it and click the **Align Left** button.

To key text aligned at the right, click the **Align Right** button and key the text. If the text exists, select it and click the **Align Right** button.

Click the **Center** button to center this text.

This text is **justified**. The text is aligned at both the left and right margins except for the last line of a paragraph. The last line of the paragraph may end at some point other than the margin.

1. Open a new blank document.

2. Key the four ¶s shown on the previous page, aligning them as shown.

3. Save as **tm-drill13**.

Spacing

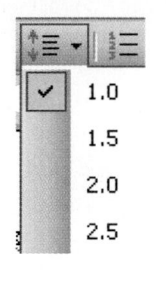

Word's default line spacing is single. When paragraphs are single-spaced, the first line of the paragraph is normally not indented. However, a blank line is added between paragraphs to distinguish them and improve readability. Double-spacing leaves a blank line between each line. Therefore, it is necessary to indent the first line of each double-spaced paragraph to indicate the beginning of the paragraph. To indent the first line, press the TAB key.

To change line spacing:

1. Position the insertion point in the paragraph in which you want to change the line spacing. If more than one paragraph is to be changed, select all the paragraphs.

2. Click the down arrow on the Line Spacing button, and selected the desired spacing.

1. Open **Drill 14** from the data files.

2. Change the lines spacing of each of the ¶s to single spacing.

3. Remove the ¶ indentions from each ¶.

4. Check to see that a blank line appears between each ¶. If not, insert a blank line.

5. Save as **tm-drill14**.

Cut, Copy, and Paste

The **Cut** feature removes text or an image from a document and places it on the Office Clipboard. The **Copy** feature places a copy of text or an image from a document on the Clipboard. The **Paste** feature transfers a copy of the text or image from the Clipboard to a document.

To move text to a new location:

1. Select the text to be copied. Click **Cut** on the Standard toolbar.

2. Move the insertion point to the new location. Click **Paste**.

To copy text to a new location:

1. Select the text to be copied. Click **Copy** on the Standard toolbar.

2. Move the insertion point to the new location. Click **Paste**.

Office Clipboard

Text or objects cut or copied are stored on the **Clipboard**. The Clipboard stores up to 24 items. To paste an item from the Clipboard, click the down arrow next to the item and select **Paste**. All items on the Clipboard can be pasted or deleted. When an item is pasted in a document, the Paste button smart tag provides options for formatting the text that has been pasted. You can keep the formatting of the source document (document from which it was cut or copied) or that of the destination document (document to which you are pasting).

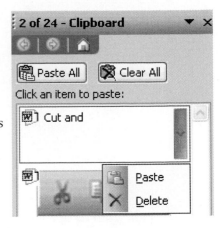

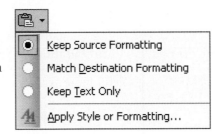

DRILL 15   CUT, COPY, AND PASTE

1. Open **Drill 15** from the data files.

2. Select **Cut and** in the first heading and cut it. The heading is **Paste**.

3. Select the heading **Paste** and the ¶ that follows it.

4. Move the selected copy below the last ¶.

5. Key a line across the page.

6. Copy both ¶s and paste them below the line.

7. Save as **tm-drill15**.

Bullets and Numbering

Bullets and **Numbering** are used to create lists of items. Numbers are used for a sequence of steps or points that should be in a certain order. Bullets are used for a list when the order does not follow a sequence. Single-space bulleted or numbered items if each item consists of one line. If more than one line is required for any item, double-space between items.

To create bullets or numbers:

1. Key the list without bullets or numbers. Select the list and click the **Bullets** button or the **Numbering** button on the Formatting toolbar.

2. To add or remove bullets or numbers, click the **Bullets** or **Numbering** button.

Supplies Needed:
1. Notebook
2. Pen
3. Textbook

Steps to Create a Numbered List:
1. Key the list.
2. Select the list.
3. Click the Numbering button.

1. Key the first list below SS; do not key the bullets.
2. Select the list and click the **Bullets** button.
3. Key the second list SS.

4. Click the **Numbering** button.
5. Save the document as **tm-drill16**.
6. Preview and print the document.

Software applications:
- Word processing
- Spreadsheet
- Presentation
- Database

Registration Steps:
1. Complete the application.
2. Check space availability list with program manager.
3. Pay fees.
4. Pick up program supplies.

Center Page

The **Center Page** command is used to center a page vertically. Use Show/Hide to see if any extra hard returns are at the beginning or end of the document. Delete extra hard returns before centering the page.

To center a page vertically:

1. Position the insertion point on the page to be centered.
2. From the File menu, select **Page Setup**.
3. Click the **Layout** tab.
4. Click the **Vertical alignment** down arrow. Select **Center**; then click **OK**.

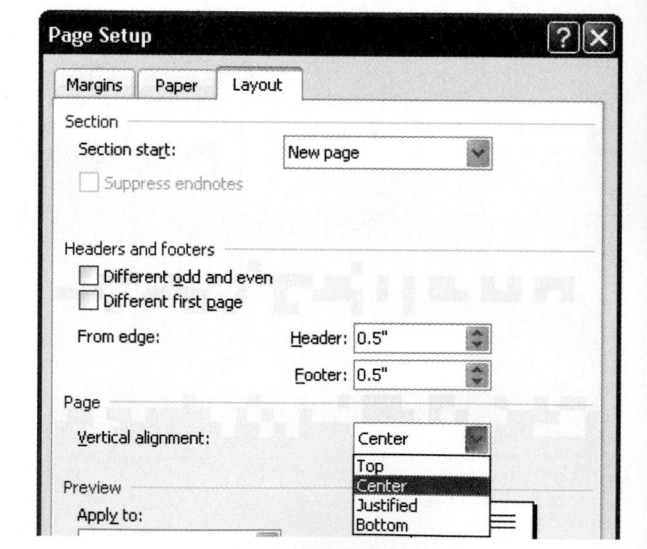

1. Open **tm-drill16** and save it as **tm-drill17**.
2. Remove any hard returns at the beginning or end of the document.

3. Center the page vertically.
4. Resave the document, preview, and print.

Margins

Default margins are 1" top and bottom and 1.25" for left and right.

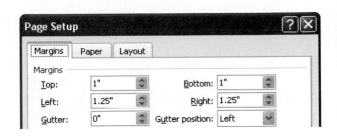

To change margins:

1. From the File menu, select **Page Setup**.
2. Click the **Margins** tab.
3. Click the arrows to change the margins as desired.

DRILL 18   MARGINS

1. Open **Drill 18** from the data files.
2. Change the top margin to 2".
3. Change side and bottom margins to 1".

4. Save as **tm-drill18**.
5. Preview and print.

Date and Time

The date and time can be inserted into documents using the **Date and Time** command from the Insert menu.

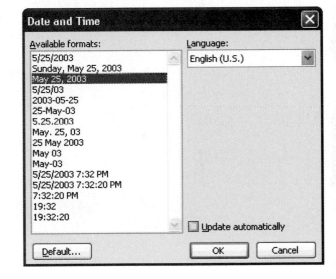

To insert the date and/or time:

1. Choose **Date and Time** from the Insert menu.
2. Choose the format from the Available formats box. Standard business format is month-day-year.
3. To update the date each time the document is opened, click the **Update automatically** box.

DRILL 19   DATE AND TIME

1. Open a new blank document.
2. Key your name on the first line and right-align the text.
3. A double-space below your name, insert the date in standard business format. Update the date automatically.

4. A double space below the date, insert the time using hour-minute-second AM/PM format.
5. Save as **tm-drill19**.

Tabs

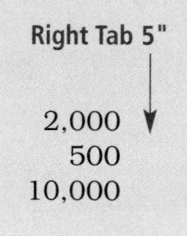

Tabs are used to indent paragraphs and align text vertically. Pressing the TAB key aligns text at the tab stop. *Word* has five tabs: left tab, right tab, center tab, decimal tab, and bar tab. Tabs can be set and cleared on the Horizontal Ruler. The numbers on the ruler indicate the distance in inches from the left margin. The small gray lines below each half-inch are default tab stops. The Tab Alignment button on the left edge of the ruler indicates the type of tab. To change the tab type, click the **Tab Alignment** button.

To set a tab: Click the alignment button; choose the type of tab; click the ruler where you want to set the tab.

To delete a tab: Click the tab marker and drag it straight down off the ruler.

To move a tab: Click the tab marker and drag the tab to its new location.

DRILL 20

1. Display the Horizontal Ruler if necessary (**View, Ruler**).

2. Set a left tab at 2" and a right tab at 5".

3. Key the drill below.

4. Save as **tm-drill20**.

Left Tab 2"	Right Tab 5"
↓ Jones	2,000 ↓
Smith	500
Brown	10,000

Increase/Decrease Indent

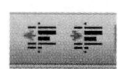

The **Indent** feature moves all lines of a paragraph to the next tab, whereas TAB only moves the first line to the next tab. You can indent a paragraph by clicking the Increase Indent button or by moving the indent marker on the Horizontal Ruler. Note the indent markers shown below are moved .5" from the left and right margins.

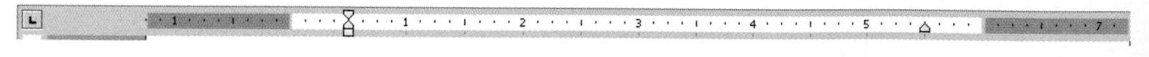

With a hanging indent, the first line begins at the left margin and the remaining lines are indented. Move the left indent marker on the Horizontal Ruler to format a paragraph with a hanging indent.

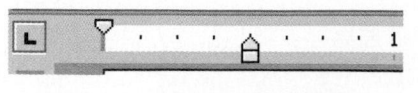

1. Open a new blank document.

2. Key the first ¶ below. Indent from the left.

3. Leave a blank line; then key the second ¶.

4. Use Decrease Indent to return this ¶ to the left margin.

5. Key the third ¶ with a hanging indent.

6. Save as **tm-drill21**.

Note that this paragraph is indented from the left. Each line of the paragraph begins at the same position. An easy way to indent a paragraph is to click the paragraph and click the indent button. The left indent will continue with the next paragraphs until you click the Decrease Indent button.

To return to the left margin, click the Decrease Indent button and key this paragraph without indenting it.

To key with a hanging indent, leave the paragraph marker at the left margin and move the indent marker to .5". This paragraph illustrates the hanging indent feature. Note that the first line begins at the left margin and the remaining lines are indented.

Tables

Tables can be created using the Table button on the Standard toolbar or using the Table menu. Position the insertion point where you want the table to appear.

To create a table using the Table menu:

1. From the Table menu, choose **Insert** and then click **Table**.

2. Click the up or down arrows to specify the number of rows and columns. Click **OK**. The table displays.

To create a table using the Table button:

1. Click the **Insert Table** button on the Standard toolbar; a drop-down grid displays.

2. Click the left mouse button, and drag the pointer across and down to highlight the number of columns and rows in the table. The table displays when you release the left mouse button.

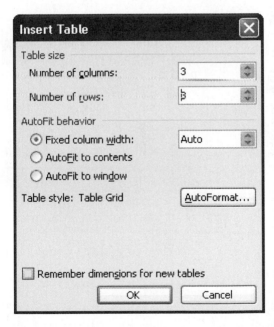

DRILL 22 TABLE

1. Open a new blank document.

2. Key the title; select it and format it using 12-point, all caps, bold type, and center. Leave a blank line after the title.

3. Position the insertion point at the left margin and create a 3-column, 4-row table.

4. Key the table shown below.

5. Save as **tm-drill22**.

SPORTS PROGRAMS AVAILABLE

Men	Women	Both Men and Women
Football	Volleyball	Basketball
Baseball	Softball	Golf
Cross Country	Crew	Tennis

Spelling and Grammar

Word places a red wavy line under misspelled words and a green wavy line under potential grammar errors. Clicking the right mouse button in a marked word displays a shortcut menu with suggested replacements to correct the error. The Spelling and Grammar Status button on the status bar also informs you if there is an error in the document. The check indicates no errors; the x indicates errors in the document.

DRILL 23 SPELLING AND GRAMMAR

1. Open a new blank document.

2. Key the following sentence; do not correct errors.

   The increease in cost will effect our budget.

3. Position the insertion point in *increease* and right-click the mouse. Select the correct spelling, *increase*.

4. Position the insertion point in *effect* and right-click the mouse. Select the correct grammar, *affect*.

5. Save as **tm-drill23**.

Find and Replace

Find and **Replace** are functions used to locate and replace text, graphics, and formatting. The More button on Find and Replace displays a list of search options.

To find and replace text:

1. Click **Edit** on the menu bar; then click **Replace**. If you just want to locate text, click **Find**.

2. Enter the text you want to find in *Find what* and text you wish to replace in *Replace with*.

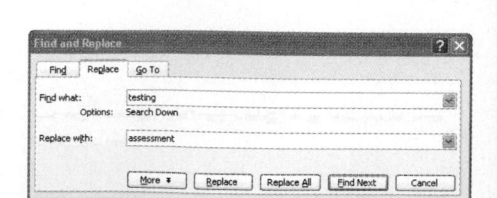

3. Click **Replace** to find and replace the next occurrence or **Replace All** to replace all instances.

DRILL 24 FIND AND REPLACE

1. Open **Drill 24** from the data files.

2. Find *testing* each time it appears and replace it with *assessment*.

3. Save as **tm-drill24**.

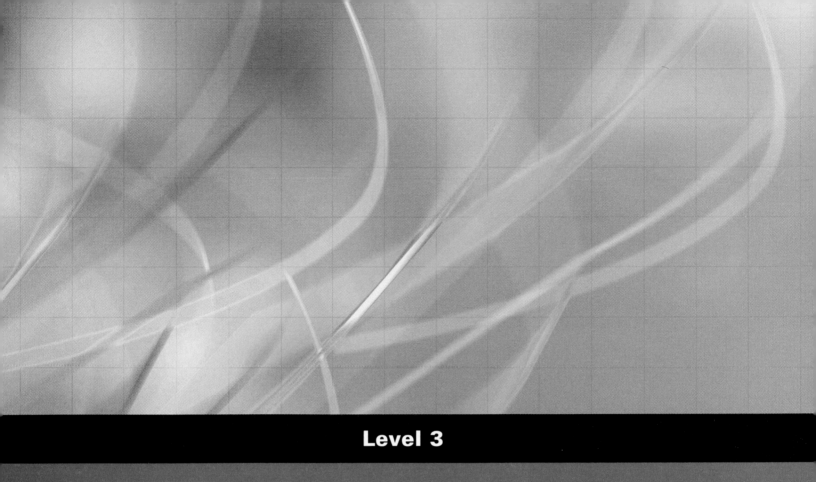

Level 3

Mastering Document Design

OBJECTIVES

DOCUMENT DESIGN SKILLS
To format business correspondence with special features.

To enhance report formats with elements that add structure, provide a consistent image, and increase readability.

To format tables, forms, and financial documents.

WORD PROCESSING SKILLS
To apply many of the basic competencies.

COMMUNICATION SKILLS
To produce error-free documents and apply language arts skills.

KEYBOARDING
To improve keyboarding speed and accuracy.

TIP

Reach to the first and third rows with a minimum of hand movement; keep hands quiet; don't bounce on the keys.

Key two 3' or one 5' writing; key with fluency and control.

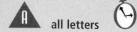 all letters

Rows 3, 2, 1

1 you we quip try pot peer your wire put quit wet trip power toy to
2 salad fad glad lass lag has gall lash gas lad had shall flag half
3 comb zone exam man carve bun oxen bank came next vent zoo van cab

4 we try to; you were; put up your; put it there; you quit; wipe it
5 Gail asked Sissy; what was said; had Jake left; Dana sold a flag
6 Zam came back; can Max fix my van? a brave man, Ben came in a cab

7 Peter or I will try to wire our popular reports to Porter or you.
8 Ada Glass said she is glad she had half a kale salad with Dallas.
9 Zack drove a van to minimize expenses; Ben and Max came in a cab.

Writing 41

		gwam	3'	5'
Sports are very big business today; that is, those sports competi-			4	3	62

Sports are very big business today; that is, those sports competi- 4 | 3 | 62
tions in which men participate are very big business. What about 9 | 5 | 65
sports for women? At the professional level, women have made real 13 | 8 | 67
progress in golf and tennis; they, as well as their sponsors, can 18 | 11 | 70
make big money in both of these events. The other sports for women 22 | 13 | 73
still are not considered to be major revenue sports. The future 26 | 16 | 75
may be much better, however, because sports for women at all levels 31 | 19 | 78
are gaining in popularity. Programs that are designed to help 35 | 21 | 81
young girls develop their athletic skills and interest are having 40 | 24 | 83
an impact. The result is that girls now expect to play for organ- 44 | 26 | 86
ized clubs as well as in school programs just as boys do. Club 48 | 29 | 88
sports often will lead to varsity teams. 51 | 31 | 90

Many people wonder how much impact the current emphasis on 55 | 33 | 92
gender equity will have on sports at the college level. Most 59 | 35 | 95
people agree that this new emphasis is very positive for women. 63 | 38 | 97
Some people feel, though, that it either has had or could have a 68 | 41 | 100
negative impact on sports for men. They believe that resources 72 | 43 | 103
that would have been spent on sports such as football, basketball, 77 | 46 | 105
and baseball for men are now being spent on the Olympic sports for 81 | 49 | 108
women. Overall, most people believe that both men and women who 85 | 51 | 111
have the ability to excel in an athletic event as well as in the 90 | 54 | 113
classroom should have the opportunity and should be encouraged to 94 | 56 | 116
do so. Success for both women and men is better than success for 98 | 59 | 118
either. 99 | 59 | 119

3' | 1 | 2 | 3 | 4
5' | 1 | 2 | 3

Skillbuilding and Editing Review

- Improve keyboarding skills.
- Review setting and changing margins.
- Review inserting bullets and numbering.
- Review alignment.
- Review using indent.
- Review using font attributes.

LESSON 61 Skillbuilding and Editing Review

SKILLBUILDING

61a
Warmup
Key each line twice SS.

alphabet	1	Quickly quiz veterans for kinds of whims and big jig experiences.
figures	2	Why add 17%, 26%, and 47%, when others (380, 95) will do as well?
adjacent	3	Miss too many meetings called for noon and you will need to call.
easy	4	Do you see the new dog and cats that play in the yard each night?

| 1 | 2 | 3 | 4 | 5 | 6 | 7 | 8 | 9 | 10 | 11 | 12 | 13 |

61b

Timed Writings
Key two 1' writings at your top rate.
Key two 1' writings at your control rate.

 all letters

gwam   2'

Most men and women in executive positions accept travel as a   6 | 50
part of corporate life.   At the same time, executives try to keep   13 | 57
time spent on the road to a minimum.   Top management usually   19 | 63
supports the efforts to reduce travel time as long as effective-   25 | 70
ness is not jeopardized.   One of the reasons for support is that   32 | 76
it is quite expensive for executives to travel.   Other reasons   38 | 82
are that traveling can be tiring and frequently causes stress.   44 | 89

2' | 1 | 2 | 3 | 4 | 5 | 6 |

SPECIFIC FINGERS

Key each set of lines twice;
DS between groups.

1st
1 fun gray vent guy hunt brunt buy brunch much gun huge humor vying
2 buy them brunch; a hunting gun; Guy hunts for fun; try it for fun

2nd
3 cite decide kick cider creed kidded keen keep kit idea ice icicle
4 keen idea; kick it back; ice breaker; decide the issue; sip cider

3rd
5 low slow lax solo wax sold swell swollen wood wool load logs doll
6 wooden dolls; wax the floor; a slow boat; saw logs; pull the wool

4th
7 quip zap Zane zip pepper pay quiz zipper quizzes pad map nap jazz
8 zip the zipper; jazz at the plaza; Zane quipped; La Paz jazz band

1. Key three 1' writings on each paragraph.
2. Key one 5' or two 3' writings.

Option: Practice as a guided writing.

		gwam	
1/4'	1/2'	3/4'	1'
8	16	24	32
9	18	27	36
10	20	30	40
11	22	33	44
12	24	36	48
13	26	39	52
14	28	41	56
15	30	45	60
16	32	48	64
17	34	51	68
18	36	54	72

  all letters

Writing 40

gwam 3' | 5'

How much power is adequate? Is more power always better   4 | 2 50
than less power? People often raise the question in many differ-   8 | 5 52
ent instances. Regardless of the situation, most people seem to   12 | 7 55
seek more power. In jobs, power is often related to rank in an   17 | 10 57
organization, to the number of people reporting to a person, and   21 | 13 60
to the ability to spend money without having to ask someone with   25 | 15 63
more power. Most experts indicate that the power a person has   30 | 18 65
should closely match the responsibilities (not just duties and   34 | 20 68
tasks) for which he or she can be held accountable.   37 | 22 70

Questions about power are not limited to jobs and people.   41 | 25 72
Many people ask the question in reference to the amount of power   45 | 27 75
or speed a computer should have. Again, the response usually   50 | 30 77
implies that more is better. A better approach is to analyze how   54 | 32 80
the computer is to be used and then try to match power needs to   58 | 35 82
the types of applications. Most people are surprised to learn   62 | 37 85
that home computer buyers tend to buy more power than buyers in   67 | 40 87
offices. The primary reason is that the computers are used to   71 | 43 90
play games with extensive graphics, sound, and other media appli-   75 | 45 93
cations. Matching the needs of the software is the key.   79 | 47 95

3' | 1 | 2 | 3 | 4 |
5' | 1 | 2 | 3 |

61c

Drill Practice
Key each set of drills 3 times;
then repeat the timed writing
on the previous page.

1st finger

5 fog the turn for yet gun bright got gut nor just fun you give Bob
6 burns turn fern fight found girl granny from Juan hunt minute him
7 The brave boy found his neighbor giving Juan taffy to go hunting.

2nd finger

8 ice ore keep kind kitten echo dickens chicken I kneel nick icicle
9 Pat saw pop swap pizza with Adam as he zipped past the pool hall.
10 Ike etched kittens, chickens, and icicles on Dee's knee with ink.

3rd and 4th fingers

11 swap zone we poll was lap pa asp zap wad sap saw wax papa sow wow
12 as pax own sass is well all pan will ax sew pot Paul few loop Pam
13 Debra averages six fewer servings of sweet dessert during Easter.

left hand

14 crazed bass averages dessert cedar badger affect braggart detects
15 beware greatest feet effects gag faster bazaar assess drawers ads
16 grease estate carafe awarded exerted get careers agrees beads ear
17 In my opinion, today anyone can play pool or monopoly with Jimmy.

right hand

18 honk million kimono pumpkin yolk poplin oil lumpy homily hoop lip
19 pill nylon million puppy uphill yoyo ninny opinion lion polio mum
20 Jimmy minimum pupil holly imply kinky monopoly pool union you ohm
21 Their neighbor's mangy dog and lame duck slept by a box of rocks.

balanced hand

22 neighbor papa tight shantytown usual worn downtown fork ensign am
23 coalfield ape fishbowl disorient ivory giant leprosy neurotic may
24 problem rogue whale theory ornament quench mandible jangle mentor
25 Their big naughty dog would torment us and ambush the wheelchair.

| 1 | 2 | 3 | 4 | 5 | 6 | 7 | 8 | 9 | 10 | 11 | 12 | 13 |

COMMUNICATION

61d

Standard Procedures for Proofreading and Saving a Document

1. Use Spelling and Grammar to check spelling when you have completed the document.
2. Proofread the document on-screen to be sure that it makes sense.
3. Preview the document, and check the overall appearance.
4. Create a new folder for each module to hold the exercises keyed in the module (**Module 10 Keys**).
5. Save the document with the exercise or drill name (**61e-d1**) in the module folder.
6. Print the document.
7. Compare the document to the source copy (textbook), and check that text has not been omitted or added. Revise, save, and print if necessary.

DRILL 2

ADJACENT KEYS

Key each set once; repeat entire drill.

Goal: To eliminate persistent errors on side-by-side keys.

as/sa
1 has sale fast salt was saw vast essay easy say past vast mast sap
2 We saw Sam; Sal was sad; Susan has a cast; as Sam said; as I said

er/re
3 were there tree deer great three other her free red here pert are
4 we were there; here we are; there were three; here are three deer

io/oi
5 point axiom prior choir lion boil toil billion soil action adjoin
6 join a choir; prior to that action; millions in a nation rejoiced

op/po
7 polo drop loop post hope pole port rope slope power top pony stop
8 rope the pony; drop the pole; power at the top; hope for the poor

rt/tr
9 trail alert train hurt tree shirt trap smart trim start tray dirt
10 trim the tree; start the train; dirt on the shirt; alert the trio

ew/we
11 few we stew were pew went dew web sew wept crew wear brew wet new
12 we were weak; few were weeping; the crew went west; we knew a few

gh/ui
13 sight quit laugh suit might ruin ghost guide ghastly guilt ghetto
14 a ghastly suit; quit laughing; recruit the ghost; might be guilty

DRILL 3

OUTSIDE REACHES

Key each set once. DS between groups.

Goal: To key with a maximum of one error per line. (Letters are often omitted in outside reaches—concentrate.)

a/p
1 tapioca actual against casual areas facial equally aware parallel
2 impower purpose people opposed compute pimple papyrus pope puppet
3 Perhaps part of the chapter page openers can appear on red paper.

s/w
4 class sash steps essential skills business discuss desks insisted
5 wow wayworn away awkward wrong awaits wildwood waterworks wayward
6 The snow white swan swayed as the waves swept the swelling shore.

z/l
7 hazard zip zero zeolite freezer zoom zealous z-axis zodiac sizing
8 likely indelibly, laurel finally leaflet regularly eloquently lily
9 A New Zealand zoologist was amazed as a zebra guzzled the zinias.

x/?
10 fax oxford exert excite examples xylan exercise oxygen exact taxi
11 When? Where? Which? For her? How much? What color? To whom?
12 After examining the x-rays, why did Dr. Ax exempt an exploratory?

DRILL 4

ALPHABETIC SENTENCES

Key each line once with good rhythm. Keep fingers curved and upright over the keys.

1 Judge McQuoy will have prizes for their next big track meet.
2 Jack may provide some extra quiz problems for the new group.

3 Gary Quazet mended six copies of books and journals we have.
4 Jack quibbled with a garrulous expert on Zoave family names.

5 Jake will study sixty chapters on vitamins for the big quiz.
6 Max asked Quin to provide a jewel box for the glossy zircon.

7 This judge may quiz the Iowa clerks about extensive profits.
8 Meg Keys packed and flew to Venezia to acquire her next job.

61e-d1
Document with Tabs

1. Center the main heading **NEW COMPUTER LAB HOURS** at about 2"; then DS and key the text below.
2. Set left tabs at 1.25" and 3.25" to key the columns of text. Save as **61c-d1** and print.

State budget cuts and reduction of revenue to our district require that the computer lab, located on the first floor of the Business/CIS building, reduce the number of hours of operation.

The new lab hours will be effective beginning Monday, May 1, 200-.

Monday	9:00 a.m. to 8:00 p.m.
Tuesday	10:00 a.m. to 9:00 p.m.
Wednesday	8:30 a.m. to 7:30 p.m.
Thursday	9:00 a.m. to 3:00 p.m.
Friday/Saturday	Closed

Please announce the new lab hours to all your students so they can adjust their schedules accordingly. The new hours will be posted on the lab doors and on the sign-in terminals.

61e-d2
Edit Document

TIP

Review "Proofreaders' Marks" in the Reference Guide.

1. Open **61e-d1**. Change the paragraphs to DS. The column text remains SS. Insert a tab at the beginning of each paragraph.
2. Change the closing hour on Thursday to 9:00 p.m. Delete Friday/Saturday.
3. Move the line beginning with "The new lab hours . . ." and the columns of text to a DS below the last paragraph.
4. Search for the word *lab* and replace it with *laboratory*. Save as **61c-d2**.

61e-d3
Document with Proofreaders' Marks

1. Set 2" side margins; then key the copy below. Make the changes as shown.
2. Create a 2-column, 5-row table a DS below the last ¶, and key the column text shown in **61e-d1**.
3. Center the document vertically on the page. Save as **61e-d3**.

I have received numerous complaints from staff members over the past few weeks regarding their telephone messages. I was told that many of the phone messages contained misspelled names of callers, incorrect telephone numbers, and the date and time the message was taken was often not filled in. It is important that our sales and support staff recieve complete and acurate telephone messages.

The telephone company will be providing a Customer Service Seminar from 9:00 - 12:00 on Friday, May 15th in conference room 2. Please arrage for all your office staff to be present. I have arranged for switchboard coverage during these hours.

Writing 37: **85** *gwam*

Business letters can be defined by their goals; for example, 12 4 60
a letter of inquiry, a reply letter, a promotion letter, a credit 25 8 65
letter, or other specialized letter. While you learn to compose 38 13 69
these letters, just keep each letter's individual goals always in 52 17 74
front of you. If you fix in your mind a theme, pattern, and 64 21 78
ideal for your writing, composing good business letters may 75 25 82
emerge as one of the best tricks in your bag. 85 28 85

Competent business writers know what they want to say—and 12 32 89
they say it with simplicity and clarity. Words are the utensils 25 37 93
they use to convey ideas or to convince others to accomplish some 38 41 98
action. The simple word and the short sentence usually are more 51 45 102
effective than the big word and the involved sentence. But don't 64 50 106
be afraid of the long or unusual word if it means exactly what 77 54 111
you intend to say in your business letter. 85 57 113

Writing 38: **90** *gwam*

Although many of us are basically comfortable with sameness 12 4 64
and appear to dislike change, we actually prize variation. We 24 8 68
believe that we are each unique individuals, yet we know that we 38 12 72
are really only a little different; and we struggle to find 50 16 76
"sense of self" in how we think and act. Our cars, too, built 62 21 81
on assembly lines are basically identical; yet when we purchase 75 25 85
one, we choose model, color, size, and style which suits us 87 29 89
individually. 90 30 90

Also many people expect to find security by buying things 12 34 94
that are in keeping with society's "image" and "status." But 24 38 98
what we think of as "status" always changes. The wise buyer will 37 42 102
buy those items that give most in utility, comfort, and satisfac- 50 47 106
tion. Status should just be a thing we create in ourselves, not 63 51 111
a thing created for us. Common sense should guide us in making good 77 55 115
decisions—and if our "status" is increased thereby, well, why not? 90 60 120

Writing 39: **95** *gwam*

Normally, customers do not abandon a firm because of a mistake. 13
All firms will make mistakes at one time or another. The way a 26
problem is resolved is far more crucial than the fact that a 38
problem existed. More customers leave a firm and take their 50
business to a competitor because they get upset with an employee 63
than for any other reason. The key qualifications for a customer 76
service employee are superb human relations skills and knowledge 89
of the product or service. 95

1'	1	2	3	4	5	6	7	8	9	10	11	12	13
3'		1			2			3			4		

SKILLBUILDING

62a
Warmup
Key each line twice SS.

alphabet	1	With zeal the boy quickly jumped over the x-ray, avoiding a fall.
figures	2	Invoice #13579 for $24.80 will be released on or before 06/15/03.
adjacent reaches	3	Were we going to open the voice track before we check any others?
easy	4	I will call you this week to see if you can act in our new plays.

| 1 | 2 | 3 | 4 | 5 | 6 | 7 | 8 | 9 | 10 | 11 | 12 | 13 |

62b
Technique Builder
Improve keyboarding technique.
Key each pair of lines 3 times.
Key at a controlled rate.

az	5	Zen and Ozzie zealously played the anthem in the Aztec Jazz band.
	6	Batz went to Phoenix, Arizona to take a math quiz that he missed.
by	7	Boyd drove by the Blue Bayou to bypass the road block at the Bay.
	8	By daybreak, Mary will stop by to bake a birthday cake for Jayne.
cx	9	Please carry the X-ray from exit C to exit X for Cece and Xavier.
	10	Carol can meet Xian at the exit doors following the movie Exodus.
dw	11	Don walked the dog at dawn when he dwelled in his downtown condo.
	12	Did Dwight drive Wendy to the new drive-in or the new drive-thru?
figures	13	The 12 teams spent $3,489.00 on groceries for the 567 boy scouts.
	14	Judy's 13 puzzles had 60,789 pieces, but 524 pieces were missing.

| 1 | 2 | 3 | 4 | 5 | 6 | 7 | 8 | 9 | 10 | 11 | 12 | 13 |

gwam 3'

62c
Timed Writings
Take two 1' writings and two 3'
writings at your control rate.

 A all letters

One of the most important skills needed for success on the	4 | 42
job is listening. However, this is a skill that takes hours of	8 | 46
practice. You can maximize your effectiveness by learning and	12 | 50
using techniques for effective listening. People can listen two	17 | 55
or three times faster than they can talk. Use the difference be-	21 | 59
tween the rate at which a person speaks and the rate at which you	25 | 63
can listen to review what the person has said and to identify the	30 | 68
main ideas communicated. This active style of listening helps	34 | 72
you avoid the tendency to tune in and out of a conversation.	38 | 76

3' | 1 | 2 | 3 | 4 |

Writing 34: **70 gwam**

gwam 1' 3'

Foreign study and travel take extra time and effort, but 11 4 50
these two activities quickly help us to understand people. Much 24 8 55
can be learned from other cultures. Today, business must think 37 12 59
globally. Learning about the culture of others is not a luxury. 50 17 63
Even the owner of a small business realizes that he or she cannot 64 21 68
just focus on the domestic scene. 70 23 70

Many examples can be used to show how a local business may 11 27 74
be influenced by global competition. A hair stylist may be re- 24 31 78
quired to learn European styles because customers may want to try 38 36 83
a style just like they saw on their travels. Or salons may want 51 40 87
to offer other services such as facials that people have tried 63 44 91
while they were traveling abroad. 70 47 93

Writing 35: **75 gwam**

gwam 1' 3'

Getting a job interview is certainly a triumph for the job 12 4 54
seeker. Yet anxiety quickly sets in as the applicant becomes 24 8 58
aware of the competition. The same attention to details that was 37 12 62
used in writing the successful resume will also be needed for the 51 17 67
interview. Experts often say that the first four minutes are the 64 21 71
most crucial in making a strong impact on the interviewer. 75 25 75

First, people focus on what they see. Posture, eye contact, 12 29 79
facial expression, and gestures make up over half of the message. 26 33 84
Next, people focus on what they hear; enthusiasm, delivery, pace, 39 38 88
volume, and clarity are as vital as what is said. Finally, 51 42 92
people get to the actual words that are said. You can make a 63 49 96
good impression. But, realize, you have just four minutes. 75 50 100

Writing 36: **80 gwam**

gwam 1' 3'

Would a pitcher go to the mound without warming up? Would 12 4 57
a speaker go to the podium without practice? Of course not! These 25 8 62
experts have spent many long hours striving to do their best. 38 13 66
Similarly, the performance of business employees is rated. The 51 17 70
manager's evaluation will include a record of actual performance 64 21 75
and a list of new goals. A good mark in these areas will demand 77 26 79
much hard work. 80 27 80

Many work factors can be practiced to help one succeed on 12 30 84
the job. Class attendance and punctuality can be perfected by 24 35 88
students. Because work is expected to be correct, managers do 37 39 92
not assign zeros. Thus, students must learn to proofread their 49 43 96
work. A project must also be completed quickly. Students can 62 47 101
learn to organize work and time well and to find ways to do their 75 52 105
work smarter and faster. 80 53 107

1'	1	2	3	4	5	6	7	8	9	10	11	12	13
3'		1			2			3			4		

62d-d1
Document with Bullets

1. At about 2.1", center and bold the heading **PROTECT YOUR COMPUTER**; then strike ENTER twice before keying the paragraphs below.

2. Align-justify the first and last paragraphs.

3. Use **Increase Indent** to indent the bulleted items to 1"; align the numbered paragraphs at the left margin.

4. Right-align your name and the current date DS below the last paragraph; save as **62d-d1** and print.

Connecting your PC to the Internet means that you need to have antivirus software and a firewall. Not having this protection is similar to leaving the front door of your home open when you go away on vacation, just inviting anyone in. You might be lucky and not have any intruders, but there is still the risk.

Some ways that you can help keep your computer safe and protected are:

- install a firewall on every computer
- use a firewall that is bidirectional
- use an antivirus software

There are two types of firewalls that can be installed to provide your computer with adequate protection. Choose the one that will best suit your needs.

1. **Hardware firewalls.** A hardware firewall needs to be installed between the terminal or network and the Internet. The firewall can be set to block or allow all packets passing in and out through various ports. Hardware firewalls are much preferred over software firewalls because they do not impede the end user. The major disadvantage of a hardware firewall is the cost; it can easily cost thousands of dollars.

2. **Software firewall.** A software firewall is much less expensive and often can be downloaded from the Internet free of charge. Software firewalls are often loaded on computers used in the home and small businesses.

Once you have installed your virus software and firewall, make sure that you get the updates and patches to the software on a regular basis. This is extremely important with the virus software, as new viruses are constantly being created. Most virus software are updated weekly, but some are updated as often as daily.

Student Name
Current date

62d-d2
Edit Document

1. Open **62d-d1**.

2. Change the paragraphs to DS; tab at the beginning of each ¶. SS the bulleted lines and the numbered paragraphs.

3. Align the numbered paragraphs at .5" (select the ¶s and click the **Increase Indent** button twice).

4. Change the heading to 14-point font and delete one hard return above the heading to make the document fit on one page. Save as **62d-d2**. Print.

Writing 31: **55** *gwam*

A crucial life skill is the ability to put things in proper perspective. Individuals often fail to realize that many things are just not worth fighting about. A quick way to know whether an issue is worth fighting for is to look at the situation from a long-term perspective.

If you will care five or six years from now that you defended an issue, it is a principle worth defending. If you will not even remember, the situation does not justify the effort required for defending it. The odds of winning are also important. Why fight a losing battle?

	1'	3'
	12	4	41
	25	8	45
	38	13	50
	51	17	54
	55	18	55
	11	22	59
	24	26	63
	36	31	67
	49	35	72
	55	37	74

Writing 32: **60** *gwam*

Why do we remember some things and forget others? Often, we associate loss of memory with aging or an illness such as Alzheimer's disease. However, the crux of the matter is that we all forget various things that we prefer to remember. We tend to remember things that mean something special to us.

For many people, recalling dates is a difficult task; yet they manage to remember dates of special occasions, such as anniversaries. Processing requires one not only to hear but to ponder and to understand what has just been said. We recall things that we say and do longer than things we hear and see.

	1'	3'
	12	4	44
	24	8	48
	37	12	52
	50	17	57
	60	20	60
	12	24	64
	25	28	68
	36	33	72
	49	37	77
	60	40	80

Writing 33: **65** *gwam*

Humor is very important in our professional and our personal lives. Fortunately, we realize that many things can and do go wrong. If we can learn to laugh at ourselves and with other people, we will get through the terrible times. Adding a little extra laughter can help put the situation in proper perspective much quicker.

Maintaining our sense of humor lets us enjoy our positions to a greater degree. No one is perfect, and we cannot expect perfection from ourselves. However, the quality of our performance is greater when we do the things we like. We realize our prime time is devoted to work. Thus, it is important that we enjoy this time.

	1'	3'
	12	4	47
	25	8	52
	37	12	56
	50	17	60
	63	21	64
	65	22	65
	12	26	69
	24	30	73
	37	34	77
	50	38	82
	62	42	86
	65	43	87

1'	1	2	3	4	5	6	7	8	9	10	11	12	13
3'		1			2			3			4		

SKILLBUILDING

63a
Warmup
Key each line twice SS.

alphabet	1	We analyzed why my quick proxy fight was not over the objectives.
figures	2	Follow players number 18, 92, 40, and 57 to room 36 for more fun.
shift key	3	Mr. Jeff Smith called Ms. Helene Snow on Monday, April 15, in NY.
easy	4	He puts half the money he earns into the boxes and half in banks.

| 1 | 2 | 3 | 4 | 5 | 6 | 7 | 8 | 9 | 10 | 11 | 12 | 13 |

63b
Technique Builder
Improve keyboarding technique.
Key at a controlled rate.

home row	5	A lad has been hard at work all day; Sal and Dallas had to help.
	6	Sally and Jill also had Les Fasladd fill the large salad dishes.
third row	7	Take Wes to the plane to see if Patty is ready for a quick tour.
	8	Ray and Roy took a trip to walk with two pretty twins in Queens.
first row	9	Vic and Ben came to show Manny the excellent new victory banner.
	10	Benny is excited about the new banners that help bring in money.
right hand	11	Start grading the tests before the exercises for Ted and Saddie.
	12	Dale and Dave are trading recipes for salsa, salads, and cookies.
left hand	13	Pay Kip for the many long hours he put in joining the old lines.
	14	Jill likes how my mom opens up her home to many homeless people.

| 1 | 2 | 3 | 4 | 5 | 6 | 7 | 8 | 9 | 10 | 11 | 12 | 13 |

63c
Timed Writings
Take two 3' writings. Strive for good control.

  all letters

	gwam	3'	5'
If you wish to advance in your career, you must learn how to	4	2	37
make good decisions. You can develop decision-making skills by	8	5	39
learning to follow six basic steps. The first three steps help	13	8	42
you to see the problem. They are identifying the problem, ana-	17	10	44
lyzing the problem to find causes and consequences, and making	21	13	47
sure you define the goals that your solution must meet.	25	15	49
Now, you are ready to solve the problem with the last three	29	17	52
steps. They include finding alternative solutions to the prob-	33	20	54
lem, analyzing each of the alternatives carefully to locate the	37	22	57
best solution, and putting the best solution into action. Once	41	25	59
you have implemented a plan of action, check to make sure that	46	27	62
it meets all of your objectives. If it does not, then determine	50	30	64
if the problem is with the solution or with the way it is being	54	33	67
implemented. Always keep all options open.	57	34	69

| 3' | 1 | 2 | 3 | 4 |
| 5' | 1 | 2 | 3 | |

Skill Builders 5

Save each drill as a separate file. Save as **SB5-d1**, etc. (Skill Builders 5, Drill 1).

DRILL 1

PROGRESSIVE WRITINGS

1. Set the timer for 1'.
2. Practice each ¶ in a set until you can complete it in 1' with no more than one error.
3. Take a 3' writing; strive to maintain your 1' rate.
4. Move onto the next set. Notice that each set progresses by 5 words.

  all letters

Writing 28: **40 *gwam***

	gwam	1'	3'

"An ounce of prevention is worth a pound of cure" is really — 12 — 4 — 31
based on fact; still, many people comprehend this statement more — 25 — 8 — 35
for its quality as literature than on a practical, common-sense — 38 — 12 — 39
philosophy. — 40 — 13 — 40

Just take health, for example. We agonize over stiff costs — 12 — 17 — 44
we pay to recover from illnesses; but, on the other hand, we give — 25 — 22 — 48
little or no attention to health requirements for diet, exercise, — 38 — 26 — 53
and sleep. — 40 — 27 — 53

Writing 29: **45 *gwam***

	gwam	1'	3'

Problems with our environment show an odd lack of foresight. — 12 — 4 — 34
We just expect that whatever we may need to support life will be — 25 — 8 — 38
available. We rarely question our comforts, even though they may — 38 — 13 — 43
abuse our earth, water, and air. — 45 — 15 — 45

Optimism is an excellent virtue. It is comforting to think — 12 — 19 — 49
that, eventually, anything can be fixed. So why should we worry? — 25 — 23 — 53
A better idea, certainly, is to realize that we don't have to fix — 38 — 28 — 58
anything we have not yet broken. — 45 — 30 — 60

Writing 30: **50 *gwam***

	gwam	1'	3'

Recently, a friend of mine grumbled about how quickly papers — 12 — 4 — 37
accumulated on her desk; she never seemed able to reduce them to — 25 — 8 — 42
zero. She said some law seemed to be working that expanded the — 38 — 13 — 46
stack today by precisely the amount she reduced it yesterday. — 50 — 17 — 50

She should organize her papers and tend to them daily. Any — 12 — 21 — 54
paper that needs a look, a decision, and speedy, final action — 24 — 25 — 58
gets just that; any that needs closer attention is subject to a — 37 — 29 — 62
fixed completion schedule. Self-discipline is the key to order. — 50 — 33 — 67

1'	1	2	3	4	5	6	7	8	9	10	11	12	13
3'		1			2			3			4		

63d-d1
Editing Review

1. Position the main heading at approximately 2" and key the text below.
2. Save as **63d-d1**. Print. Leave the document on the screen and continue with **63d-d2**.

Looking for a new computer? ←———— caps, bold, center, 22-point font
DS
Fewer and fewer buyers are buying a new desktop computer when the time comes to replace their old one. Laptops have become the "way to go," as the price gap between the 2 has gotten smaller. The decrease in price has resulted in consumers shedding their 60-pound desktop computers in favor of the smaller, lighter laptop computers.

What are consumers looking for in a laptop computer?

- Batteries with a longer life—laptop computers that can be used away from a power outlet as long as possible.

- Powerful microprocessors—with advances in technology, consumers want laptops that have more processing power to meet the requirements of the high-end applications that are becoming more and more common.

- DVD players—with more and more software becoming available on DVDs, users are requiring the ability to play DVDs and *burn* DVDs on the laptop.

Since battery life is a major concern for consumers, manufacturers have been developing some power-saving steps on laptops that can extend the battery time. Axiom has created SlowDoze, which drops the speed of the processor when it is running on battery power. JumpStart shuts down the processor during periods of inactivity, and instantly turns it back on when it is necessary.

Visit our Web site for more information ←——— bold, italics, center, 16-point font

http://www.laptops-r-us.com   ←——— bold, center, red, 18-point font

63d-d2
Editing Review

1. Open **63d-d1**.
2. Change the left and right margins to 1".
3. Spell out the number 2 in the first paragraph.
4. Italicize *SlowDoze* and *JumpStart* in the last paragraph.
5. Change the bullets to numbers.
6. Save as **63d-d2**. Print.

Change left and right margins to 1"; arrange the document so that it fits on one page. Use the following heading lines. Signature line: **Respectfully submitted, Alice Liu, Secretary**. Save as 120c-d7.

Sterling Heights Community Hospital
August 10, 200-
Advisory Board Meeting Minutes

	words
heading	17

Presiding: Jacinto A. Campo, Administrator   25

Participants: Shawn Hartman, Assistant Administrator;   36
Terry Olson, Community Relations; John Kaplan, Director of   48
Marketing; Ron Volson, Human Resources; Lisa Summons,   59
Director of Education; Susan Phillips, Director of Nursing   71

Board Members: Vincent Perez, City of Sterling Heights;   82
Captain Wayne Anderson, Wayne County Sheriff Station;   93
Robert Le, American Heart Association; Cynthia Cross,   104
Buxton Medical Supplies; Nancy Ricardo, General Motors   115
Corp.   116

Administrator Jacinto Campo welcomed all new board members   128
and guests to the first official advisory board meeting.   140
Introductions were made around the table.

All advisory committee members and participants toured   155
the hospital guided by Jacinto Campo. Facility improve-   162
ments were discussed during the tour. Areas targeted for   176
remodeling this year were also pointed out.

Bylaws for the advisory board were distributed and   186
discussed. Mr. Campo expressed the hospitals desire to get   200
involved in the community. The advisory board input will be critical.   215

Bullet these items

Current hospital projects were discussed: Bears   225
Program, MOMS Hospital feedback methods.   241
(Maternal Obstetrical Medical Services)

Plaques were presented to each of the advisory board   250
members and pictures were taken. The next advisory board   262
meeting is scheduled for   . October 16, 200-.   270

63e

Opposite-Hand Combinations
Concentrate as you key each line for accuracy.

> **TIP**
>
> Key fluently, without rushing.

br/rb
15 break barb brawn orbit brain carbon brakes barbecue brazen barber
16 Barbara Brady brought us a new brand of barbecue to eat at break.

ce/ec
17 cease decide cent collect cell direct cedar check center peck ice
18 Cecil recently received a check for his special barbecue recipes.

mu/um
19 mull dumb must human mud lumber mulch lump mumps slump music fume
20 Bum Muse must have dumped too much muddy mulch on the bumpy lawn.

nu/un
21 nut sun fun nurse gun sinus number punch nuzzle pound lunch until
22 Uncle Gunta, a nurse, was uneasy about numerous units unionizing.

gr/rg
23 grade merge grand purge great large grab organ green margins gray
24 Margo, our great grandmother, regrets merging those large groups.

ny/yn
25 Wayne any shyness many agony balcony Jayne lynx penny larynx myna
26 Wayne and Jayne fed many skinny myna birds on that sunny balcony.

63f

Timed Writings
Take one 5' writing. Strive for good control.

  all letters

	gwam	1'	5'

The job market today is quite different than it was a few years ago. The fast track to management no longer exists. Entry-level managers find that it is much more difficult to obtain a promotion to a higher-level position in management than it was just a few years ago. People who are in the market for new jobs find very few management positions available. In fact, many managers at all levels have a difficult time keeping their current management positions. Two factors seem to contribute heavily to the problem. The first factor is the trend toward self-managed teams. The second factor is that as companies downsize they often remove entire layers of management or an entire division.

12 | 2
24 | 5
36 | 7
49 | 10
61 | 12
74 | 15
87 | 17
99 | 20
112 | 22
124 | 25
136 | 27
140 | 28

Layoffs are not new; but, what is new is that layoffs are affecting white-collar workers as well as blue-collar workers. Coping with job loss is a new and frustrating experience for many managers. A person who has just lost a job will have concerns about personal security and welfare, and the concerns are compounded when families are involved. The problem, however, is more than just an economic one. Job loss often damages an individual's sense of self-worth. An individual who does not have a good self-concept will have a very hard time selling himself or herself to a potential employer.

12 | 30
24 | 33
38 | 35
50 | 38
63 | 40
75 | 43
87 | 45
100 | 48
112 | 50
120 | 52

```
1' |  1  |  2  |  3  |  4  |  5  |  6  |  7  |  8  |  9  |  10  |  11  |  12  |  13  |
5' |        1        |              2              |           3           |
```

120c-d5
Create Billing Form

1. Change the left and right margins to .75". Create a 5-column, 7-row table.
2. Merge Row 1 and create a heading similar to the illustration. Row 1 contains all the copy from the top of the page through *This bill is due and payable within 21 days*.
3. Key the invoice shown below. Insert appropriate form fields (**ff**) to accommodate the type of information to be filled in.
4. Protect the form. Save as **120c-d5** and print.

*P*acific *N*ewport *M*edical *G*roup
3160 Redhill Ave. • Newport Beach, CA 90630 • (714) 555-0112

BILLING STATEMENT
This bill is due and payable within 21 days.

Date	Services Rendered	Charges	Insurance Payment	Balance Due
(ff-patient name) *(ff-street address)* *(ff-city, state, zip)*		Account # *(ff-acct. #)*	Balance Due Past Due Total Balance	

120c-d6
Complete Billing Form

1. Open **120c-d5** and save it as **120c-d6**. Fill in the form with the name, address, and account number, as well as the services and charges shown below.
2. Unprotect the form to fill in the rest of the form.
3. Use the math feature to write a formula that will calculate Balance Due in Column E (Charges – Insurance Payment). Display the Balance Due with a dollar sign and two decimal places. Use the Sum Above feature to insert the Balance Due in Cell E7.
4. Insert decimal tabs to align the numbers. You will need to align the numbers manually in Cell E7.
5. Calculate Total Balance (Balance Due + Past Due). Save and print.

6-22-xx	Office visit	65.00	50.00
6-27-xx	Lab test/X-ray	185.00	160.00
7-06-xx	Consultation	200.00	125.00

Cheryl Bocanegra, 793 Haven Ln., Costa Mesa, CA 92626 Acct. # 09431   Past Due: $60.00

Letter and Memo Mastery

- Format block and modified block letters with special features.
- Create e-mail and format interoffice memos.
- Use memo templates for efficiency.
- Prove keyboarding skills.

LESSON 64   Block Letter Format

SKILLBUILDING

64a
Warmup
Key each line twice SS.

alphabet 1 Judging by that quick quiz quality, were my extra videos helpful?
1st/2nd fingers 2 Using a good browser to connect to the Internet will please Benny.
figure/symbol 3 Their new garden (10' wide x 23' long) will cost 48% of $13,695.72.
long words 4 Expect physiological or psychological reactions to unusual works.

| 1 | 2 | 3 | 4 | 5 | 6 | 7 | 8 | 9 | 10 | 11 | 12 | 13 |

gwam 1' | 3'

64b

Timed Writings
Take a 1' writing on each paragraph and a 3' writing on both paragraphs.

  all letters

Do you ever "goof off" for an hour or more with a television | 12 | 4
program or a visit on the telephone and realize later that you | 25 | 8
haven't actually enjoyed your leisure? Each nagging little vision | 38 | 13
of homework or chores to be completed always seems to result in | 51 | 17
taking the edge off your pleasure. And then you must hurriedly | 64 | 21
complete whatever you postponed. Why do so many people end up | 76 | 25
rushing around in a frenzy, trying to meet their deadlines? | 88 | 29

First, do not waste time feeling guilty. Check with your | 12 | 33
friends who always seem ready for a good time but are also ready | 25 | 38
for unexpected quizzes. Learn their secrets to managing time. | 37 | 42
Knowing that there are sixty seconds in every minute and sixty | 50 | 46
minutes in each hour, you can schedule your activities into the | 63 | 50
time available. Second, learn to set priorities. You can achieve | 76 | 55
your plans and enjoy your leisure as well. | 85 | 58

1' | 1 | 2 | 3 | 4 | 5 | 6 | 7 | 8 | 9 | 10 | 11 | 12 | 13 |
3' | 1 | 2 | 3 | 4 |

Body of letter:

Thank you for volunteering to be on the advisory committee for the County Medical Rescue Mission. I am sure that this will be a very rewarding experience for you and your company. The County Medical Rescue Mission served over 1,500 low income and homeless people during the past year.

I am enclosing a copy of the last advisory committee minutes to give you an idea of what was discussed at the last meeting. A copy of the agenda for the next meeting, scheduled for August 16, 200-, is also enclosed.

We look forward to seeing you on August 16th.

120c-d3
Name Badges

1. Use the mail merge feature to create name badges for the advisory committee members in **120c-d2**.
2. Use Avery 5883 Name Badge. Include the speaker's name, job title, and company name on each badge. Make the font large enough so that it is easily visible.
3. Save as **120c-d3**. Print.

120c-d4
Format Report with Styles and Footnotes

1. Open **Frogkick Island**. Save as **120c-d4**.
2. Format this document as a SS leftbound report. Change the spacing after the paragraphs to 6 points.
3. Main heading: Center, initial caps, Heading 1 style.

   Side headings: Heading 2 style.

   Paragraph headings: Place on line above ¶, make initial cap, remove period, and apply Heading 3 style.
4. **a.** Insert footnote 1 at the end of the first paragraph:

   International Government Publication, *2000 Census Report* (Washington, D.C.: International Government Press, 2001) p. 92.

   b. Insert footnote 2 at the end of the first paragraph under the side heading **Government**:

   ***Frogkick Island Ordinances* (New York: Majestic Publishing House, 2002) p. 1035, §2015.**
5. Insert a header that contains your name at the left margin and the page number at the right followed by a ¾-point line; the header will appear on all pages except the first.

   Student Name   **2**
6. Insert these references on the last page of the report; then save the report and print.

   Crane, Thomas B. *Unique Trips Around the World.* London: Versaille Publishing Co., 2002.

   Peterson, Angelica S. *Undiscovered Travel Adventures.* Singapore: International Printing Association, 2002.

64c
Basic Letter Review

Business Letter Review

The following letter parts are basic to all business letters. Review the block-format model letter on page 248. In a block-style letter, all lines begin at the left margin.

Letter Parts

Businesspeople expect to see standard letter parts arranged in the proper sequence. The standard parts are listed below. Other parts may be included.

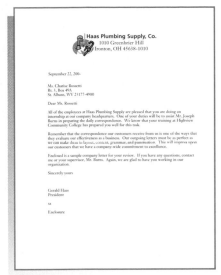

Letterhead. Stationery printed at the top with the company name, logo, full address, and other elements such as trademark symbols, phone numbers, fax numbers, and e-mail address. As a general rule, allow 1.5" for the letterhead.

Dateline. The date is the month (spelled out), day, and year that the letter is prepared. Remember that letters may be used as legal documents, so correctness of the date is very important. Press ENTER four times after the date. The dateline should be positioned about 0.5" below the letterhead. Therefore, position the date about 2" (press ENTER six times). If the letter is short (two paragraphs or about 100 words), center the page vertically.

Letter address. The complete address of the recipient of the letter. The letter address usually includes the personal title, first name, and last name of the recipient followed by the company name, street address, and city, state, and ZIP Code. Press ENTER twice after the letter address.

Salutation. The word *Dear* followed by the personal title and last name of the recipient (*Dear Mr. Nibert*; *Dear Professor Glenn*). Use the first name of the recipient only if there is a close relationship between the sender and recipient (*Dear Sue*). Press ENTER twice after the salutation.

Body. The text that makes up the message of the letter. Single-space the paragraphs and double-space between paragraphs. Press ENTER twice after the last paragraph.

Complimentary closing. A phrase used to end a letter. Capitalize only the first letter. Press ENTER four times after the complimentary close to allow space for a written signature.

Name and title of writer. Key the first and last name of the sender. The sender's personal title (Dr., Ms., Mrs., Mr.) may be included if the first name does not clearly indicate gender (e.g., Ms. Lee Jones). Use a comma to separate the title if it's on the same line as the name. Do not use a comma if the title is on a separate line. Press ENTER twice after the name or title.

William Karlet, Coordinator   or   *William Karlet*
                                                            Coordinator

Reference initials. When the letter is keyed for another person who is the originator of the letter, the typist includes his/her initials in lowercase below the signature line. In the textbook, *xx* is a reminder to key your reference initials. If the originator of the letter also keys the letter, reference initials are not included. Press ENTER twice after the reference initials if additional letter parts follow.

Enclosure notation. An enclosure notation indicates that something is included in the envelope with the letter. Read each letter and add an enclosure notation if needed. The notation may include a description of the items.

Enclosure   or   *Enclosure: Application form*   or   *Enclosures: 3*

1. Key the first line of the heading on approximately line 2". DS and bold the heading.
2. Set a left tab at .5" and a right leader tab at 6.0".
3. Key the agenda. Save as **120c-d1**. Print.

PACIFIC NEWPORT MEDICAL GROUP

ANNUAL BOARD OF DIRECTORS MEETING

July 15, 200-

Agenda

1. *Call to Order...Dr. Paul De La Rosa, President*
2. *Review of Previous Minutes...................................Melanie Leyda, Secretary*
3. *State of the Corporation Address.......................................Richard Pham, Controller*
4. *Technology Update ....Dr. Lisa Lee*
   Nuclear Medicine...Dr. Steven Coast
   Ultrasound Lab ....Dr. David Beem
5. *Quality Assurance...Claire Zehner, RN*
6. *HIPAA Privacy Regulations ....Susan Smith, Director of Education*
7. *Goal Setting...Adam Rogers, Chief Operating Officer*

1. Use mail merge to create the following letter. Supply all necessary letter parts. The letter is from you, Administrative Assistant.
2. Save the merged letters as **120c-d2**. Print the main document and the merged letters.

Recipients:

Mr. Jacinto Campo, Administrator, Sterling Heights Community Hospital, 5252 Hospital Rd., Newport Beach, CA 90630.

Ms. Betty Gross, Public Relations Coordinator, American Hospitals Association, 9754 Campus Dr., Buena Park, CA 90620

Ms. Loretta Pascua, Manager, Rehabilitation Specialist, 9217 Champion Way, Tustin, CA 92782

Haas Plumbing Supply, Co.
1010 Greenbrier Hill
Ironton, OH 45638-1010

Dateline   September 22, 200- ↓ 4

Letter
address   Ms. Charise Rossetti
Rt. 3, Box 49A
St. Albans, WV 25177-4900   ↓ 2

Salutation   Dear Ms. Rossetti   ↓ 2

All of the employees at Haas Plumbing Supply are pleased that you are doing an internship at our company headquarters. One of your duties will be to assist Mr. Joseph Burns in preparing the daily correspondence. We know that your training at Highview Community College has prepared you well for this task. ↓ 2

Body   Remember that the correspondence our customers receive from us is one of the ways that they evaluate our effectiveness as a business. Our outgoing letters must be as perfect as we can make them in layout, content, grammar, and punctuation. This will impress upon our customers that we have a company-wide commitment to excellence. ↓ 2

Enclosed is a sample company letter for your review. If you have any questions, contact me or your supervisor, Mr. Burns. Again, we are glad to have you working in our organization.   ↓ 2

Sincerely yours   ↓ 4   **Complimentary Close**

Writer's
Name   Gerald Haas
Title   President ↓ 2

Reference
initials   xx ↓ 2

Enclosure
notation   Enclosure

Block Letter with Open Punctuation

LESSON 120 | Assessment

SKILLBUILDING

120a
Warmup
Key each line twice SS;
DS between 2-line groups.

alphabet 1 Zack Q. Davis just left a very brief message with six nice poems.
figures 2 Jan bought 27 toys at $3.98 each, a total of $107.46 plus 5% tax.
adjacent reaches 3 We are going to build a store on a very quiet point west of here.
easy 4 Tod and I may visit the ancient chapel and then go to the island.
| 1 | 2 | 3 | 4 | 5 | 6 | 7 | 8 | 9 | 10 | 11 | 12 | 13 |

120b
Timed Writings
Key one 3' and one 5' writing.
Strive for good accuracy.

 all letters

gwam 3' | 5'

A successful organization tries to put the right employee in 4 | 2 | 51
the right job. The process of selecting employees raises many 8 | 5 | 53
questions that frequently are very perplexing. A key issue 12 | 7 | 56
that must be balanced deals with the rights of the individual 16 | 10 | 58
who is seeking a position and the rights of the organization that 21 | 12 | 61
is hiring a person to fill a position. Laws specify the types of 25 | 15 | 64
information that can be asked in the hiring process to ensure 29 | 18 | 66
that bias is not a factor in hiring. However, most firms do 33 | 20 | 69
strive to be fair in the hiring process. The issue that many 37 | 22 | 71
employers struggle with is how to determine who will be the 41 | 25 | 73
right employee for a particular job that is available. 45 | 27 | 76

The ability to predict an individual's performance on the 49 | 29 | 78
job is very important. Assessing an individual in the hiring 53 | 32 | 80
process to determine how he or she will perform on the job, 57 | 34 | 83
however, is a very difficult task. Most techniques measure the 61 | 37 | 85
potential or the way that a person can perform, but the way a 66 | 39 | 88
person can perform may differ drastically from the way the person 70 | 42 | 90
will perform when he or she is hired. Past performance on a job 74 | 45 | 93
may be the best measure of future performance, which is why firms 79 | 47 | 96
seek individuals with experience. 81 | 49 | 97

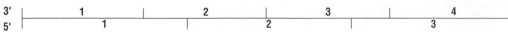

APPLICATIONS

120c
Assessment
Timed Production: 40'

On the signal to begin, key the documents in sequence. When time has been called, proofread all documents again and correct any errors you may have overlooked. Reprint if necessary.

Punctuation Style

Letters may use either open punctuation or mixed punctuation. **Open punctuation** uses no punctuation after the salutation or complimentary closing. **Mixed punctuation** adds a colon after the salutation and a comma after the complimentary closing.

Word Processing Tips for Letters

Dateline: Begin the dateline at about 2" as shown on the status line. Due to variations in fonts, you may not be able to work exactly at 2". You may also center the letter vertically on the page as long as there is at least 0.5" below the letterhead. (If longer letters are centered vertically, the dateline or letter address may print in the letterhead area.) Short letters look better centered on the page.

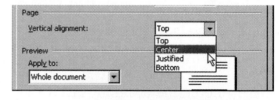

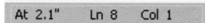

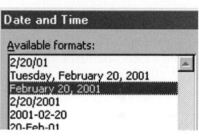

Use the Date and Time feature to insert the date. Use the Month, day, year format; do not select Update automatically (**Insert**, **Date and Time**).

Margins: Use default margins.

Reference Initials: *Word* automatically capitalizes your reference initials. To format them in lowercase, click the smart tag above your initials and choose **Undo Automatic Capitalization**.

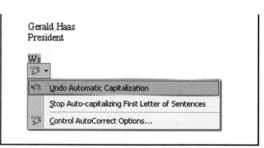

DRILL 1   BLOCK LETTER

1. Open **64Hightower** from the data files.

2. Add or adjust letter parts as needed, including the date.

3. Make the necessary adjustments so that all the lines begin at the left margin and the spacing between the letter parts is correct.

4. Position the date so that the letter is formatted attractively on the page. Be sure that if a letterhead were present, the dateline would not print in this area.

5. Save the letter as **64c-drill1**.

APPLICATIONS

64d-d1
Block Letter

1. Key the block letter on the previous page with open punctuation. Position the date line at approximately 2" (if necessary, deselect Update automatically).

2. Change the *xx* to your initials. Be sure that your initials are both lowercase.

3. Save the document as **64d-d1** and print.

Project, *continued*

Supplementary services. Meal and beverage services are frequently contracted, in addition to the transportation package. For example, box meals and cold drinks on the return flight after the game are usually a part of athletic charter flight packages. Equipment handling is also a part of the package. Tickets, convention packages, and other services provided usually are arranged through travel partners when they are part of a charter flight contract.

Market Analysis

The Southeast market was targeted first because of limited jet charter service available in the geographic area. Another determining factor was the intense interest in and support of athletics, particularly college football in the Southeast. Successful charters to games at other institutions created demand from those institutions for their travel schedule. The most profitable section of the market stems from the athletic connections.

Emerging markets. An emerging market is being created by women's athletic programs. This market is fueled by the current gender equity emphasis in college athletics. Court decisions and athletic regulations focus on equal treatment of men's and women's sports. Other emerging markets are the resort (particularly tennis, golf, beach, and ski resorts) and casino charters that are arranged by the resorts to bring in customers at a relatively low cost.

Competition. Only one other charter air service in the Southeast competes in the same niche market in which Pommery competes with all jet service. Several smaller charter air service companies try to compete with relatively large turboprop aircraft. The market clearly demands jet service. Pommery's market share is conservatively estimated to be 65 percent of the market in the Southeast.

Market expansion. The real challenge is to increase the size of this niche market through promotional activities and strategic alliances with travel partners. Pilot projects have produced promising results and are being evaluated as part of the growth strategy.

Pro Formas—2004–2006

Pro formas for 2004, 2005, and 2006 are based on the addition of two jet aircraft within the next 18 months. Revenue and expenses are in current dollars.

(Insert Pro Forma Statement of Income from 117-d6.)

Ownership

Five million common shares have been authorized. Of the authorized shares, 2,802,654 shares have been issued. Common stock ownership is diverse as noted in the following groupings.

(Insert the table from 117-d7 here.)

1. Format the following letter in block style with open punctuation. Since this letter is short, align it at the vertical center of the page.
2. Add your reference initials. Save as **64d-d2** and print.

Current date ↓ 4

Ms. Alice Noe
4723 Glacier Dr.
Selden, NY 11784-4723 ↓ 2

Dear Ms. Noe ↓ 2

Due to an unavoidable change in his schedule, Dr. Skyler will be unavailable to see patients during the first week in November. Since your next regularly scheduled appointment is during this week, we would like to give you the opportunity to reschedule your appointment for a later date. If rescheduling your appointment is impossible, we will be glad to make arrangements for you to see one of the other physicians in the medical group. ↓ 2

We apologize for any inconvenience. Please call our office at 555-0102 as soon as possible to reschedule your appointment. ↓ 2

Sincerely yours ↓ 4

Frederick Limerick
Office Manager ↓ 2

1. Format the letter in block style and open punctuation; center vertically. Send the letter from yourself to **Sylvia Gianchin, Redmon Publishers, 5280 Circle Pt., Long Beach, CA 90840-0792**.
2. Add letter parts and apply correct spacing. Do not include reference initials since you are both the originator and the typist. Save as **64d-d3** and print.

The Institute for Appalachian Studies will be having a seminar this spring entitled "Women of the Mountains". Elizabeth Sugerfoot, author of *Rural Life in Modern Appalachia*, will be our keynote speaker, and we know that the attendees will be clamoring for her exciting book. Enclosed is our purchase order with shipping instructions for 100 copies.

If you have questions regarding this order, please call me between 10 a.m. and 2 p.m. on Thursday or Friday. We will need these books delivered to the convention center during the first week of December. The center will be able to store them until the seminar, but they will not have storage space available before the first week in December.

Sincerely yours

Student Name, Coordinator

Pommery Air Service, Inc.
Business Plan

Pommery Air Service, Inc. (Pommery), since it was founded as a Delaware corporation in January 1999, has operated as a niche player in the charter air segment of the airline industry.

Industry

Three distinct segments comprise the charter air service industry:

- Small, local charter operations designed to provide point-to-point transportation for groups of fewer than 20 people in turboprop aircraft.

- Occasional charter flights provided by major passenger airlines.

- Small niche markets that target specific types of clientele.

Pommery operates exclusively in the third segment of the industry, offering contract charter flights and event charter flights. The overall charter air service industry is highly competitive. The most intensive competition exists in the other two segments of the charter air service. Pommery's board of directors and management agree that Pommery cannot and should not try to compete with the major passenger airlines for numerous reasons. They also agree that Pommery cannot compete with the small, local charter services because of the cost structure involved in providing jet air service exclusively.

The Service

Pommery provides event charter flights and contract charter flights throughout the United States. About 85 percent of the flights originate east of the Mississippi River, and almost 65 percent of flights originate in the Southeast.

Event charter flights. These flights are called event charters because they exist to transport passengers to attend specific events that are occurring. The range of events spans from those that occur one time or once in a significant period of time to regularly scheduled events. Examples of one-time events include charters to attend Olympic events, Mardi Gras, or a world-class art exhibition or musical production.

Seasonal events are those that occur regularly during a specified period of time. Athletic events comprise a high percentage of seasonal events. Charter flights to a ski resort or to a nearby city on weekends during the season to watch professional football, basketball, or baseball games would be an example. The flight is made available to a number of participating travel agency partners who reserve a number of seats on these charter flights for their clientele.

Regularly scheduled charters include special packages (usually weekends) to fixed destinations such as Las Vegas, a Gulf Coast casino and resort, or a country music/golf weekend in Myrtle Beach. These events are generally marketed through participating travel agency partners.

Contract charter flights. Contract charter flights often overlap with event charter flights. The primary difference is that the contract charter flights are with specific organizations or individuals. For example, a contract may be issued with an athletic department to take its football team and band to a game. The contract is with that athletic department. On the other hand, an event charter flight may go to the same football game with passengers from several travel agency partners and an alumni group.

Companies also use charter flights to take groups to conventions, meetings, and other business activities. Travel agencies often contract for charter flights between destinations on vacation packages.

LESSON 65 · Block Letter with Special Letter Parts

SKILLBUILDING

65a
Warmup
Key each line twice SS.

alphabet	1	The dizzy boxer's mad opponent jabbed quickly with his fat glove.
figures	2	I received 128 books, 7,349 magazines, and 560 newspapers yearly.
1st/2nd fingers	3	Prepare for the future by studying, working, and playing at home.
shift key	4	Mr. Sam Keatley gave the letters and memos to Ms. Charlene Jones.

| 1 | 2 | 3 | 4 | 5 | 6 | 7 | 8 | 9 | 10 | 11 | 12 | 13 |

65b
Skillbuilding
Key each group 3 times; work at a controlled rate.

double letters	5	Janna allowed me to borrow her oval office to answer my messages.
	6	Cobb swallowed the big blue pills with a tall glass of green tea.
	7	Will you commit some time this summer to vacuum for Miss Ferraez?
direct reaches	8	June and I received a number of calls from NYCE Mutuals Thursday.
	9	The brave youngster doubts his cute brown bunny can run and jump.
	10	Bryce bragged about his decision to build huge muscles by summer.
adjacent reaches	11	Yulana was to polish the three silver trays, sweep, and mop well.
	12	Some of the people hoped to quit working by three this afternoon.
	13	Polly was quick to offer her opinions and to make fast decisions.

COMMUNICATION

65c
Compose Journal Entry

1. In a new document, key your name at the left margin and insert the date using the Date and Time feature on the line below. Compose a paragraph that answers the following questions:

   - Why do you think business letters include the date at the beginning of the letter?
   - Why would companies require a common style for business letters, i.e., block letter style with open punctuation?
   - What personal business letters will you be required to write in the months ahead?
   - How do you think this module will assist you in preparing those letters?

2. Save as **65c** and print.

DOCUMENT DESIGN

65d

Special Letter Parts

In Lesson 64, you reviewed the standard letter parts that are present in each business letter. Other special features may be included, depending on the needs of the document. When special parts are added to a letter, they cause the letter to move down farther on the page. If you center the page vertically, always preview the letter to be sure that it is not positioned too high on the page.

Document 8
Report

Key the Pommery Business Plan, shown on the following pages, according to the directions below. Save as **117-119-d8**.

1. Format the leftbound report as follows:
   a. Spacing—SS; set spacing at 6 points following the paragraph
   b. Main heading—Heading 1 style, centered, main words initial cap
   c. Side headings—Heading 2 style
   d. Paragraph headings—Place above the paragraph, make each word initial cap, remove period, and apply Heading 3 style

2. Tables: Insert tables from Documents 6 and 7 as indicated.

3. Headers: Insert the page number at the right, followed by a ¾-point graphic line (bottom border) header on all pages except the first.

4. Footers: Insert a ¾-point graphic line (top border) footer followed by *Pommery Air Service, Inc.* at the left margin and the current date at the right margin. Place on all pages. Example:

Pommery Air Service, Inc.   July 3, 2004

Document 9
Table of Contents

1. Key a Table of Contents for the Pommery Business Plan. Apply Heading 1 style to the main heading. Key side headings at the left margin; indent for the paragraph headings. Indent the main heading of each table.

2. Include leader tabs and page numbers. Center the page number *ii* in the footer.

3. Save as **117-119-d9** and print.

Table of Contents

Industry 1

The Service 1
    Event charter flights 1
    Contract charter flights 2
    Supplementary services 2

Market Analysis 2
    Emerging markets 2
    Competition 3
    Market expansion 3

Pro Formas—2004-2006 3
    2004, 2005, and 2006 Pro Forma
    Statement of Income 3

Ownership 4
    Stock Ownership 4

Document 10
Title Page

Create an attractive title page using *WordArt*.

1. Insert the logo.

2. Insert a page border.

3. Use the current date.

4. Save as **117-119-d10**.

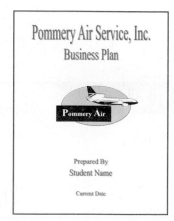

65d

An **attention line** is used to direct a letter to a specific individual, position, or department within an organization. It is keyed as the first line of the letter address. Whenever an attention line is used, the correct salutation is *Ladies and Gentlemen.*

> Attention Accounting Department
> Chou and Chou Furniture Company
> First St. and First Ave.
> Olympia, WA 99504-6480

A **subject line** provides the reader with a short description of the purpose of the letter. It is placed between the salutation and the body of the letter. Double-space before and after the subject line. The subject line may be keyed using initial caps or all caps. It may be preceded by the word *subject*.

> Dear Mr. Jones:
>
> Subject: Projected Sales Figures
>
> The sales figures for the first quarter have been released.

A **copy notation** is used to indicate that someone other than the receiver will get a copy of the letter. It is keyed a double space below the reference initials or the enclosure notation (if there is one). Key **c** to indicate copy; then press TAB and key the name(s).

> John Mastrangelo, President
>
> xx
>
> Enclosure
>
> c   Norman Elswick
>   Sheila Solari

A **postscript**, often used to emphasize information, is keyed a double space below the last notation in a letter. It is not necessary to begin with *PS*. Do not indent the postscript unless paragraphs in the letter are indented.

> John Mastrangelo, President
>
> xx
>
> Enclosure
>
> Use modified block for whenever

A **blind copy notation** indicates that a person(s) is receiving a copy of the letter without the addressee's knowledge. A blind copy notation is keyed a double space after the reference initials, enclosure notation, or copy notation (if any). The blind copy notation appears on copies, but not on the original.

> John Mastrangelo, President
>
> xx
>
> Enclosure
>
> bc   Norman Elswick
>   Sheila Solari

Appears on copies, but not on the original

Document 6
Table with Formulas

1. Merge Row 1 and increase height to .45". Key the title in 12-point, all caps, and bold.

2. Write a formula to calculate Operating Profit / Loss = (Operating Revenue – Operating Expense).

3. Write a formula to calculate Net Income / (Loss) = (Operating Profit – Non-Operating Expense).

4. Apply 15% shading to Row 1. Save as **117-119-d6**.

2004, 2005, AND 2006 PRO FORMA STATEMENT OF INCOME			
	2004	**2005**	**2006**
Operating Revenue	$44,438,400	$61,466,400	$78,874,400
Operating Expenses	41,144,600	53,190,000	68,898,400
Operating Profit/(Loss)			
Non-Operating Expense	671,200	709,800	1,673,600
Net Income/(Loss)			
Cost Per ASM	.1019	.0721	.0868
Yield	.1647	.1621	.1575
Operating Margin	7.4%	13.5%	12.6%

Document 7
Table with Sum Above and Decimal Tab

1. Merge Row 1 and increase height to .45". Key title in 12-point, all caps, and bold.

2. Use Sum Above to obtain the totals in Row 8.

3. Use a decimal tab to align the numbers in Column C.

4. Apply Table List 7 format; do not apply special formats to the last column. Save as **117-119-d7**.

STOCK OWNERSHIP		
Group	**Shares**	**% of Stock Issued**
Employees	586,268	20.9
Senior officers	353,146	12.6
Outside directors	651,700	23.3
Business community	640,000	22.8
Founders	571,540	20.4
Total		

65e-d1

Block Letter with Subject Line and Copy Notation

1. Format the following letter in block style with open punctuation. Use your judgment in centering the letter attractively on the page.

2. Add the subject line **Volusia Community Goals Conference—January 30**.

3. Send a copy of the letter to the lead facilitator mentioned in the letter.

4. Save as **65e-d1**. Print.

	words
January 10, 200-|The Honorable Alice Vinicki|P.O. Box 249|Volusia,	13
FL 32174-3852|Dear Senator Vinicki	20

Your positive response to deliver the keynote address at the Volusia — 34
Community Goals Conference on Saturday, January 30, was received — 47
with much excitement by the Goals Conference Planning Committee. — 60
Thank you, Senator Vinicki, for your commitment to this community — 74
effort. Mr. Roger Bourgeois, director of the United Planning Institute, — 88
is the lead facilitator of the goals conference and will introduce you at the — 104
opening session beginning at 9 a.m. in the Vinicki Exhibit Hall of — 117
the Volusia Convention Center. — 124

Hotel accommodations have been made for you at the Riverside Suites — 137
for Friday, January 29; confirmation is enclosed. Mr. Bourgeois and I — 151
will meet you at the hotel restaurant at 7:30 a.m. for breakfast and — 165
to escort you to the convention center. A copy of the conference program — 180
and an outline of the issues to be discussed in the various breakout — 194
groups are also enclosed for your review. — 202

We look forward to your address and to your being a key player in our — 216
goals conference. — 220

Respectfully yours|Ms. Le-An Nguyen, President|Chamber of Commerce| — 234
xx|Enclosures — 236

65e-d2

Block Letter with Subject Line and Blind Copy Notation

1. Format the following letter in block style with open punctuation. Center the letter vertically on the page.

2. Add an appropriate subject line. Save as **65e-d2** and print.

3. Add a blind copy notation for Carol Winstead and print the copy for Ms. Winstead.

January 10, 200-|Ms. Denise McWhorter|HandPrints, Inc.|	11
92 E. Cresswell Road|Selden, NY 11784|Dear Ms. McWhorter	24

Booth 24, your first choice, had been reserved for you — 35
for the annual craft fair on May 15-17. Your booth was ex- — 46
tremely popular last year, and we are very pleased to have you — 59
participate in the fair again this year. — 67

Our standard agreement from is inclosed. Please sign — 78
the form and return it to us by April 15. Your booths will — 90
have a large table and a minimum of two chair. If you need — 102
anything else for the booth please let us know prior to the — 114
opening of the fair. — 119

Sincerely|Ms. Jennifer A. Reed| resident|xx|Enclosure — 129

Pommery Facts

Pommery Air Service, Inc.

Headquarters
P.O. Box 8473
Hopkins, SC 29061-8473

(803) 555-0123
Fax (803) 555-0124

www.pommeryair.com

Mission Statement

Pommery Air Service Inc. is a charter air service headquartered in Hopkins, South Carolina. Pommery s mission is:

- To provide its charter customers with safe, reliable jet transportation, quality service, outstanding value, and low costs.

- To provide an environment for its employees that fosters teamwork and customer focus and rewards integrity and productivity.

- To deliver superior value to its shareholders.

The Company

Pommery Air Service, Inc., a Delaware corporation founded in January 1999, currently has a fleet of four 737 jet aircraft. Pommery provides air service to almost 60,000 passengers per month. The mix is almost equally divided among business trips, athletic functions, and leisure travel.

An experienced, highly competent management team leads Pommery Air Service, Inc. Management emphasizes teamwork, empowerment, and productivity. Employee stock options provide incentives to employees to focus on quality and profitability.

Pommery Air Service, Inc. became profitable in its tenth month of existence and continues to be profitable. The company operates as a lean, efficient organization. Costs per available seat mile (ASM) have dropped from 14 cents to 10 cents.

Yield per revenue passenger mile increased from 12 cents to 16 cents.

The Market

Pommery Air Service, Inc. provides charter flights to destinations throughout the United States. The primary market, however, is defined by origination point rather than destination point. Approximately 65 percent of all flights originate in the Southeast. The secondary market by origination point is the Northeast.

The Services

Pommery Air Service, Inc. provides two types of charter services: event charter flights and contract charter flights. Both event and contract charter flights include an array of services depending on the needs of the customer. Supplementary services available with both charter and event flights include: meal and beverage services; local transportation; event tickets; side trips; conference facilities, including logistical support; and a host of special activities.

The Strategy

Pommery Air Service, Inc. strives to become the dominant air charter service in the eastern United States. Pommery s core competencies involve providing safe, high-quality jet air services that are cost effective. All other services provided are designed to facilitate and enhance the continual development of the core competencies.

To implement this strategy, Pommery Air Service, Inc. must expand. Expansion requires the addition of two jet aircraft within 18 months.

65e-d3

Block Letter with Attention Line, Subject Line, and Copy Notation

1. Key the following letter in block letter style with open punctuation. Supply a complimentary closing.
2. Position letter attractively on the page. Save as **65e-d3**. Print.

	words
May 15, 200-|Attention Frequent Flyer Service Center|Atlanta	14
International Airport|P.O. Box 84410|Department 129|Atlanta, GA	27
30320-8441|Ladies and Gentlemen	33

Request for Redemption of Frequent Flyer Award	43

Please redeem an award of 30,000 miles from my frequent flyer account   57
#2521-70442. Award #D731 is being redeemed as a round-trip ticket to   71
Honolulu, Hawaii, with a departure on Thursday, August 15, and a return   84
on Monday, August 19, 200-. Flight information is listed below: 99

Thursday, August 15	**Monday, August 19**	106
Depart Jackson, Mississippi	Depart Honolulu, Hawaii	116
7:10 a.m.	6:05 p.m.	120
Flight #5315	Flight #178	125

Please mail a certificate to the business address listed on the letterhead.   140
Your agent, Azida Hamff, has instructed me to submit this certificate to   155
an airline agent by June 15 to receive my airline tickets. I will be sure to   168
follow these instructions and look forward to benefiting from my first fre-   183
quent flyer award.   189

Dr. Frances Hamilton, Professor|xx|bc Robert Heflin, Travel Department   203

65e-d4

Block Letter with Subject Line and Copy Notation

1. Key the following block letter for **Alexandria H. Skiwski, Technical Manager**.
2. Add any missing letter parts. Send a copy to **Todd West, Account Manager**.
3. Save as **65e-d4**. Print.

Current date | Mr. Jamie Kurman, Jr. | P.O. Box 7390 | Counderspot, PA   15
16315-0985 | Dear Mr. Kurman: | Scanner Recommendations   24

Your assessment, Mr. Kurman, is right on target. The payback period for a   39
scanner would be about six months. We are pleased to provide you with our   54
recommendations.   58

Your test generation software handles both text and graphics; therefore, an   73
intelligent OCR should be purchased. The enclosed analysis provides speci-   88
fications, price information, and our recommendations for both the scanner   103
and the software.   107

Please call us at 1-800-555-0139 to schedule a demonstration of the OCR   121
scanner. We look forward to hearing from you.   131

closing   149

Document 4
Mail Merge

1. Insert the **letterhead** file and use mail merge to create a letter to each member of the board of directors. Sign the letter from you, Administrative Assistant. Supply necessary letter parts.

2. Print the main document and the merged letters. Save the merged letters as **117-119-d4**.

Members of the Board of Directors:

Natalie Bass, Airline Consultant, RTA and Associates, 3829 Quincy Ave., Denver, CO 80237-2756

Herman Davis, Chief Financial Officer, Financial Securities, Inc., 3979 El Mundo, Houston, TX 64506-2877

Betsy Burge, President, Associated Travel Services, 3958 Highland Dr., Sterling, CO 80751-1211

Joseph Perkins, Senior Vice President, River Industries, 7463 St. Andrews, Dallas, TX 75205-2746

Kimberly Hess, Professor, Business Administration, Central University, 3744 Main St., Oakdale, LA 71463-5811

Body of Letter:

A copy of the Pommery Air Service Business Plan is enclosed. Please review the plan carefully and be ready to vote on final approval at the board meeting next Friday. Note that this item appears on the agenda sent to you last week.

If you have any questions prior to the meeting, please call me. All of the changes recommended by the board at the last meeting have been implemented in the plan.

Document 5
Newsletter

1. In a new document, change the top and side margins to .6".

2. Insert the **logo** file, as shown on the next page. Use *WordArt* to key the banner heading. Insert the same graphic line that appears in the letterhead. Increase the width of the graphic line so that it stretches across the page.

3. Insert a continuous section break.

4. Use a three-column format with a line between columns for the newsletter. Set the width of the columns as follows: Column 1, **1.5**"; Columns 2 and 3, **2.4**".

5. Key **Pommery Air Service, Inc.** in 12-point and bold. Key the remainder of the text in Column 1 in 10-point.

6. Key the text in Columns 2 and 3 in 11-point font; set the spacing to 6 points after paragraphs. Apply Heading 2 style to the headings. Use justify alignment.

7. Make adjustments to the banner heading, if needed to make the newsletter attractive; it should fit on one page.

8. Save as **117-119-d5**. Print.

LESSON 66 — Modified Block Letter Format

SKILLBUILDING

66a
Warmup
Key each line twice SS.

alphabet	1	The Lake View magazine of junior boxers may have clean equipment.
figures	2	She found 4,721 cats, 9,038 kittens, and 56 frightened bluebirds.
shift key	3	Mr. Paul Wilkes called Ms. Angie Pace on Friday, March 15 in OH.
double letters	4	Bill looked down the hall for a happy bookkeeper named Jill Mill.

| 1 | 2 | 3 | 4 | 5 | 6 | 7 | 8 | 9 | 10 | 11 | 12 | 13 |

66b
Timed Writing
Key one 3' writing and one 5' writing.

  all letters

	gwam	3'	5'
The technology used in offices today requires employees to	12	4	58
be flexible and to be willing to learn new ways to accomplish the	25	8	62
work that they do. Too often workers try to adapt the new	38	13	66
technology to the old procedures rather than modify the way they do	51	17	70
work to maximize the advantages of the technology. Although most	64	21	75
people think they can adapt to change very easily, the truth is	77	25	79
that change is very frustrating for most people. The majority of the	90	30	83
changes in offices caused by technology are difficult to make	103	34	88
because many things have to change at the same time. A change in	116	39	92
hardware or software requires changes in the way work is done as	129	43	97
well as learning to use the new software or hardware. These	141	47	101
changes might be easier to implement if they could be made	154	51	105
gradually rather than simultaneously.	161	54	107

3'	1	2	3	4
5'	1	2	3	

DOCUMENT DESIGN

66c

Modified Block Letter Review

The only difference between the block and modified block style letters is the placement of the dateline, complimentary close, and the writer's name and title. These lines begin at the horizontal center of the page. See the modified block letter on page 257. Note that it applies mixed punctuation.

Begin the letter by setting a left tab at the center of the page. Determine the center by dividing the line length by two (6" ÷ 2" = 3"). Set a left tab at 3".

Press TAB before keying the dateline, complimentary close, name, and title of the sender.

Note: If the letter has already been keyed and you are changing it to modified block format, select the entire document and then set the tab.

Document 1
Create Logo

1. Use the Oval shape from the Drawing toolbar to draw an oval approximately 2" wide.

2. Fill the oval with Gold color.

3. Insert a clip art of an airplane. Size the airplane to look approximately like the illustration below.

4. Use the text box or the rectangle to key the box containing *Pommery Air*. Make the box black and the lettering white. Increase the size of the *P* and *A* to 20 point, bold.

5. Group the three items (hold down the CTRL key as you click each item; then select **Group** from the Draw menu).

6. Change the layout of the drawing canvas so that it is in back of the text. Do this by clicking the canvas border to select it; then click the **Format** menu and select **Drawing Canvas**. Click the **Layout** tab and select **Behind text**. Save as **logo** and print.

Document 2
Create Letterhead

1. In a new document, change the side margins to 1" and the top margin to .5".

2. Insert the file **logo** (**Insert, File, Logo, Insert**).

3. Key the letterhead as shown below; use 11-point font and italics.

4. Insert a graphic line below the logo. Change the width of the line to 6.5" so that it stretches across the entire letterhead. (Select the line; click **Format, Horizontal Line, Width** 6.5".)

5. Save as **letterhead** and print.

P.O. Box 8473, Hopkins, SC 29061-8473
(803) 555-0123 fax (803) 555-0124
www.pommeryair.com

Document 3
Create Fax Cover Sheet

1. Open the Business Fax template. (In *Word 2003*, click **File** and then **New**, and then click **On my computer** in the Task Pane. Next, click the **Letters and Faxes** tab.)

2. Delete the picture of the facsimile machine (select the picture and press DELETE). Insert the Pommery logo in its place (**Insert, File, Logo, Insert**).

3. If a text box displays asking for the company name and address, delete it. Add the company address and phone number in the box.

4. Key the word **FACSIMILE** in a large bold print in the box. Arrange the logo, address, telephone number, and the word *FACSIMILE* attractively in the box.

5. Key the fax number in the From box at the right.

6. Save as **pommery business fax** and print.

Envelopes

Word will automatically copy the letter address from the letter on the screen to the envelope (**Tools, Letters and Mailings, Envelopes and Labels**).

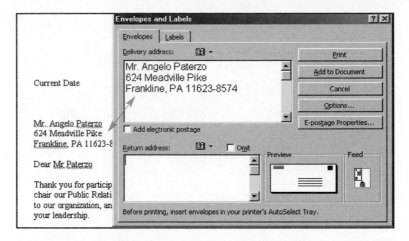

If the return address is not preprinted on the envelope, it is necessary to key a return address. When you complete the information for the envelope, you can either print the envelope, or choose **Add to Document** and print the envelope followed by the letter.

DRILL 1 — MODIFIED BLOCK LETTER

1. Open **64Hightower** from the data files.

2. Change the letter to modified block style with mixed punctuation (colon after the salutation and a comma after the complimentary closing). (Do not indent paragraphs.)

3. Position the date so that the letter is formatted attractively on the page. Be sure that if a letterhead were present, the dateline would not print in this area.

4. Add or adjust letter parts and spacing between parts as needed.

5. Save it as **66c-drill1**.

DRILL 2 — ENVELOPE

1. Open **66c-drill1**.

2. Generate an envelope for the letter.

3. Attach the envelope to the letter.

4. Save the document as **66c-drill2**.

APPLICATIONS

66d-d1
Modified Block Letter

1. Key the modified block letter on page 257 with mixed punctuation. Note that it includes an attention line, subject line, and blind copy notation.

2. Center the page vertically.

3. Save the letter as **66d-d1**. Preview the letter to be sure the vertical placement is appropriate if a letterhead were present. Print.

4. Add a blind copy notation for Mr. David, save, and reprint.

5. Create an envelope and attach it to the letter. Save the job again as **66d-d1a**.

Pommery Air Service, Inc.

- Integrate formatting and word processing skills.

LESSONS 117–119 | Business Plan

SKILLBUILDING

117–119a
Timed Writing
Take one 3' and one 5' writing.

all letters

An effective job search requires very careful planning and a   3   2 42
lot of hard work. Major decisions must be made about the type of   8   5 45
job, the size and the type of business, and the geographic area.   13   8 48
Once all of these basic decisions have been made, then the com-   17   10 50
plex task of locating the ideal job can begin. Some jobs are   21   13 53
listed in what is known as the open job market. These positions   25   15 55
are listed with placement offices of schools, placement agencies,   30   18 58
and they are advertised in newspapers or journals.   33   20 60

The open market is not the only source of jobs, however.   37   22 62
Some experts believe that almost two-thirds of all jobs are in   41   25 65
what is sometimes called the hidden job market. Networking is   46   27 67
the primary way to learn about jobs in the hidden job market.   50   30 70
Employees of a company, instructors, and members of professional   54   32 72
associations are some of the best contacts to tap the hidden job   58   35 75
market. Much time and effort are required to tap these sources.   63   38 77
But the hidden market often produces the best results.   66   40 80

```
3' |    1       |    2       |    3       |    4       |
5' |        1        |        2        |        3        |
```

Monica A. Carter
Communication Consultant
100 Main St.
Clinton, MS 39056-0503

July 11, 200-

Attention line Attention Office Manager
Professional Document Designs, Inc.
9345 Blackjack Blvd.
Kingwood, TX 77345-9345

Ladies and Gentlemen: **Mixed punctuation**

Subject line Subject: Modified Block Style Letters

Modified block format differs from block format in that the date, complimentary close, and the writer's name and title are keyed at the center point.

Paragraphs may be blocked, as this letter illustrates, or they may be indented 0.5" from the left margin. We suggest using block paragraphs so that an additional tab setting is not needed.

We recommend that you use modified block style only for those customers who request it. Otherwise, we urge you to use block format, which is more efficient. Please refer to the model documents in the enclosed *Communication Experts Format Guide*.

Sincerely,   **Mixed punctuation**

Monica A. Carter
Communication Consultant

xx

Enclosure

bc   Lyndon David, Account Manager   **Blind copy notation—not on original**

Modified Block Letter with Mixed Punctuation

Module 18: Checkpoint

Answer the questions below to see if you have mastered the content of this module.

1. Legal documents prepared for court are keyed on _____.
2. Legal documents contain a double ruling in the _____ margin and a single ruling in the _____ margin.
3. A(n) _____ form is completed by the person delivering the papers.
4. _____ contain information regarding the name, address, and purpose of the company, as well as the share structure.
5. Medical offices keep recorded notes of the patient's office visit called _____.
6. Patients sign a(n) _____, which allows a physician or medical facility to release information in their medical records.
7. A(n) _____ is a summary of your qualifications that is presented to potential employers.
8. A list of names, addresses, and telephone numbers of people who are willing to comment on you are called _____.
9. A letter indicating the job you are seeking, stating your key qualifications, and requesting an interview is called the _____ _____.
10. A(n) _____letter should be sent to companies that have not responded to a resume that was mailed one month before.

Performance Assessment

Document 1
Create Lease Form

Document 2
Fill in Lease Form

1. Key the heading on line 2", DS. Insert form fields as indicated. Protect the form, and save it as **Checkpoint18-d1** and print.
2. Fill in the form with the following information: (1) **Molnar Inc.**; (2) **June 26, 200-**; (3) **4 Griffin Dr.**; (4) **Harbor City**; (5) **Wayne**; (6) **Michigan**; (7) **5**; (8) **July 1, 200-**; (9) **June 30, 200-**; (10) **11:59 p.m.**; (11) **60,000.00**; (12) **1,000.00**; (13) **July 1, 200-**; (14) **first**.
3. Save it as **Checkpoint18-d2** and print.

LEASE AGREEMENT BETWEEN
HUTTON PROPERTY MANAGEMENT, LESSEE
AND
(ff1), LESSOR

This lease agreement was entered into on (**ff2—date**), between Hutton Property Management, lessee, and (**ff1**), lessor.

Lessor leases to lessee the premises located at (**ff3—address**), (**ff4—city**), (**ff5—county**) County, (**ff6—state**).

The term of this lease agreement is (**ff7—number**) years, beginning on (**ff8—date**), and terminating on (**ff9—date**), at (**ff10—time**). The total rent under this lease agreement is $(**ff11—amount**). Lessee shall pay lessor the above-specified amount in installments of $(**ff12—amount**) each month, beginning on (**ff13—date**), with succeeding payments due on the (**ff14**) day of each subsequent month during the term of the lease agreement.

_____   _____
Lessor   Lessee

66d-d2
Modified Block Letter

1. Key the following letter in modified block style with mixed punctuation.
2. Create a subject line. Use appropriate spacing and supply any missing letter parts.
3. Save the letter as **66d-d2** and print.

Sarah Atkinson | 1234 Elm Ln. | Bronx, NY 10466-1234

Thank you for your interest in our dogs. As you know, there are two varieties of collies. The rough-coated collie and the smooth-coated collie both make excellent family pets.

Our kennel, Quality Collies, regularly has rough-coated collies available. We generally have smooth-coated puppies available only in the spring.

Enclosed is a photograph of our most recent litter. You will certainly agree that these quadruplets are adorable. Contact our office (555-0198) Monday through Saturday to arrange a time for you to visit our kennel and see these exquisite puppies for yourself.

Sincerely yours | Sally Moss, Owner | Enclosure

66d-d3
Modified Block Letter

1. Open **66c-drill1**. Remove Mr. Bucciantini as the recipient of the letter. Instead, use the attention line **Marketing Department**.
2. Read the letter and create an appropriate subject line.
3. Add a blind copy notation to **Candice Kinneer** and **James O'Brien**.
4. Preview the letter. Change the font size to 11 point to make the letter fit on one page; assume the letterhead is 1.5" deep.
5. Save it as **66d-d3** and print. Did the letter fit on one page?

66d-d4
Modified Block Letter

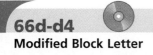

1. Open **66Global** from the data files.
2. Read the letter and create an appropriate subject line. Make adjustments so that the letter fits on one page.
3. Save the letter as **66d-d4**.
4. Generate an envelope and add it to the letter. Save it as **66d-d4a**.

116c-d1
Pleading Form with Table List of Trial Exhibits

1. Activate the **Superior Court** Pleading Wizard. Click **Finish** to close the Wizard, and then fill in the following List of Trial Exhibits. Use the table feature; remove borders and underline column heads.

2. Save as **116c-d1** and print.

LEE & DURAND, LLP
ATTORNEYS AT LAW
James W. Lee, Esq.
State Bar Number 202256
8578 Main St., Suite 202
Huntington Beach, CA 92646-1801
Telephone: (714) 555-0174
Attorneys for Plaintiffs

Donald Hurt, et al., Plaintiffs   vs.   Susan Reckless, et al., Defendants.
Case No. 01 CC05144   PLAINTIFFS' LIST OF TRIAL EXHIBITS

Exhibit Number	Description	Date Identified	Date Admitted
1	City of Costa Mesa Police Department Accident Report dated February 15, 200-		

Dated this 19th day of June, 200-

By _____
JAMES W. LEE
Attorneys for Plaintiffs

116c-d2
SOAP Note

1. Open **Soap Note Form** and save it as **116c-d2**.

2. Fill in the form with the following information: **Lucas, Steve**; **# 22653**; age **42**; allergies: **None known**; Meds: **Nexium**; T: **99.0**; P: **80**; R: **15**; B/P: **118/76**; C/O: **Pain left elbow**; Date: **4-10-xx**.

S	Pt injured left elbow two days ago in fall from rollerblades. Complains of pain on outside of elbow, superficial.
O	No inflammation; slight hematoma; limited ROM on left elbow FLEXION.
A	Treatment: lateral epicondyle 15 minute hot pack every day for a week and help with passive ROM. Ask pt to apply a hot pack at home once a day. Diagnosis: Lateral epicondylitis on left.
P	Pt will return twice a week to reduce pain and increase ROM.

Letters with Special Features

SKILLBUILDING

67a
Warmup
Key each line twice, striving for good technique.

alphabet	1	Liz Bowhanon moved very quickly and just played exciting defense.
figures	2	I fed 285 cats, 406 dogs, 157 birds, and 39 rabbits at a shelter.
1st/2nd fingers	3	Jimmy or Vick sent my fur hat this summer, but I did not need it.
easy	4	An authentic ivory tusk may be key to the ancient island rituals.

| 1 | 2 | 3 | 4 | 5 | 6 | 7 | 8 | 9 | 10 | 11 | 12 | 13 |

67b
Timed Writings
Key two 1' writings at your top rate. Key two 3' writings at a controlled rate working for good accuracy.

  all letters

gwam 1' | 3'

Technical, human, and conceptual skills are three types	12	4 35
of skills all supervisors are expected to have. The skills are	25	8 40
quite different, and they vary in importance depending on the level	37	12 44
of the supervisor in an organization. Technical skills	50	16 48
refer to knowing how to do the job. Human skills relate to	62	20 52
working with people and getting them to work as a team. Concep-	74	25 56
tual skills refer to the ability to see the big picture as well	87	29 60
as how all the parts fit together.	94	31 63

1' | 1 | 2 | 3 | 4 | 5 | 6 | 7 | 8 | 9 | 10 | 11 | 12 | 13 |
3' | 1 | 2 | 3 | 4 |

67c
Letter Part Drills

1. Key a 30" writing on each drill, keying each line as quickly as possible.

2. Press ENTER the correct number of times between letter parts.

3. DS and key the drill again as many times as possible before the time expires.

Drill A
Current date

4

Dr. J. K. Villivakkam
1000 Honey Tree Dr.
Starkville, MS 39759-1000

Dear Dr. Villivakkam:

Drill B
Sincerely,

4

Ms. Janice A. Minor
Sales Manager

xx

Enclosures

c   J. Thomas Dixon

SKILLBUILDING

116a
Warmup
Key each line twice SS.

alphabet	1	Di quickly won several junior prizes at the Foxburgh swim trials.
figures	2	From July 13 to 20, the extension numbers will be 45, 67, and 89.
shift/lock	3	Ms. Ing keyed the notations REGISTERED and CERTIFIED in ALL CAPS.
easy	4	Did he visit a city to handle the authentic enamel dish and bowl?

| 1 | 2 | 3 | 4 | 5 | 6 | 7 | 8 | 9 | 10 | 11 | 12 | 13 |

116b
Timed Writing
Key one 3' and one 5' writing.

	gwam	3'	5'
Individuals who conduct interviews often make snap judg-	4	2	41
ments. In fact, the decision to hire or not to hire an applicant	8	5	43
is usually made in the first five minutes of the interview. The	12	7	46
rest of the time is used to verify that the decision made was the	17	10	49
correct one. The wisdom of making a decision so early should be	21	13	51
questioned. When a quickly made decision is analyzed, generally	25	15	54
the result is that the decision is influenced heavily by the	30	18	56
first impression the person makes.	32	10	58
You can learn to make a good first impression in an inter-	36	21	60
view; all you have to do is be on time, dress appropriately,	40	24	62
shake hands firmly, establish eye contact, relax, smile, and show	44	26	65
that you have excellent communication skills. Doing all of this	48	29	68
may seem very difficult, but it really is not. Making a good	53	32	70
impression requires careful planning and many hours of practice.	57	34	73
Practice gives you the confidence you need to be able to do the	61	37	75
things that make an excellent impression.	64	38	77

3'	1	2	3	4
5'	1	2	3	

APPLICATIONS

116c
Assessment

On the signal to begin, key the documents in sequence. Check spelling after keying each document. Preview before printing. When time has been called, proofread all documents again; identify errors.

67d

Special Letter Parts

Additional special features help communicate clear and effective messages. Learn the purpose of these features.

A **reference line** such as Re: Order No. R1084 directs the reader to source documents or to files. Do not confuse a reference line with a subject line; the purposes are different. Key the reference line a DS below the letter address.

> Route 2, Box 332
> Natchez, MS 39120-1452
> **DS**
> Re: Order No. R1084
> **DS**
> Dear Mr. Allison
>
> Demand for two of the items (Stock Nos. 3856C and 9257D) that you ordered has been so great that we've had to place

A **mailing notation** such as FACSIMILE, OVERNIGHT, CERTIFIED, SPECIAL DELIVERY, or REGISTERED provides a record of how the letter was sent. Other notations such as CONFIDENTIAL or PERSONAL indicate how the recipient should treat the letter.

Key special notations in ALL CAPS at the left margin a DS below the dateline. On the envelope, key notations that affect postage right-aligned below the stamp (about line 1.3"). Key envelope notations that pertain to the recipient below the return address.

> April 2, 200- **DS**
> CONFIDENTIAL
> **DS**
> Dr. Spencer A. Blakeney
> Golden Triangle Clinic
> P.O. Box 10984
> Tullahoma, TN 37388-1267
>
> Dear Dr. Blakeney

> December 14, 200-
> **DS**
> CERTIFIED
> **DS**
> Attention Division 2 Manager
> Clinard Security Services
> 207 Hollyhill Ave.
> Downers Grove, IL 60515-0357
>
> Ladies and Gentlemen

> Dwight Reed
> 389 Highway 17
> Maysville, KY 41056-2332
>
>
>
> CERTIFIED
>
> Attention Division 2 Manager
> Clinard Security Services
> 207 Hollyhill Ave
> Downers Grove IL 60515-0357

Follow-Up Letters

Successful job hunters understand the importance of writing winning resumes and application letters and the value of writing follow-up letters. Key these letters on quality paper, use an acceptable letter style, and proofread to ensure an error-free document. Applicants may also write any or all of the following letters:

- Follow-up letter to companies that have not responded to the resume (mailed two weeks to one month later).
- Thank-you letter after the interview (mailed the day of or the day after the interview).
- Thank-you letter to references.
- Job acceptance or job refusal letters.

APPLICATIONS

114–115b-d1
Application Letter

1. Open **fisher-lthd** from the data files. Save it as **114-115b-d1**.
2. Position the insertion point at the end of the document. Key Scott's application letter, which is shown on p. 444, block style with open punctuation. Remove the hyperlink within the letter (right-click and select **Remove Hyperlink**). Do not key any sentences in bold. Save and print.

114–115b-d2
Thank-You Letter
1. Use the **fisher-lthd** file to create the letter.
2. Save and print.

Thank you for taking time to talk with me about the position as a junior graphic designer at *Financial News*.

I appreciated the comprehensive tour and the information you provided about the Graphic Design Department. This group of professionals is very fortunate to be equipped with the most up-to-date hardware and software and an outstanding staff development program. Consequently, your subscribers are the real winners.

Mr. Stanberry, I would like the opportunity to work at *Financial News* and to contribute to the popularity and success of this outstanding newspaper. I am eager to receive a call from you.

Sincerely | Scott T. Fisher

114–115b-d3
Reference Letter
1. Use the **fisher-lthd** file to create the letter to Dr. Michael Jenkins.
2. Save and print.

Dr. Michael Jenkins, Academic Advisor | College of Arts and Communication | Cother University | Mobile, AL 36617-1001

Thank you for writing the letter of recommendation for my application to *Financial News*. Mr. Stanberry called today and offered me the position as a junior graphic designer.

I appreciate very much the time that was devoted to writing such a detailed letter listing my accomplishments. Thank you for encouraging me to compete in the National Collegiate Graphic Design Association contest. That early involvement in the profession and my success were edges in my selection.

Dr. Jenkins, I look forward to sharing with you my first experiences as a graphic designer. Sincerely | Scott T. Fisher

To add notations to an envelope:

1. Click the **Add to Document** button; click **View**, **Print Layout** to switch to Print Layout View.

2. Position the insertion point on line 1.3". Click the **Right Align** button. Key the mailing notation, i.e., **SPECIAL DELIVERY**.

3. Position the insertion point on line 1.5". Key the recipient's notation—i.e., **CONFIDENTIAL**—at the left margin. Save and print.

DRILL 1   ENVELOPE WITH NOTATIONS

1. Open **66c-drill1**. Save as **67d-drill1**.

2. Generate an envelope for this letter.

3. In Print Layout View, key the mailing notation **SPECIAL DELIVERY** at the right on line 1.3".

4. Key the recipient notation **PERSONAL** on line 1.5" at the left margin.

5. Save and print the envelope only.

APPLICATIONS

67e-d1
Modified Block Letter with Notations

1. Format the modified block letter; use mixed punctuation.

2. Add the mailing notation **CERTIFIED** and the reference line **Re: Order No. S3835**.

3. Move the last paragraph to the end of the letter and format as a postscript; save as **67e-d1**. Generate an envelope. Save as **67e-d1a**.

	words
Current date|CERTIFIED|Dr. Carol Metzger, Instructor|Merritt Business	15
College|319 North Jackson St.|Jacksonville, FL 32256-0319|Dear Dr.	32
Metzger:	34

Your TIME+ personal manager software was shipped to you this morning by next-day air service. We realize that your time is valuable, and installing incorrect software is not a good use of your time. However, we are glad to learn that your students benefited from your demonstration of the software.

48 62 77 91 94

Easy-to-follow instructions for installing the new software over the current software are enclosed. You will also note on your copy of the invoice that you were billed originally for the TIME software. The TIME+ software is $99 more; however, we are pleased to provide it at no extra cost to you.

109 124 139 155

An additional bonus for choosing TIME+ is the monthly newsletter, *Managing Time with TIME+*. You should receive your first copy by the first of the month.

168 183 186

Sincerely yours,\|Ms. Veronica Scrivner\|Customer Service Manager\|xx\| Enclosure\|c Eric Shoemaker

198 204

67e-d2
Edit Letter

1. Open **67e-d1** and save it as **67e-d2**.

2. Reformat as a block letter with open punctuation.

3. Save and print the letter.

DOCUMENT DESIGN

114–115a
Application Letters

The purpose of an application letter is to obtain an interview. Application letters vary, depending on how you learned of the position. You want to show that your skills match the position requirements. A good strategy for writing an application letter is to: 1) establish a point of contact if possible, 2) specify the job you are seeking, 3) convey your key qualifications, 4) interpret your major qualifications in terms of employer benefits, and 5) request an interview.

Plain paper or personal stationery—never an employer's letterhead—may be used for an application letter. Your application letter must include your return address. You can create your own letterhead or use the personal business letter format that places your address immediately above the date. Block or modified block format may be used.

Scott T. Fisher

1001 Hogan St., Apt. 216A ● Mobile, AL 36617-1001 ● (251) 555-0103 ● sfisher@cu.edu

Current date

Establish a point of contact if possible

Mr. Coleman Stanberry
Financial News
706 Kentwood St.
Honolulu, HI 96822-6218

Dear Mr. Stanberry

State the job you are applying for

My bachelor's degree with double majors in graphic design and information technology and my graphic design work experience in the United States and Japan qualify me as a **junior graphic designer for your international newspaper**.

Convey key qualifications

As a result of my comprehensive four-year program, I am skilled in the latest Office suite as well as the current versions of desktop publishing and graphics programs. In addition, my **excellent research and writing skills** played a very important role in the Cother University Design Award I received last month. **Being able to locate the right resources and synthesize that data into useful information for your readers** is a priority I have practiced in my positions at the Cother University College Alumni Office and the Cother University Library.

State how the employer will benefit from your qualifications

My technical and communication skills were applied as well as I worked as the assistant director and producer of the *Cother University Alumni News*. **I understand well the importance of meeting deadlines and also producing a quality product that will increase newspaper sales**. Additionally, my intern experience in Japan provides me with a global view of international business and communication.

Request an interview

After you have reviewed the enclosed resume as well as my graphic design samples located on my Web page at http://www.netdoor.com/~sfisher, **I would look forward to discussing my qualifications and career opportunities with you** at *Financial News*.

Sincerely

Scott T. Fisher

Enclosure

1. Format the block letter; use open punctuation.
2. Compose an appropriate subject line and correct salutation.
3. Send a blind copy to the intern mentioned in the letter. Save as **67e-d3**.
4. Generate an envelope with the special notation. Save as **67e-d3a**.

words

Current date | CONFIDENTIAL | Merritt College | Attention Ms. 16

Louise Brown, Director | 750 East Wolfe Rd | Vienna, Wv 22

26105-0750 25

Thank you for the opportunity to participate as an 38
~one of your technology majors,~
employer in your internship program. Paul Zieger worked 90 56
~addition~
hours this summer and was an excellent ~edition~ to our 67
n
department. His final project was a interactive tutorial of 80

the Merritt College library. This tutorial provides an 91

electronic tour of the library, including the layout of the 103
~its holdings,~
library and specific directions on locating certain materials. 119

¶Paul has agreed to work (for us part-time) during the fall 130
are
semester. Our initial plans ~is~ for him to work with faculty 143
ing
in setting up and conduct private demonstrations for classes. 156

In addition he will write a second tutorial for the graduate 168

library. ¶ *Please send another excellent intern next semester.* 181

Sincerely | Daniel E. Romano, Director | Library Services | xx 192

1. Open **67e-d3** and save it as **67e-d4**.
2. Reformat as a modified block letter with mixed punctuation.
3. Reformat the last paragraph as a postscript.
4. Save and print the letter.

1. Compose a letter for **Paul Zieger** to **Merritt College** to the attention of **Registrar** requesting an official copy of his transcript. The transcript should be sent to **Mr. Daniel E. Romano, Director, Library Services, Merritt College**. See the address in Document 3. Paul was enrolled from June 2001 to present. Enclose $5 for the transcript.
2. Format the letter in block letter style with open punctuation. Center this short letter vertically on the page and add the special notation **FACSIMILE**.
3. Add the reference line **Re: Paul Zieger ID No. 55-43-2001**.

SCOTT T. FISHER

Temporary Address (May 30, 200-)
1001 Hogan St., Apt. 216A
Mobile, AL 36617-1001
(251) 555-0103
E-mail: sfisher@cu.edu

Permanent Address
583 Post Oak Rd.
Savannah, GA 31418-0583
(912) 555-0171
Web page: http://www.netdoor.com/~sfisher

CAREER OBJECTIVE	To obtain a graphic position with an opportunity to advance to a management position.
SUMMARY OF ACHIEVEMENTS	Bachelor's degree with double major in graphic design and information technology; certified in major software applications and one programming language. Related work experience in two organizations.
EDUCATION	**B.S. Graphic Design and Information Technology** (double major), Cother University, Mobile, Alabama. May 200-. GPA: 8.8/4.0.

—3.5" tab

SPECIAL SKILLS	Environments:	Microsoft Windows and Macintosh
	Software:	Microsoft Office 2003, QuarkXpress, PhotoShop, Freehand, Dreamweaver
	Certifications:	C++ and MOS (Microsoft Office 2003 Suite)
	Languages:	Java, JavaScript, Visual Basic Script, C++
	Keyboarding skills:	70 words per minute

EXPERIENCE	**Cother University Alumni Office**, Mobile, Alabama. Assistant editor and producer of the *Cother University Alumni News*, 2002 to present.

- Designed layout and production of six editions; met every publishing deadline.
- Received the "Cother University Design Award."
- Assisted editor in design of Alumni Office Web page (http://www.cu.edu/alumni/).

HONORS AND ACTIVITIES	Dean's Scholar (3.5 GPA or higher); President, Cother University Graphic Design Association; Recipient of "Cother University Leadership Award."
REFERENCES	Available upon request

68a
Warmup
Key each line twice SS.

alphabet 1 Frances Zwanka exited very quietly just prior to the big seminar.
figures 2 Please call 235-9167 or 294-3678 before 10:45 a.m. on January 18.
adjacent reaches 3 Louis, Sadi, Art, and a few other people were going to a concert.
easy 4 Vivian may go with a neighbor or with me to work on an amendment.
| 1 | 2 | 3 | 4 | 5 | 6 | 7 | 8 | 9 | 10 | 11 | 12 | 13 |

68b
Proofreading

1. Open **68b** from the data files and print.

2. Compare the printed letter to the source copy shown below. Mark any errors using the proofreaders' marks on page REF3.

3. Make the marked corrections; save as **68b-revised** and print. Submit the marked copy and the corrected printout to your instructor.

January 23, 200-

                 Press ENTER 4 times

Ms. Audra Meaux
2689 Marsalis Ln.
Hot Springs, AR 71913-0345

Dear Ms. Meaux

Thank you for agreeing to serve as chair of the Hospitality Committee for the National Technology Association Convention on April 3-6 in Phoenix, Arizona.

The enclosed guidelines outline the responsibilities and timelines of the Hospitality Committee. Please read them carefully and call me at (602) 555-0137 if you have any questions. You will need about 25 individuals to work with you on this committee. After you have organized this group, please mail me a complete roster including names, addresses, phone and fax numbers, and e-mail addresses.

Ms. Meaux, thank you for your professionalism and willingness to serve.

Sincerely   **Press ENTER 4 times**

Ryan Messamore
Vice President of Sales

xx

Enclosure

COMMUNICATION

113a
Creating Resumes

A **resume** is a summary of your qualifications; it is the primary basis for the interviewer's decision to invite you for an interview. Prior to preparing a resume, complete a self-analysis, identifying your career goals and job qualifications. Most resumes contain some or all of the following:

- **Identifying information:** Your name, telephone number, address, e-mail address, and Internet address. Students may need to list both a temporary and a permanent address.
- **Career objective:** The type of position you are seeking. Let the employer know you have a specific career goal.
- **Summary of achievements:** Summary of your most important achievements, strengths, or unique skills.
- **Education:** Diplomas or degrees earned, schools attended, and dates. Include majors and grade-point averages when it is to your advantage to do so.
- **Experience:** Job titles, employers, dates of employment, a brief description of the positions, and major achievements. Emphasize achievements rather than activities. Use active voice and concrete language; for example, *Handle an average of 200 customer orders a week*. List information in the same order for each position.
- **Honors and activities:** Specific examples of leadership potential and commitment.
- **References:** Generally do not include references on your resume. On a separate sheet of paper, list the names, addresses, and telephone numbers of several people who are willing to provide a reference for you. Use former employers, school advisors, former instructors, or a friend who is working in the field. Obtain their permission before you list them. Take the list with you to an interview.

Items within the sections of the resume are arranged in reverse chronological order (most recent experiences listed first). Which section is presented first? From your self-analysis, you will determine which one of your qualifications is the strongest. If work experience is stronger than education, present work experience first. A recent college graduate would present education first.

A major consideration in preparing an effective resume is the overall attractiveness of the resume. Use high-quality paper and print it on a laser printer using effective layout design that will allow your resume to appear professionally created.

Applicants may also submit resumes electronically by posting to corporate Web pages, personal Web pages, or job banks on the Internet. Saving the document as a Web page allows you to view your resume as it will appear in a Web browser.

APPLICATIONS

113b-d1
Resume

1. In a new document, change the side margins to 1" and key the resume on the following page.
2. Select Arial for the Identification section and the headings. Select Times New Roman for the body. Use 11-point font so that it will fit on one page.
3. Format the body as a 2-column table. Set a second tab in Column 2 for about 3.5".
4. Save as **resume**. Save it again as a Web page. View the resume using your browser.
5. Open the *Word* document **resume**. Remove the hyperlinks to the e-mail and Web page addresses since you will print this resume (right-click and select **Remove Hyperlink**). Save again and print.

113b-d2
Resume

Look for an ad or job description for a position for which you would qualify; then use the guidelines above to write a resume for the position. Save it as **113b-d2**.

Two-Page Letters

Letters that are more than one page in length require special layout considerations. Use letterhead paper only for the first page. For additional pages, use plain paper that matches the letterhead in quality and color. Be sure that there are at least two lines of text from the final paragraph of the body of the letter on the last page with the closing lines.

Follow these steps to format multipage letters:

1. Position the date on the first page approximately 2" from the top of the page or 0.5" below the letterhead.

2. On the second and following pages, use a 1" top margin and the same side margins as the rest of the letter.

3. Create a header for the second and following pages (suppress the header on the first page, click the **Page Setup** button on the Header and Footer toolbar, and select **Different first page** in the Page Setup dialog box).

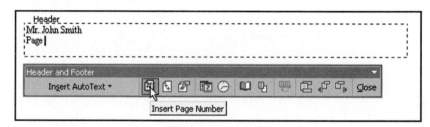

4. At the left margin of the header box, key the name of the recipient and press ENTER.

5. Key the word **Page** and space; then use the automatic page numbering feature on the Header and Footer toolbar to insert the page number and press ENTER.

6. Insert the date and press ENTER to leave a blank line between the header and the body of the letter.

> Mr. Jay Bloss
> Page 2
> October 10, 200-
>
> a reply by the end of the week will give us ample time to process your request.

Correct style. At least two lines of the last paragraph are on the page.

1. Open **68Collins** from the data files.

2. Add standard letter parts and adjust spacing as needed. Position the date at approximately 2". Change the font to 12-point Times New Roman.

3. Add an appropriate header for the second page and suppress it on the first page. Be sure the font matches the letter.

4. Add a copy notation to **Susan Wyman**. Note that the letter ends with a postscript.

5. Save the letter as **68c-drill1**.

112c-d3
Completing a Consent for Release of Information Form

1. Open **Release of Information Form**. Save it as **112c-d3**.

2. Fill in the form using the following information:

   I, **Hector Martinez**,

   ☒ receive information from

   NAME: **Dr. Phillip Simpson**

   AGENCY: **Blue River Medical Group**

   ADDRESS: **9062 Decanteur Ave.**

   CITY: **Sterling Heights, MI 48310**

   Information concerns 1. **Louisa Martinez, daughter**; 2. **Richard Martinez, son**

   Information requested is ☒ All of the above

   Release of information will terminate on (**insert a date that is approximately 60 days from the current date**)

3. Save and print.

112c-d4
Completing a Disclosure Statement

TIP
It may be helpful to display the gridlines in the table when filling in the amounts (**Format, Borders and Shading, Borders** tab, **Grid**).

1. Open **Disclosure Statement** and save it as **112c-d4**.

2. Fill in the form using the following information:

   Patient: **Patricia Cheshire**

   Parents or Responsible Party: **Susana Cheshire, mother**

   Address: **67 Raven Ln., Irvine, CA 92623**

3. Unprotect the form and insert the following information in the table. Use a decimal tab to align the numbers in Column B. Use the math feature to calculate the total. The total should display with a dollar sign and two decimal places.

PROFESSIONAL FEE	
Limited Treatment:	$2,015.00
Phase I:	525.00
Phase II:	400.00
Full Treatment (Single Phase):	
Retainer Fee:	
Retainer Visit Fee:	
Finance Charge:	
Total	

4. Protect the form again and insert the following information in the ¶ below the table.

   Initial payment: **$1,440.00**; Balance: **$1,500.00**; payable at **$500.00** per month for **three** months. Retainer fee **$220.00** is due on debanding . . .

5. Check to see that the page breaks in an appropriate place. Save and print.

68d-d1
Two-Page Letter

1. Key the following two-page letter in block style.

2. Add the necessary letter parts. Create a header for the second page; use the Search Committee name in the header. Add the subject line **Assistant Professor of Curriculum Position**.

3. Save the letter as **68d-d1** and print.

Current Date | Attention Chairperson | College of Education Search Committee | Lynn State University | 323 University Ave. | Albuquerque, NM 87105-1742

It is my pleasure to apply for the position of Assistant Professor as advertised in the *Bulletin of Educational Positions.* As you can see from my enclosed resume, I have extensive experience in the area of curriculum design and instruction. I am excited about the prospect of using my knowledge and experience in this area to strengthen your program.

In my current position with the State Board of Education, I am responsible for overseeing the curriculum development for all Business Education programs at the secondary level throughout the state. I meet regularly with secondary teachers, content specialists, advisory boards, industry representatives, and state legislators. These contacts provide me with a variety of viewpoints concerning the construction of curriculum. Without considering all of the available sources of input, it would be impossible to develop a curriculum that would address the needs of today's workforce.

In addition to supervising curriculum development, during the past five years I have been loaned to three other states to help with their curriculum development. Each assignment gave me the opportunity to use and expand my expertise in my field. These experiences in particular are significant when considering the knowledge base that I can bring to the classroom.

I also have classroom experience at the secondary level. After obtaining my bachelor's degree, I taught Business Education for Finton Public Schools. During the five years that I held this position, I completed both my master's and doctorate degrees. After completing these degrees, I taught for two years at Shadowland Community College. These invaluable experiences of developing curriculum for and teaching in both secondary and postsecondary schools will make it possible for me to personally guide the future teachers being trained by Lynn State University to a point where they are prepared to excel at whatever teaching level they seek.

I look forward to hearing from you to discuss your faculty needs. I can be reached at 505-555-0199 Monday through Friday. Your advertised position and my curriculum development experiences certainly appear to be a good fit. | Sincerely yours | Ms. Betheny Isner | Enclosure

112c-d2
Disclosure Statement

1. In a new document, change the side margins to 1" and top margin to .6" and insert the **letterhead** file.

2. Key the form shown below. Use text form fields (*tff*) as needed, and apply Table List 7 format to the table.

3. Change the height of Row 1 to .45" and center the heading. Change the height of Rows 2–9 to .3" and center the text vertically in the cells.

4. Place a heading at the top of the second page as follows:
   DISCLOSURE STATEMENT/CONSENT TO TREATMENT
   Page 2
   Insert current date code

5. Protect the form and save it as **Disclosure Statement**.

Insert medical letterhead file here

DISCLOSURE STATEMENT AND CONSENT TO TREATMENT

Federal law requires this disclosure statement pursuant to Regulation Z, Truth-in-Lending Act for Professional Services

Confirmation of arrangements for the orthodontic management of:

Patient: (*tff*)

Parents or Responsible Party: (*tff*)

Address: (*tff*)

FINANCIAL ARRANGEMENTS:

The undersigned hereby agrees to the following financial arrangements:

PROFESSIONAL FEE
Limited Treatment:
Phase I:
Phase II:
Full Treatment (Single Phase):
Retainer Fee:
Retainer Visit Fee:
Finance Charge:
Total

Initial payment of (*tff*) is due on the first treatment appointment. Balance of (*tff*) is payable at (*tff*) per month for (*tff*) months. Budgeting of the fee is for your convenience. Monthly remittance is not a monthly fee. Retainer fee of (*tff*) is due on debanding appointment.

A service charge of 5% per month will be made on all past due balances. If it becomes necessary to send your account to collection, the undersigned agrees to pay all costs and expenses including a reasonable attorney's fee.

I/We hereby certify we discussed the content of this contract with the physician and that I/we give INFORMED CONSENT for all necessary orthodontic treatment and related services.

| Patient Signature | Parent Signature | Physician Signature | Date |

SKILLBUILDING

69a
Warmup
Key each line twice.

alphabet	1	Mixon plays great jazz with a quintet at a club five days a week.
fig/sym	2	Errors were found on page 389 (line #17) and page 460 (line #25).
direct reach	3	Brad and Cec had a great lunch and much fun with many youngsters.
easy	4	The city may pay for half of the maps, and Jake may pay for half.

| 1 | 2 | 3 | 4 | 5 | 6 | 7 | 8 | 9 | 10 | 11 | 12 | 13 |

69b
Technique Builder

1. Key the following heading as follows:
   a. Press CTRL + 2 to change to DS.
   b. Press CAPS LOCK key. Press CTRL + B to bold. Key **TO:**.
   c. Press CAPS LOCK key to turn off caps lock.
   d. Press CTRL + B to turn off bold.
   e. Repeat Steps a-e for remaining lines. Press CTRL + 1 to change to SS.
2. Try to complete in 30' or less. Key as many times as possible.

TO:	Jason Smith
FROM:	Khalilah Palmer
DATE:	(Enter date command)
SUBJECT:	Keying Efficiency

COMMUNICATION

69c
Proofread and Edit Text

1. Key the following paragraphs, correcting the marked revisions. Locate the three errors in word choice. For example, *to* may be incorrectly keyed for *too*.
2. Save as **69c** and print.

All form letters have been reviewed, revised, and approved for general use. You will receive a new copy within a few days of the correspondence manual.

Special thanks are do each of you for your help on this important project. The consultants were most complementary of the excellent corporation they received and of the quality of your suggestions for improving the letters.

1. In a new document, change the side margins to 1", change the top and bottom margins to .5", and insert the **letterhead** file.

2. Key the form shown below. Use text form fields (*tff*) and checkboxes as needed. The form should fit on one page. Save as **Release of Information Form**; print.

Insert medical letterhead file here

CONSENT FOR RELEASE OF INFORMATION

I, (*tff*) , hereby authorize Christina Greene, Psy. D. to:

☐ disclose information to

☐ receive information from

NAME: (*tff*)

AGENCY: (*tff*)

ADDRESS: (*tff*)

CITY: (*tff*)   STATE: (*tff*)   ZIP CODE: (*tff*)

This information concerns myself or the following minors of whom I am parent or guardian:

1. (*tff*)

2. (*tff*)

The information to be disclosed/requested is to be used for professional purposes only.

The information to be disclosed/requested includes the following specific items:

☐ Treatment plan   ☐ Treatment progress notes

☐ Diagnosis   ☐ Other information

☐ Opinion & recommendation (specify) _____

☐ All of the above

I understand this information will be kept confidential and disclosed only to the persons named on this release or to law enforcement as required by law (Illinois Code 16-1619) or other applicable Illinois laws, or upon appropriate court order.

Consent termination date: This release of information will remain in effect for the duration of treatment or terminate on (*tff*), a date that has been mutually agreed upon by the psychologist and myself.

Client: _____   Witness: _____   Date: _____

Memorandums

Memos, which are less formal than letters, are used for correspondence within an organization. Memos are generally prepared on plain paper and sent in plain or interoffice envelopes.

To format a memo:

1. Begin the heading approximately 2" from the top of the page. DS the heading lines and key the heading words in all caps and bold.

2. Press TAB once or twice after each heading to align the text that follows each item.

3. Press ENTER once after the last heading, change the line spacing to single, and key the body of the memo with a double space between paragraphs.

4. Press ENTER twice after the last line of the body and key the reference initials and any other notations such as attachment, enclosure, or copy notation.

Distribution Lists

When memos are sent to more than one person, key the names separated by commas after the word **TO:** or in a list. Generally, names should be in alphabetical order by last name. Some organizations prefer the names in order of rank.

TO: Maxine Cagiano, Benjamin Morgan   or   **TO:** Maxine Cagiano
                                                          Benjamin Morgan
                                                           Cynthia Yost

When the memo is being sent to a large number of people, use a distribution list.

1. After the heading word **TO:**, key a reference to a distribution list at the end of the memo.

2. At the end of the memo, key the words **Distribution list** or the name of the group (for example, *Project Managers*) followed by a colon.

3. TAB to begin the first name. Key each name on a separate line (aligned at the tab) in alphabetical order.

Distribution list:
     Maxine Cagiano
     Benjamin Morgan
     Naomi Peyton
     Heather Lewis
     Cynthia Yost

Two-Page Memorandums

If a memo is more than a single page, follow the same guidelines for long letters.

1. Leave a 1" top margin on second and succeeding pages.

2. Create a header that includes the recipient's name, page number, and date on separate lines, and suppress the header on the first page.

3. Press ENTER once after the date to leave a blank line between the header and the body of the memo.

SKILLBUILDING

112a
Warmup
Key each line twice SS.

1 gait focal appendix bile colic pedal hernia dyspnea anorexia drug
2 test arid uria tissue benign adenitis renal jaundice sinus apical
3 cystitis dilate vital scan penicillin sputum pelvic saline tonsil
4 tubal flap aural chronic mucosa mitral nodes sputum codeine femur

| 1 | 2 | 3 | 4 | 5 | 6 | 7 | 8 | 9 | 10 | 11 | 12 | 13 |

DOCUMENT DESIGN

112b

Consent for Release of Information Form

Medical records are the property of the physician. He/she is legally and ethically obligated to keep them confidential unless a Release of Information form has been signed by the patient. In some cases, insurance companies and federal and state agencies are exceptions to the right of privacy and privileged communication. This means they may request medical information even without the consent of the patient.

Disclosure Statement

The Truth-in-Lending Act, also known as Regulation Z of the Consumer Protection Act, covers credit agreements that involve more than four payments. This act requires that the physician and patient discuss, sign, and retain copies of a disclosure statement, which is a written description of the agreed terms of payment.

69e-d1
Memorandum with Distribution List

1. Key the following memo, but do not key the letterhead. Save as **69e-d1**.

2. Print a copy for each person on the list. Place a check mark next to the name of each person who will receive the memo. (*Example*: Place a check mark next to Samuel Gibbs on the first copy, next to Angela Sansing on the second copy, etc.)

2" top margin

Acme Technologies

Interoffice Memo

TO: Distribution List
                                    DS
FROM: Acme Mexican-American Achievers Committee
                                    DS
DATE: April 15, 200-
                          DS
SUBJECT: Mexican-American Achievers
                                    DS

Default side margins

For the past three years Acme has nominated a deserving Mexican-American staff member to be honored as a Mexican-American Achiever. This career development program seeks to expose, educate, and enlighten young adults to various opportunities found in the corporate sector. Adult Mexican-American Achievers serve as volunteer counselors, tutors, confidants, and advisors to youth.

Mara Pena was the first recipient for Acme. Lydia Valquez was the recipient the second year, and last year Acme sponsored an At Large participant chosen by the Youth in Business Association (YBA). This year we should like to nominate an Acme staff member.

The nominating criteria established by the YBA are as follows:

• A current Acme employee who has been employed for at least two years.

• An individual who is willing to volunteer at least one year of service to the program.

• An individual recently completing a special leadership role by representing our company on a community service project.

Please make your nomination on the attached form and forward it to Human Resources by **Thursday, April 20**.
                                    DS
xx
      DS
Attachment

Distribution List:
Tab ──▶ Samuel Gibbs
        Angela Sansing
        Collin Sheridan
        Joan Wang

---

1. Open **Soap Note Form** and fill in the form with the information for each document. NOTE: *Pt* is a common abbreviation for patient. Spell out the word "patient" when keying the notes.

2. Save Document 3 as **111b-d3** and Document 4 as **111b-d4**; print.

Field Names	Document 3	Document 4
Last Name	Jones	Pham
First Name	Sarah	Loriana
Patient No.	10680	31048
Age	20	27
Allergies	None	Bee stings
Meds	None	None
T	99.5	98.5
P	84	62
R	20	15
B/P	130/87	112/72
C/O	Cough	Pain in right knee
Date	6/9/--	6/21/--

DOCUMENT 3 SOAP NOTE BODY

S	Pt complains of cough and head congestion for the past 48 hours, shortness of breath, lethargy, and low appetite.
O	Pt coughing up green sputum. Lungs clear, ears clear. Lymph nodes enlarged bilateral neck. Bilateral tonsils enlarged. CXR-WNL, PPD negative. CBC—elevated white count.
A	Acute upper respiratory infection.
P	Pt is to take 333 Mg. E-Mycin, one tablet every 8 hours for one week. Increase fluids, increase rest. Pt is to remain off from work for 3 days. Recheck in one week or sooner, if needed.

DOCUMENT 4 SOAP NOTE BODY

S	Pt complains of pain in the right knee; tripped and fell 6/17/--.
O	Inflammation/hematoma on right anterior medial patella; decreased ROM right knee, with flexion, extension.
A	Diagnosis: Pre-patellar bursitis. Treatment: R.I.C.E. on right patellar anterior medial with ice pack twice a day for 4-6 weeks. Stay off right leg. ADL: rest knee; ice right anterior knee morn/night; elevate.
P	Stay off right leg. Rest; ice morn/night; elevate. Week 1: decrease pain; week 2: increase ROM.

1. Key the two-page memo. Use the following information for the heading:

   TO: Electronic Presentations Class; FROM: Linda T. Walters, Instructor; DATE: Current date; SUBJECT: Library Research

2. DS between numbered items.

3. Add an appropriate second-page header. Save as **69e-d2** and print.

The library research assignment described in this memo comprises 10 percent of your total grade. Read the directions carefully, follow the enclosed format, and mark the deadline on your calendar. If you have questions about this assignment, please call me at my office or e-mail me via the class Web page.

Prepare a critical review of five recent (2000 to present) journal articles (not the popular press) related to the following electronic presentation issues.

1. What design rules should be considered in creating electronic presentations?

2. What delivery skills are needed when using electronic presentation software?

3. What copyright issues should be considered when creating electronic presentations?

4. What advanced features of *PowerPoint* are available to make a powerful electronic presentation?

5. What speaking skills are necessary when delivering a presentation (with or without visual aids)?

6. What helpful advice would be given to new presenters who will design their own presentations?

7. What resources are available to assist the presentation designer?

See the Web sites provided in the syllabus. Your online databases at the University Library are excellent. For many articles, you are able to choose full- text articles with full citations. Be sure to choose a combination of journals and magazines. Beware of Web sites that are not scholarly but rather someone's opinion.

Discuss, summarize, and evaluate each article separately. Submit this assignment in a three-ring folder—not notebook. Be sure you have labeled the outside of the folder with your name and the title *Library Research.* Mail to Linda T. Walters, 307 Springdale Drive, Ellisville, MS 39437. This assignment must be postmarked Monday, March 17. You are also required to post the electronic file to the drop box labeled *Library Research.* Remember when naming your file, use one word. The drop box will be open only up to the deadline—March 17 at 11 p.m.

The required format is enclosed. Be sure to read it carefully and follow it.

Good luck on this project. I look forward to reading outstanding research in these areas of electronic presentations.

111b-d1
Letterhead

In the next two documents, you will create the form shown on the previous page. In Document 3, you will fill in the form.

1. In a new document, change the top margin to .6" and the side margins to 1".

2. Insert clip art that will be appropriate for a medical office. Change the height of the clip art to 1.25". Do not change the width; it will automatically reset in proportion to the height.

3. Change the layout of the picture to **In Front of Text** (select the picture, select **Picture** from the Format menu, and click the **Layout** tab).

4. Press TAB twice to move the insertion point to the right of the picture. Key **Quality Care Medical Center**, as shown on the previous page.

5. Arrange the address and telephone number (shown on the previous page) attractively in the letterhead.

6. Add a graphic line below the picture. Save as **medical letterhead**.

111b-d2
SOAP Note Form

1. In a new document, change the top margin to .6" and the side margins to 1", and then insert the **medical letterhead** file (**Insert, File**).

2. Create a field for each item in the SOAP note shown on the previous page. Make all fields text fields with unlimited length unless otherwise indicated in the table below.

Field Name	Field Type	Maximum Length	Format
Patient No.	number	5	0
Age	number	2	0
T	number	5	0.00
P	number	2	0
R	number	2	0
B/P	number	3/2	0
Date	date		m/d/yy

3. Insert a graphic line before beginning the body of the SOAP notes.

4. Create a table for the body of the SOAP notes. All rows will have a height of 1". Center text vertically in the cells. Set width of Column B to 6".

5. Center the letters *S O A P* in Column A. Apply a larger bold font to the letter *S* in SOAP. Use Format Painter to copy the formatting to the rest of the letters. Insert an unlimited text field in each row of Column B.

6. Key the physician signature line in the footer.

7. Apply Arial Black font to the heading (select only the heading letters and the colon that follows). Use Format Painter to apply the format to all the headings.

8. Use Times New Roman font when keying the fill-in information.

9. Protect the form, save it as **Soap Note Form**, and print.

Memo from Template

70a
Warmup
Key each line twice SS.

alphabet	1	Maxwell paid just a quarter for a very big cookie at the new zoo.
fig/sym	2	Lunches for the 14 customers cost $77.37 ($67.28 x 15% = $10.09).
3rd/4th fingers	3	Quinn will oppose an opinion of Max about a jazzy pop show we saw.
easy	4	Angie, the neighbor, paid to go to the island and fish for smelt.

| 1 | 2 | 3 | 4 | 5 | 6 | 7 | 8 | 9 | 10 | 11 | 12 | 13 |

70b

help keywords
templates

Templates

A **template** is a master copy of a set of predefined styles for a particular type of document. Templates are available for formatting documents such as a memo, fax, or letter. A template can be used exactly as it exists, or it can be modified or customized and saved as a new template. The tabs on the Templates dialog box indicate the variety of templates that *Word* has available. You can also attach a template to a document.

To use an existing template:

1. Click **New** on the File menu.

2. In the New Document pane, under New from template, click **General Templates**.

3. In the Templates dialog box, click the desired tab, such as **Memos**.

4. Select the desired memo style, such as **Contemporary, Elegant,** or **Professional**.

5. If necessary, click **Document** under Create New.

6. Click **OK**. Follow the directions on the template to key the desired document.

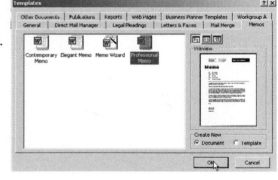

Select *Company Name Here* and key the company name.

Click where the template specifies to add heading information.

Select the body of the memo, and replace with your text.

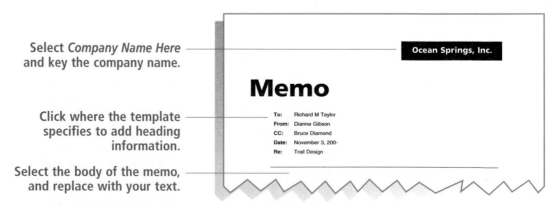

SOAP Notes and Medical Letterhead

DOCUMENT DESIGN

111a

Letterhead

Medical forms contain the name and address of the medical facility at the top of all the forms. In this lesson, you will follow the directions in 111b-d1 on p. 436 to create a letterhead that will be inserted at the top of all the medical forms.

SOAP Note Form

All medical offices keep recorded notes of the patient's office visit, which are commonly called SOAP notes. SOAP notes contain the patient's complaints, the physician's findings, and the physician's assessment and plan for treatment. The letters *S O A P* stand for:

S—SUBJECTIVE (what the patient tells the physician)

O—OBJECTIVE (the physician's findings as a result of a physical exam or evaluation)

A—ASSESSMENT (the physician's diagnosis or impression of the problem)

P—PLAN (the planned treatment for the patient)

Letterhead ——

SOAP Note Form ——

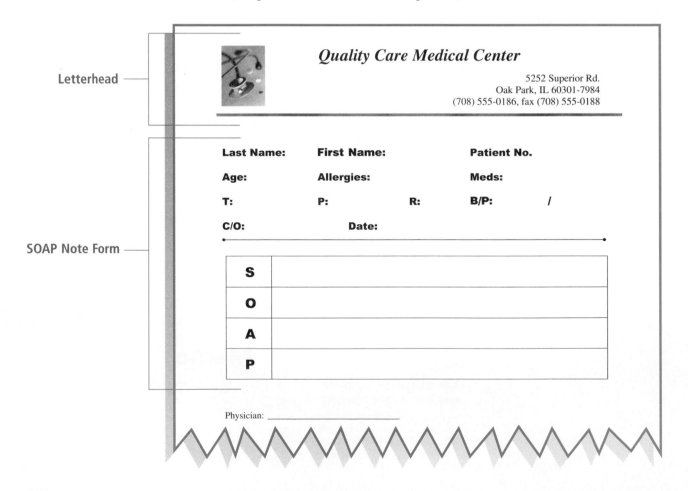

70c-d1
Memo

1. Create the following memo using the Professional Memo (do not use the Memo Wizard).
2. Add the company name **Ocean Springs, Inc.**
3. Save as **70c-d1**; print.

To: Richard M. Taylor | From: Student Name | CC: Bruce Diamond | Date: Current date | Re: Trail Design

Last week, Madilyn signed the contract for the trail design for Phase 1 of our Georgetown property. NatureLink was selected as the contractor. This firm was chosen because of its extensive experience in selecting interpretative sites, designing trails, and installing boardwalks to protect wetlands and environmentally sensitive areas.

The first onsite meeting is scheduled for November 10. We plan to meet at the main entrance at 10:30 a.m. to tour the property and review the procedures that NatureLink plans to use in designing the trails near the red cockaded woodpecker (RCW) habitat. Since the RCW is an endangered species, we want to balance the desires of ecotourists to observe these birds and the need to protect them.

Please let me know if you plan to participate in the initial meeting with NatureLink.

70c-d2
Memo

1. Create the following memo using the Contemporary Memo.
2. Include the following in the heading: **TO: Marvell Hodges; FROM: Student Name, Coordinator; DATE: Current date; CC: Jacob White, Human Resources Manager; SUBJECT: August 8-9 Workshop**
3. Save as **70c-d2**; print.

Over seventy-five teachers have preregistered to participate in the Electronic Presentation Workshop scheduled for August 8-9 at Ferguson Community College. We are very pleased with the overwhelming response to this offering.

The workshop will begin at 8 a.m. and conclude by 5 p.m. each day. Please come to Room T38 of the Continuing Education Building. You may make your housing reservation today by calling (601) 555-0142. I look forward to an outstanding learning experience.

110c-d2
Table on Pleading Form

Schedule A, illustrated below, is a portion of a long document prepared for court that shows the receipts, disbursements, and assets on hand for estates in probate. This document, like all documents prepared for court, is created on a pleading form.

1. Open the **Los Angeles County** pleading template you created in Lesson 109. When the Pleading Wizard dialog box displays, click the **Finish** button.
2. Schedules are placed at the back of legal documents; therefore, you will not need the information that is displayed on the first page of court documents. You will delete the text that is on the first page and use only the line numbering on the form. Choose **Select All** from the Edit menu, and then press the DELETE key to delete all the text from the pleading page.
3. Key the heading as shown.
4. Strike ENTER twice and create a 3-column, 6-row table. Key the table.
5. Use the math feature to insert the total. The total should display with a dollar sign and two decimal places, and it should be in bold print.
6. Set a decimal tab in Column C to align the numbers. Center and underline column heads.
7. Remove the table grid (**Format**, **Borders and Shading**, **Borders** tab, click **None** and **Apply to Table**).
8. Remove the page number from the footer and key **SCHEDULE A** in its place.
9. Save as **110c-d2** and print.

SCHEDULE A

RECEIPTS

Date	Item	Amount
03/22/--	Medical reimbursement from Medicare	$ 147.00
04/07/--	Accrued interest on savings account at People's Bank	225.00
04/28/--	Rent payment from Mazo property tenant	995.00
05/01/--	Dividend from Jefferson Electric Stock	89.00
05/15/--	Dividend from Alaska Oil Stock	116.50
05/30/--	Accrued interest from savings account at credit union	315.00
	TOTAL RECEIPTS	

110c-d3
Fill in Articles of Incorporation

1. Open **110c-d1**. Fill in the form as follows: (1) **Quality Care Medical Center**; (2) **providing medical care**; (3) **Andrew Wainscott**; (4) **5561 Golden Lantern**; (5) **Laguna Niguel**; (6) **92677**; (7) **Ten Thousand (10,000)**; (8) **David M. Smith, Incorporator**.
2. Save as **110c-d3** and print.

LESSON 71 Review E-Mail

SKILLBUILDING

71a
Warmup
Key each line twice SS.

alphabet	1	Liz Page quickly found six major errors in the book she reviewed.
figures	2	Chapters 7, 18, 19, and 23 had 65 pages; the others had 40 pages.
space bar	3	Ty saw us as we got in a new car to go to the zoo; he did not go.
easy	4	Is the problem with the ancient chapel or the chapel at the lake?

| 1 | 2 | 3 | 4 | 5 | 6 | 7 | 8 | 9 | 10 | 11 | 12 | 13 |

71b
Technique Builder

first finger	5	to kite flat byte joyful hitter night vacuum tab yummy vague earn
	6	Babbs hung a gorgeous hanging on the first floor by the fountain.
	7	Annabelle gave her baby daughter big hugs and put her in the bed.

second finger	8	dike kind cider insider decided child creek cracked deadlock kite
	9	Dicky screamed and cried as Mickey cracked the huge chicken eggs.
	10	Tired divers tried to no avail to rescue the sinking cargo liner.

fourth finger	11	sap soap spots salsa poppy squares people wool swoosh assess pass
	12	Sally knew pool, zymoscope, x-axis, wassail, Lallan, and swallow.
	13	Palisade apologized to sloppy Wally for the lollipops and apples.

DOCUMENT DESIGN

71c

E-Mail Review

Memorandums sent electronically are called **e-mail**. Accurately key the recipient's e-mail address and supply a specific subject line. The sender's name and date are automatically added by the e-mail software.

The following three examples of commonly used e-mail software screens illustrate that while each is different, they all have locations for the recipient's address, the subject line, and the message.

Attachments: Documents can be sent electronically by attaching the document files to the email. The attachment can be saved and opened. To attach a file, click the Attach button or icon browse to locate the file. A window will open to search for the file. When you locate the file, click on the file name. Click Open, Insert, or Attach to attach the document; procedures will vary depending on the e-mail service.

Formatting: Do not add bold or italic or vary the fonts. Do not use uppercase letters for emphasis. Use emoticons or e-mail abbreviations with caution (e.g., ;- for wink or BTW for by the way). SS the body of an e-mail. DS between paragraphs.

America Online

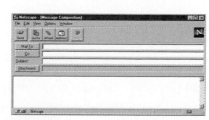

Netscape

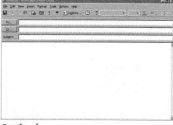

Outlook

1. In a new document, key **Name:** followed by 2 spaces. Click the **Text Form Field** button. Strike ENTER twice.

2. Key **Student Number:** followed by 2 spaces. Click the **Text Form Field** button. Click the **Form Field Options** button. Change the type of field to *Number* and the maximum length to 6. Strike ENTER twice.

3. Key **Gender:** followed by 2 spaces. Click the **Check Box Form Field** button followed by 2 spaces. Key **Male**. Press TAB twice. Click the **Check Box Form Field** button followed by 2 spaces. Key **Female**. Strike ENTER twice.

4. Key **Class Standing:** followed by 2 spaces. Click the **Drop Down Form** button. Click the **Form Field Options** button. In the Drop Down Item box, key **Freshman** and click the **Add** button. Add **Sophomore**, **Junior**, and **Senior** to the items in the Drop Down List. Click **OK**.

5. Click the **Protect Form** button. Test the form by filling in information about yourself. Press TAB to move to the next field.

6. Save as **110a-drill1**. Print.

DOCUMENT DESIGN

110b

Articles of Incorporation

Articles of Incorporation contain information regarding the name, address, and purpose of the company, as well as the share structure. The document may differ for medical, nonprofit, professional, and municipal corporations.

Key the Articles of Incorporation. DS between paragraphs. Leave a space about 3" square in the upper-right corner of the first page for the filing stamp of the Secretary of State. Use plain paper.

3" square space for filing stamp →

ARTICLES OF INCORPORATION

I

The name of this corporation is (*ff1*).

II

The purpose of the corporation is to engage in the profession of (*ff2*) and any other lawful activities (other than the banking or trust company business) not prohibited to a corporation engaging in such profession by applicable laws and regulations.

III

The corporation is a professional corporation within the meaning of Part 4, Division 3, Title 1, California Corporation Code.

IV

The name and address in the State of California of this corporation's initial agent for service of process are:

Name: (*ff3*)

Street Address: (*ff4*)

City: (*ff5*)   California   ZIP: (*ff6*)

V

The corporation is authorized to issue only one class of stock; and the total number of shares which the corporation is authorized to issue is (*ff7*).

_____

(*ff8*)

APPLICATIONS

110c-d1
Articles of Incorporation

1. Strike ENTER to place the insertion point on approximately line 2.9".

2. Key the document shown above, inserting appropriate form fields (*ff*). Protect the form and save it as **110c-d1**.

71d-d1
E-Mail Message

1. Key the e-mail message below to your instructor.
2. Key the subject line as **Assignment 3**.
3. Send the message.

Task 1: List five things to consider when choosing an appropriate e-mail password.

1. Do not choose a password that is named after a family member or a pet.
2. Do not use birth dates as a password.
3. Choose a combination of letters and numbers; preferably, use UPPERCASE and lowercase letters, e.g., TLQ6tEpR.
4. Do not share your password with anyone.
5. Do not write your password on paper and leave by your computer.

Task 2: List five things to consider when composing e-mail.

1. Do not use bold or italic or vary fonts.
2. Do not use UPPERCASE for emphasis.
3. Use emoticons or e-mail abbreviations with caution (e.g., :) for smile or BTW for by the way).
4. Write clear, concise messages that are free of spelling and grammatical errors.
5. Do not send an e-mail in haste or anger. Think about the message carefully before pressing the Send button.

71d-d2

E-Mail Message with Attachment

1. Key the e-mail message below to your instructor and one student in your class.
2. Key the subject line as **Activity Report**.
3. Attach the data file **activity** (optional). Send the message.

I have completed the Activity Report required for this year's competitive events. The file Activity.doc is attached to this e-mail for your review. Please add the names of the members initiated at the February meeting and review the listing of awards received by our members. Revise the file as needed.

After you have proofread the report, please print a laser copy and give to Brenda Jones for inclusion in the national project notebook. I would also appreciate your e-mailing me the revised file for my historian records.

Remember, the reports must be postmarked by March 1.

71d-d3
E-Mail Message

1. Send an e-mail to your instructor.
2. Copy the e-mail to yourself.
3. Use the subject line and message given in **70c-d2**. (Simplify the process by opening **70c-d2** and copying the message to the e-mail screen.)

110a
Creating Forms

Legal Forms

An online form can be created so that people can fill out the forms using *Microsoft Word*. You will key the **fixed text**; information that will be supplied by others will be keyed in **form fields**. There are three types of form fields. The table below explains them and when they are used. Display the Forms Toolbar (View, Toolbars, Forms) when working with forms.

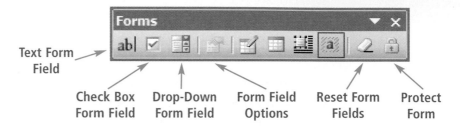

Text Form Field → Check Box Form Field | Drop-Down Form Field | Form Field Options | Reset Form Fields | Protect Form

Form Field Type	When It Is Used	Example
Text	You need the respondent to key the requested information.	Last name or telephone number
Checkbox	Respondent checks the box that applies.	❑ Male ❑ Female
Drop-down	User selects from a list of choices.	Mr. Mrs. Dr.

Form Field Options

After the field has been inserted, Form Field Options can be used to specify the parameters of the field, such as type of field and length. For example, if you are asking respondents for their social security number, you would insert a Text Form Field and then use Form Field Options to specify that the field be a number field and be limited to nine digits.

Protecting the Form

After creating the form, click the Protect Form button to prevent others from changing its contents. You cannot test the form until you protect it. If you need to edit the form, you must click the Protect Form button to unlock the form; make your changes and then click Protect Form again to lock it.

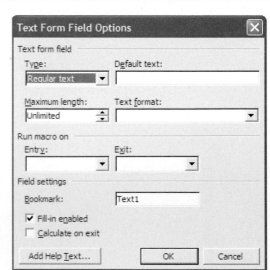

LESSON 72 — Assessment

SKILLBUILDING

72a
Warmup
Key each line twice SS.

alphabet 1 Jamie quickly apologized for submitting the complex reviews late.
figures   2 Those 1,863 bars cost $27.05 each for a total cost of $50,394.15.
easy   3 I may go to the zoo or to see you if I do not go to the new pool.
easy   4 The men may be busy, but they go to the lake to work on the dock.

| 1 | 2 | 3 | 4 | 5 | 6 | 7 | 8 | 9 | 10 | 11 | 12 | 13 |

72b
Timed Writing
Key one 3' writing and one 5' writing.

gwam   3' | 5'

How are letters and other documents produced in the modern office? They are prepared in a number of ways. Just a few years ago, with rare exceptions, a document was composed by a manager who either wrote it in longhand or dictated it. Then, one of the office staff typed it in final form. Today, the situation is quite different. Office staff may compose and produce various documents, or they may finalize documents that were keyed by managers. In some cases, managers like to produce some or all of their documents in final form.

Many people question how this dramatic change in the way documents are prepared came about. Two factors can be cited as the major reasons for the change. The primary factor is the extensive use of computers in offices today. A manager who uses a computer for a variety of tasks may find it just as simple to key documents at the computer as it would be to prepare them for office personnel to produce. The other factor is the increase in the ratio of office personnel to managers. Today, one secretary is very likely to support as many as six or eight managers. Managers who share office staff find that they get much quicker results by finalizing their own documents when they compose them.

3'		5'
4	2	52
8	5	54
13	8	57
17	10	60
21	13	62
25	15	65
29	18	67
34	20	70
36	22	71
40	24	73
44	26	76
48	29	78
52	31	81
57	34	83
61	37	86
65	39	89
70	42	91
74	44	94
78	47	96
82	49	99

3' | 1 | 2 | 3 | 4 |
5' | 1 | 2 | 3 |

APPLICATIONS

72c
Assessment

 Continue

 Check

With CheckPro: When you complete a document, proofread it, check the spelling, and preview for placement. When you are completely satisfied with it, click the **Continue** button to move to the next document. You will not be able to return and edit a document once you continue to the next one. Click the **Check** button when you are ready to error-check the test. Review and/or print the document analysis results.

Without CheckPro: On the signal to begin, key the documents in sequence. When time has been called, proofread all documents again and identify errors.

13. At the right, replace the case number with **No. SO C 87321**. Delete the words *PLEADING TITLE* and key **NOTICE OF DEPOSITION AND REQUEST FOR PRODUCTION OF DOCUMENTS AT DEPOSITION**.

14. Key **TO: ALL PARTIES AND THEIR ATTORNEYS OF RECORD** on line 17 and press ENTER twice.

15. Key the following paragraph beginning on line 19.

PLEASE TAKE NOTICE that defendants will take the deposition of plaintiff Henry Hurt on July 7, 200-, at 2:00 p.m., at the offices of Newton & Johnson, 15 Civic Center Dr., Suite 200, Santa Ana, CA 92701, before a notary public authorized to administer oaths in the State of California. The deposition will continue from day to day, excluding Saturdays, Sundays, and holidays, until completed.

16. Key **///** on numbered lines that do not contain text at the end of the page, such as on p. 1, line 26. This shows that the line was left blank by the writer.

17. On the second page of the pleading, key the following information, beginning on line 1:

PLEASE TAKE FURTHER NOTICE that plaintiff Henry Hurt is required to bring with him to the deposition the following records, documents, and things:

DS two times
1. Any and all documents which substantiate the claim for property damage.

DS two times
2. Any and all documents which substantiate the claim for loss of earnings.

DS two times
3. All photographs which in any way relate to the subject matter of this action.

18. Under the *By* line, key the following text:

BARBARA M. JOHNSON
Attorney for
Defendants JONATHAN
MOVERS and LAUREL
DELIVERIES

19. Save the document as **109b-d1** and print.

109b-d2
Create Pleading Form

1. Follow the Wizard steps in 109b-d1 to create a new pleading form for:

**SUPERIOR COURT OF THE STATE OF CALIFORNIA
FOR THE COUNTY OF LOS ANGELES**

2. Save the template as **Los Angeles County.dot**.

72c-d1
Modified Block Letter

1. Key the modified block letter with mixed punctuation for Michael Taylor, President.

2. Add the mailing notation **CONFIDENTIAL** and the subject line **Invitation to Honor Society**. Send a copy to Dr. Zimiko Tayyar. Provide the appropriate complimentary close and other notations. Center vertically on the page. Save as **72c-d1**.

3. Generate an envelope. Save as **72c-d1a**.

words

January 30, 200- | Miss Shea Patterson | 43 University Dr. | Lacombe, LA	10
70445-2536 | Dear Shea	18

Congratulations! Because of your outstanding academic record and lead- 32
ership potential in your teaching profession, you have been selected for 47
membership in Pi Omega Pi, the honorary society for undergraduate busi- 61
ness education majors. Being selected for membership in Pi Omega Pi is 75
the highest honor that a student of business education can achieve. 89

A formal initiation ceremony will be held on Tuesday, February 13, at 103
4 p.m. in Room 252 of the T. S. McKinney Building. Please complete 117
the enclosed form and return it to me by Friday, February 9. A one-time 132
initiation fee of $40 is also due by the initiation. 142

Shea, I am delighted that you have been selected as a Pi Omega Pi mem- 156
ber and look forward to your initiation on February 13. 168

72c-d2

Two-Page Block Letter

1. Open **72hightower**. Save as **72c-d2**.

2. Use the date command and position appropriately on the page.

3. Include **CERTIFIED** as the mailing notation, and add **Account USC3828GB** as the reference line.

4. Key the remainder of the letter shown below for Ms. Kathy Hossain, Manager. Provide the appropriate complimentary close and other notations. Create an appropriate second-page header. Key the last sentence as a postscript.

Our market tests indicate a great deal of interest in a tailgating package. 12
The cost for a box lunch for four is $20. The lunch will include chicken, 24
potato salad, corn on the cob, rolls, and a brownie. We could add High- 36
tower napkins, plates, plastic utensils, and souvenir mugs and sell the 45
package for $30. 55

Please review our preliminary design sketches. We will contact you in a 65
few days for your reaction to the design samples. By then, we should have 77
the final results of our marketing tests. 85

We plan to visit with you three weeks prior to the game to provide an 99
update on all of our marketing activities. 106

This game will be a bright spot for your team and your financial standing. 132
(header and notations) 150

109b-d1
Notice of Deposition and
Request for Production of
Documents at Deposition

Word's Pleading Wizard will assist in setting up the pleading form for you. Follow the steps below to create and complete a pleading template.

1. Select **New** from the **File** menu. In the Task Pane, select **General Templates** (*Word 2002*) or **On my computer** (*Word 2003*).

2. Select the **Legal Pleadings** tab in the Templates dialog box, click the **Pleading Wizard** icon, and click **OK**.

3. Click **Next** on the Pleading Wizard screen, select the option **Create a new pleading template for another court** if it is not already selected, and then click the **Next** button.

4. Key the following text in the text box on two lines:

   SUPERIOR COURT OF THE STATE OF CALIFORNIA
   FOR THE COUNTY OF ORANGE

5. Click the **Center** option, and then click **Next**. Choose **Courier New** (or another similar font). Set the line spacing for double and the lines per page to 26. Set the left margin for 1.25" and the right margin for 1". Click **Next**.

6. Set line numbers to appear on the pleading and to start the pleading at line **1**. Line numbers should start at **1** and the line numbers are to show in increments of **One**. Click **Next**.

7. Choose **Double** for the left border screen and **Single** for the right. Click **Next** to display the screen to choose the style. Select **Style 1** and then click the **Next** button.

8. Select the *Attorney and firm names* to display at the beginning of the pleading and the page numbers to display in the footer. Remove the check mark for *Summary of pleading title*. Click the **Next** button.

9. Select **Yes** for a signature block. Select **By** in the Sign With text box. Include the firm name and address above the attorney name. Include the date line before the signature.

10. Click the **Next** button and name the template **Superior Court.dot**. Click **Next** and then **Finish**. Click the **Finish** button again when the screen says that it will help you with the writing. The pleading form now displays.

11. Beginning on line 1, key the following exactly as shown. Press ENTER after each line unless otherwise specified.

    NEWTON & JOHNSON
    15 Civic Center Dr., Suite 200
    Santa Ana, CA 92701
    DS

    Telephone: (714) 555-0134   **This should start on line 3.**
    DS

    Attorneys for Defendants   **This should start on line 4.**
    JONATHAN MOVERS and
    LAUREL DELIVERIES

12. Strike ENTER as needed to place **Superior Court of the State of California** on line 8. Key **HENRY HURT, et. al.,** as the plaintiff on line 11 and key **JONATHAN MOVERS, et al.,** as the defendant on line 14.

(CONTINUED ON NEXT PAGE)

72c-d3
Memo

1. Key the memo and save as **72c-d3**.

words

TO: Technology Task Force|**FROM:** Clifford F. McCrory, Chair|**DATE:**   14
October 20, 200-|**SUBJECT:** School Board Recommendations   25

Our professional staff finalized the Technology Task Force report request-   40
ing approval of four major technology enhancements for K-14. A draft copy   55
is enclosed for your review. Please make any corrections and return the   69
draft to us within one week so that the final report can be prepared.   83

The report will be sent special delivery to each school board member no   98
later than Monday. This deadline must be followed if the item is to appear   113
on the November 15 agenda. If we do not hear from you within one week,   127
we will assume that you accept the draft as submitted.|xx|Enclosure   141

72c-d4
Memo from Template

1. Key the memo using the Professional Memo template.
2. Key **Investments, Inc.** as the company name.
3. Save as **72c-d4**.

TO: All Employees|**FROM:** Cory Johnson|**DATE:** (Insert next Monday's   12
date)|**SUBJECT:** Guidelines for Voice Mail Greeting   21

Recording an appropriate voice mail greeting is very important as we pro-   36
vide our clients with excellent and friendly service. Please study the fol-   51
lowing essential parts of an effective voice mail greeting and then study the   67
sample greeting shown below: 73

1. State your name.   77
2. Include the day and date you are recording the greeting.   89
3. Describe why you are not available to take the call.   101
4. Request caller to leave a message or directions for obtaining personal   115
   assistance.   118
5. Provide an approximate time when the call will be returned.   131

Hello, this is Cory Johnson's voice mail. It's Monday, (Insert date), and I am   147
in a meeting until 3:30. After the tone, please leave your name, phone num-   162
ber, and a detailed message. I will return your call before 5 p.m. today. For   178
immediate assistance, press 0 now. Thank you.   188

In addition to recording an appropriate message, it is equally important   203
that you update the greeting each day. Also check for voice mail messages   218
throughout the day and remember to return calls as promised in the   232
greeting.   234

72c-d5
E-Mail Message

1. Send an e-mail to your instructor that introduces yourself. Include why you are taking this class and what you hope to achieve. Create a subject line.
2. Copy the e-mail to yourself.

Legal, Medical, and Employment Applications

- Format legal office applications.
- Format medical office applications.
- Format employment application documents.

LESSON 109 — Legal Pleadings

DOCUMENT DESIGN

109a

Create Pleading Form

Legal documents that are presented for filing in court must follow specific guidelines and be keyed on pleading paper. Most documents today are keyed on standard $8\frac{1}{2} \times$ 11-inch paper; some lawyers may still use legal size paper ($8\frac{1}{2} \times 14$). Legal documents contain a double ruling, from top to bottom, at the left margin. The right margin is marked with a single ruling. The lines are numbered in the left margin. The margins for legal documents can be 1.25" on the left and 1" on the right. Some lawyers will use a 1.5" left margin and a .5" right margin. Top and bottom margins are usually 1".

Module 11: Checkpoint

Answer the questions below to see if you have mastered the content of this module.

1. What is the correct salutation written to the attention of Ms. Sarah Gray at Mountain Inn Resort?

   a. Dear Ms. Gray   b. Ladies and Gentlemen

2. For a–f below, circle the letter part that appears first.

   a. reference line or attention line   b. subject line or reference line

   c. reference initials or enclosure   d. salutation or subject line

   e. mailing notation or dateline   f. attention line or reference line

3. A _____ notation shows that a copy of the document was sent to the person(s) named without the recipient's knowledge.

Performance Assessment

Document 1
Modified Block Letter

1. Key the modified block letter with mixed punctuation for **Alberto Valenzuela, Conference Planner**, to the following address:

   Ms. Shawna Olson
   Western Regional Manager, Acune, Inc.
   5450 Signal Hill Rd., Springfield, OH 45504-5450

2. Supply an appropriate subject line. Send a copy to Susan Reading.

3. Save as **Checkpoint11-d1**; print.

Thank you for agreeing to exhibit at the National Technology Conference on May 10-12 at the Earlham Hotel in Memphis, Tennessee. We are very excited about your first-time attendance at our conference. We know our over two thousand participants will be equally as excited about the outstanding products you will have to offer them.

The exhibit hall will be available to you from 8-12 on Wednesday, May 10, for setup. You will be provided a large table with drape, two folding chairs, power supply, and a garbage can. Should you need additional assistance during the conference, please call me at my cell phone, (901) 555-0124.

Document 2
Block Letter

1. Open **Checkpoint11-d1**. Reformat as a block letter with open punctuation.

2. Add a **SPECIAL DELIVERY** mailing notation. Add the reference line **Stress Management Session**.

3. Save as **Checkpoint11-d2**.

4. Generate an envelope. Save as **Checkpoint11-d2a**.

Document 3
Memo

1. Key the message in Document 1 as a memo to **Sandra Habek** from **Alberto Valenzuela**.

2. Save as **Checkpoint11-d3**.

Module 17: Checkpoint

Answer the questions below to see if you have mastered the content of this module.

1. A(n) _____ provides detailed travel and meeting information.

2. A document used to provide a record of a meeting is _____.

3. A document detailing the business to be covered in a meeting and the order in which it will be covered is a(n) _____.

4. A document saved to the Web is saved in _____ format.

5. To preview a document saved as a Web page, you must use your _____.

6. Minutes that capture only the key decisions made in a meeting are often called _____ minutes.

7. To create a variety of different kinds of labels from one data source that can be merged with other documents use the _____ Wizard.

8. To create labels, click _____ on the Tools menu.

9. To change to a different type of label, use the _____ feature.

10. To change the name of a default field or to add or delete a field on the data source, click the _____ button.

Performance Assessment

Document 1
Agenda

Use the information at the right to prepare an agenda. Save as **Checkpoint17-d1**.

Investment Oversight Committee Meeting; June 22, 200-; 10:00 a.m.

10:00	Welcome; approve minutes of May 24, 200- meeting Ralph Green
10:15	Review of portfolio performance: domestic equity; international equity; fixed income; alternative investments Bruce Diamond
10:45	General Discussion All members
11:00	Adjournment

Document 2
Action Minutes

Use the heading information from Document 1 above and the information at the right to create action minutes. Save as **Checkpoint17-d2**.

Ralph Green presiding; members attending: John Brennan; Sharon Brown; Lynn Barrow; Mark Houser; and Bruce Diamond, consultant

Ralph Green called the meeting to order at 10:00 and welcomed all attendees. The minutes were approved as presented.

Bruce Diamond reviewed the domestic and international equity portfolios, the fixed-income portfolio, and the alternative investment portfolio in detail. He expressed concern about the small-cap domestic equity portfolio and recommended that we continue to monitor it carefully. All other accounts were on target.

The members discussed the current status of the portfolio and recommended no changes in managers or asset allocation. Members were reminded that the next meeting of the Investment Oversight Committee is on July 21 at 10:00.

The meeting was adjourned at 10:50.

Report Mastery

- Format reports with title page and table of contents.
- Format reports with notes page and references page.
- Format reports with styles, footnotes, and endnotes.
- Change number format of preliminary pages.
- Insert section breaks.

LESSON 73　Skillbuilding and Word Processing Basics

SKILLBUILDING

73a
Warmup
Key each line twice SS.

direct reaches	1	June and my brother, Bradly, received advice from junior umpires.
	2	My bright brother received minimum reward for serving many years.
adjacent reaches	3	Clio and Trey were sad that very few voters were there last week.
	4	Western attire was very popular at the massive auction last week.
double letters	5	Tommie Bennett will go to a meeting in Dallas tomorrow afternoon.
	6	Lee will meet Joanne at the swimming pool after accounting class.

| 1 | 2 | 3 | 4 | 5 | 6 | 7 | 8 | 9 | 10 | 11 | 12 | 13 |

73b
Technique Builder
Key each group 3 times; work at a controlled rate.

b	7	be bib bribe bubble baby baboon bobble cobble bonbon bogie bobbin
n	8	no nun new none noon napkin nanny ninth nonsense nothing national
b/n	9	Benny and Nate have been told to begin with bends before running.
j	10	jet joy join joke jelly jacket jackel jewel rejoice judge jonquil
f	11	of fast fief fanfare fearful fifteen flora forefoot format buffer
j/f	12	Join Jon Fondren and his staff for a fun-filled five-day journey.
y	13	yes you your yield yokes yellow yesterday phyloid reply navy away
t	14	twin total trinket triplet title ticket token meant impact tattle
y/t	15	Tom, Timothy, and Tony are triplets; Yvonne and Yvette are twins.

| 1 | 2 | 3 | 4 | 5 | 6 | 7 | 8 | 9 | 10 | 11 | 12 | 13 |

1. Prepare the following itinerary.
2. Save as **108c-d4** and print.

Itinerary for Tracy M. Westfield

July 14–17, 200–

Thursday, July 14	Boston to Bangor
8:15 a.m.	Leave Boston Airport on Coastline Flight 957 and arrive at Bangor Airport at 9:28 a.m.; Patriot Rental Car (Confirmation #218756).
10:30 a.m.	Meet with Rod Watson, Leigh Barber, Joe Coleman, and Mary Roszak of Round Rock Associates at their office—739 State St., Bangor, Maine.
4:00 p.m.	Drive to Bar Harbor (approximately 40 miles), Cliff View Hotel, 29 Eden St. (Confirmation #S536017).
Friday, July 15	Bar Harbor
10:30 a.m.	Meet with Richard Odom, Bar Harbor Medical Supply—527 West Highway 3.
2:30 p.m.	Conference for Medical Supply Professionals, Cliff View Hotel.
5:00 p.m.	Conference ends; no events scheduled for evening.
Saturday, July 16	Bar Harbor
10:30 a.m.	Conference for Medical Supply Professionals, Cliff View Hotel.
12:30 p.m.	Conference ends; no events scheduled for afternoon.
7:30 p.m.	Conference Awards Banquet
Sunday, July 17	Bar Harbor to Boston
1:30 p.m.	Drive to Bangor Airport
3:30 p.m.	Depart on Coastline Flight 648; arrive at Boston Airport at 4:28 p.m.

73c

Timed Writing
Take one 3' and one 5' timed writing; determine *gwam*; proofread and circle errors.

What characterizes the life of an entrepreneur? Those who   4 | 2 | 43
have never owned their own businesses may think owning a business   8 | 5 | 46
means being your own boss, setting your own hours, and making a   13 | 8 | 48
lot of money. Those who have run their own businesses are quick   17 | 10 | 51
to report that owning a business may be exciting and challenging,   21 | 13 | 54
but it also requires hard work, long hours, and personal sacri-   26 | 15 | 56
fice. A good idea is not the only prerequisite for a successful   30 | 18 | 59
business. A little luck even helps.   32 | 19 | 60

Many small businesses are operated as businesses from the   36 | 22 | 63
initial stages. However, some small businesses that turn out to be   41 | 24 | 65
successful are just hobbies in the early stages. The entre-   45 | 27 | 68
preneur has a job and uses the income from it to support the   49 | 29 | 70
hobby. When the hobby begins to require more and more time, the   53 | 32 | 73
entrepreneur has to choose between the job and the hobby. The   57 | 34 | 75
decision is usually based on finances. If enough money can be   62 | 37 | 78
made from the hobby or can be obtained from another source, the   66 | 39 | 80
hobby is turned into a business.   68 | 41 | 82

| 3' | 1 | | 2 | | 3 | | 4 | |
| 5' | | 1 | | 2 | | 3 | |

FUNCTION REVIEW

73d

Page Numbers

In Module 5, you learned to number pages in simple reports. If you need to review how to insert page numbers at the top right, study the instructions below.

To insert page numbers:

1. Select **Page Numbers** from the Insert menu.
2. Select **Top of page (Header)** in the Position box.
3. Select **Right** in the Alignment box.
4. Remove the check mark from the Show number on first page box.

help keywords
page numbers

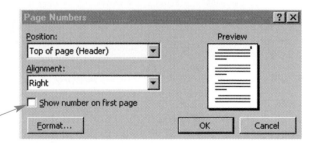

DRILL 1   PAGE NUMBERS

1. Open **benefits** from the data files. Save as **73d-drill1**.
2. Insert page numbers at the top right; do not number the first page.

3. Save and print.

1. Prepare the following minutes.
2. Save as **108c-d3** and print.

Investment Committee Meeting
April 24, 200-
Action Minutes

Presiding: Crystal Bingham

Participants: Todd Berkley, Jane Kennemur, Bert Radcliff, Julie Markham, Jerold Bradshaw, Chris Pruitt, and Sandy Westfield

Consultant: Bruce Diamond, Investment Evaluation Group (IEG)

Committee Chair Crystal Bingham called the meeting to order at 9:00, presented an overview of the meeting objectives, and introduced Bruce Diamond, who was representing our regular portfolio consultant, Fred Benjamin. She asked Bruce to summarize the results of the previous quarter. Bruce presented the written report including reports on domestic and international equity, fixed income, and alternative investments. He indicated that the portfolio results exceeded all benchmarks. The returns on the composite portfolio for the first quarter were 8.25%.

Jane Kennemur recommended that the portfolio structure be modified so that the core equity investments currently in index funds would be withdrawn and invested in actively managed funds. Bruce agreed that this move was prudent under market conditions. The committee concurred and requested that IEG complete the search for a core equity manager. Four managers need to be presented to the Committee before the final selection is made.

Jerold Bradshaw reported that the subcommittee reviewed the Investment Policy and recommended no changes. However, the change in the portfolio structure just approved would have to be incorporated in the policy. The updated policy will be sent to everybody.

James Wright reported that the Investment Oversight Committee had met monthly to monitor the investments carefully between Investment Committee meetings. The recommendation at each meeting during the past quarter had been to make no changes in the asset allocation of the portfolio or the investment managers. Monthly meetings have already been scheduled for the next quarter.

The meeting adjourned at 9:55.

Change Number Format

Preliminary pages of reports may include a title page, a transmittal letter or memo, a list of tables, a list of figures, a table of contents, and an executive summary. These preliminary pages are numbered with lowercase Roman numerals at the bottom of the page. Title pages are numbered, but the page number is suppressed. To number these pages, you will need to change the number format.

To change number format:

1. Select **Page Numbers** from the Insert menu.
2. Select **Bottom of page (Footer)** in the Position box, and **Center** in the Alignment box.
3. Click the **Format** button; click the down arrow beside Number format; select **i, ii, iii**.
4. Click **Start at,** enter the page number, and click **OK**.

DRILL 2   FORMAT PAGE NUMBERS

1. Open **preliminary** from the data files.
2. Insert the correct page numbers in the appropriate position for these preliminary pages.

3. Save as **73d-drill2** and print.

Note: In a later lesson, you will learn to use section breaks to insert page numbers for both preliminary pages and report pages in the same document file.

Line and Page Breaks

Pagination or breaking pages at the appropriate location can easily be controlled using two features: Widow/Orphan control and Keep with next.

Widow/Orphan control prevents a single line of a paragraph from printing at the bottom or top of a page. A check mark displays in this option box indicating that Widow/Orphan control is "on" (the default).

Keep with next prevents a page break from occurring between two paragraphs. Use this feature to keep a side heading from being left alone at the bottom of a page. To use Keep with next:

1. Select the side heading and the paragraph that follows.
2. Click **Format**; then **Paragraph**.
3. From the Line and Page Breaks tab, select **Keep with next**. Click **OK**. The side heading moves to the next page.

> **TIP**
>
> You can also insert a page break by pressing CTRL + ENTER or choosing **Page Break** from the Insert menu.

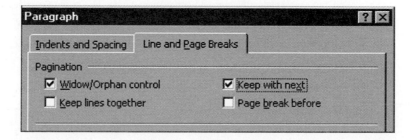

108c
Timed Production

On the signal to begin, key the documents in sequence. When time has been called, proofread the documents again and correct any errors you may have overlooked. Reprint if necessary.

108c-d1
Agenda

1. Prepare the agenda shown below. Set decimal tabs at .3" (so times align properly) and .9" and set a left tab at .6". Tab before each time and before the en dash between the times. Position the heading at about 2". Set a left tab at 1.5" and a right tab with Leader 2 at 6".

2. Save as **108c-d1** and print.

Investment Committee Meeting

April 24, 200–

Agenda

9:00 – 9:10	Welcome Overview of Meeting Objectives	Crystal Bingham
9:10 – 9:35	Quarterly Performance Report Equity–Domestic Equity–International Fixed Income Alternative Investments	Bruce Diamond
9:35 – 9:45	Investment Policy Review	Jerold Bradshaw
9:45 – 10:00	Oversight Committee Report	James Wright
10:00	Adjourn	

108c-d2
Save as Web Page

1. Save **108c-d1** as a Web page in the **Web Page** folder you set up in Lesson 104. Name the file **108c-d2**.

2. Preview in your browser and make any needed adjustments.

1. Open **73d-drill1** and save as **73d-drill3**.
2. Apply the **Keep with next** feature to the side heading left alone at the bottom of the first page.

3. Verify that Widow/Orphan control is on (✓ appears in box).
4. Save and print.

Leader Tabs

A **leader tab** displays a series of dots that lead the eye to the next column. Leaders can be combined with a left, center, right, or decimal tab. Leaders are often used in documents such as table of contents, agendas, and financial statements. Leader tabs can only be set from the Tab dialog box.

To set a leader tab:

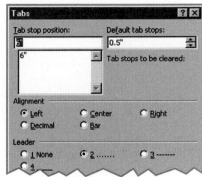

1. Click **Tabs** on the Format menu to display the Tab dialog box.

2. Enter the position of the tab in the Tab Stop Position box.

3. Choose the **Alignment** type.

4. Choose the **Leader** style, for example 2; click **Set**; then click **OK**.

1. In the Tabs dialog box, set a right leader tab at 6" using Leader style 2.
2. Key the first name at the left margin and press TAB. Note that the leaders extend to the right margin.

3. Key the title (*President*). Notice that it aligns at the right tab stop.
4. Complete the drill and save it as **73d-drill4**.

6.0" right leader tab ↓

John Sneider . . . . President

JoAnn Rouche . . . . Vice President, Education

Janice Weiss . . . . Vice President, Membership

Lotus Fijutisi . . . . Chief Financial Officer

Loretta Russell . . . . Recording Secretary

SKILLBUILDING

108a
Warmup
Key each line twice; work for fluency.

alphabet 1 Jimmy Bond quickly realized we could fix the poor girl's vehicle.
adjacent reaches 2 Last autumn, Guy and Isadore loitered here as they walked to Rio.
easy 3 Eight neighbor girls and I wish to work in the cornfield by dusk.

| 1 | 2 | 3 | 4 | 5 | 6 | 7 | 8 | 9 | 10 | 11 | 12 | 13 |

108b
Timed Writing
Take two 5' timed writings.

gwam 3' | 5'

Today, a huge number of white-collar workers use computers in	4	2
their daily work. Most of these workers also have access to the	8	5
Internet. Using the Internet for work purposes is becoming more	13	8
and more common and, most of the time, is quite effective. Some	17	10
organizations are finding, though, that a number of their workers	21	13
do abuse the Internet. The abuse tends to occur in two forms.	26	15
The first type of abuse they find is that a large number of	30	18
employees visit sites that are not related in any way to their work.	34	21
Some of the sites that workers visit contain material that is very	39	23
offensive to others. The problem is more serious when offensive	43	26
e-mails or material from Web sites are sent to other employees. In	48	29
some cases, the courts have found that these materials create a	52	31
hostile work environment. The second type of abuse is the waste of	56	34
work time. Employees who spend excessive amounts of time surfing	61	36
the Internet simply are not doing the work they are paid to do.	65	39
A number of large companies are trying to deal with this	69	41
problem by buying software that they use to track the sites that	73	44
workers access from their computers. These companies warn all of	78	47
their employees that visiting offensive sites at work can have major	82	49
consequences and might even result in job loss. They tend to be a	87	52
little more lenient on the time abuse issue and often treat the	91	54
Internet the same way that they deal with the telephone. Limited	95	57
personal use of the Internet or e-mail is not a major problem. If	100	60
the use becomes excessive, then action is taken.	103	62

3' | 1 | 2 | 3 | 4 |
5' | 1 | 2 | 3 |

Styles

The **Styles** feature enables you to apply a group of formats automatically to a document. A new *Word* document opens with the following styles attached to it: Normal, Heading 1, Heading 2, and Heading 3. Normal is the default style of 12-point Times New Roman, left alignment, single spacing, and no indent. Text that you key is formatted in the Normal style unless you apply another style.

Styles include both character and paragraph styles. The attributes listed in the Font dialog box make up the character styles. **Character styles** apply to a single character or characters that are selected. To apply character styles using the Formatting toolbar, select the characters to be formatted and apply the desired font.

Paragraph styles include both the character styles and other formats that affect paragraph appearance such as line spacing, bullets, numbering, and tab stops. The illustration below shows a list of styles that have been applied within a particular document. Character styles are listed; paragraph styles are indicated with the paragraph marker.

To apply paragraph styles using the Formatting toolbar:

1. Select the text to which you want to apply a style.

2. Click the down arrow on the Style box on the Formatting toolbar.

3. Select the desired style.

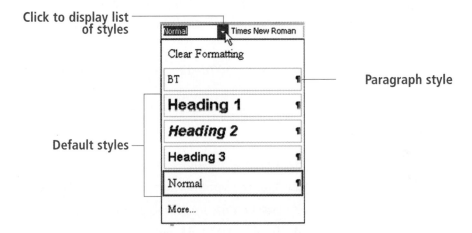

Click to display list of styles

Default styles

Paragraph style

DRILL 5   **STYLES**

1. Open a new document. Display the styles list box. Notice the default styles that are available.

2. Key your name on one line and your address below it. Select your name and apply Heading 1 style. Select your address and apply Heading 2 style.

3. Select your name again and apply Normal. Then select your name and italicize it. Display the styles list. Notice that Italic has been added as a character style.

4. Close the document without saving.

5. Open **Body Text** from the data files.

6. Apply the style **Body Text** to the document. Since there is only one paragraph, simply click anywhere within the paragraph and apply the style. The entire paragraph changes to the new style.

7. Save the document as **73d-drill5**.

Mr. Russell Adams
Trapp, Inc.
2593 Fifth St.
Dallas, TX 75221-4768
Russ
russell.adams@trapp.com

Ms. Cynthia Busch
LeVan, Inc.
2986 Sky Way
Seattle, WA 05671-4342
Cyndi
cynthia.busch@levan.com

Mr. Bradley Tate
ATA Supplies, Inc.
2155 Mack Ave.
Los Angeles, CA 90155-2074
Brad
Bradley.tate@atasupplies.com

Ms. Judith Olson
Trapp, Inc.
2593 Fifth St.
Dallas, TX 75221-4768
Judy
judith.olson@trapp.com

Mr. Donald May
SDG, Inc.
9170 Glacier Dr.
Selden, NY 11784-3579
Don
donald.may@sdg.com

Ms. Elizabeth Roth
Ashcraft, Inc.
8265 Oregon Ave.
Arvada, CO 80002-3749
Liz
elizabeth.roth@ashcraft.com

107d-d2
Name Badge Labels

1. Prepare name badge labels for all of the Customer Service Seminar participants.
2. Use the same format you used in **107c-drill2**.
3. Select a name badge label of your choice from the Avery Standard list.
4. Save as **107d-d2** and print on plain paper.

107d-d3
File Folder Labels

1. Prepare file folder labels for all of the Customer Service Seminar participants.
2. Use the same format you used in **107c-drill3**.
3. Select a file folder label of your choice from the Avery Standard list.
4. Save as **107d-d3** and print on plain paper.

107d-d4
Portfolio Labels

1. Prepare portfolio labels for all of the Customer Service Seminar participants.
2. Select **5836-Portfolio-Mtg. Creator** label from the Avery Standard list.
3. Include the address block plus the e-mail address fields.
4. Format the label by placing a double-space between the address block and the e-mail address.
5. Save as **107d-d4** and print on plain paper.

1. Open **Styles** from the data files.

2. Select the first heading (**Styles**), and apply the style **Heading 1**. Then center-align the heading and position it at about 2".

3. Select the next heading (**Built-in Styles**), and apply the style **Heading 1**.

4. Apply the style **Heading 2** to the next two headings (**Paragraph Style** and **Character Style**).

5. Apply the style **Heading 1** to the last heading (**Style Usage**).

6. Save it as **73d-drill6**. Your document should be similar to the one shown below. Print the report.

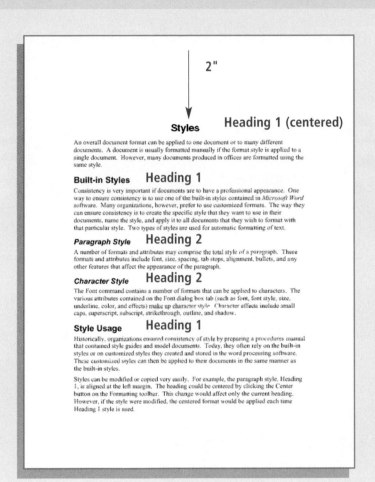

1. Key the report on page 284 SS.

2. For the tab, set tabs as follows: leader tab at 5.5" and right tab at 6.0".

3. Apply **Keep with next** feature to the side heading left alone at the bottom of the first page.

4. Insert page numbers at the top right; suppress page number on the first page.

5. Apply **Heading 1** style to the main and side headings.

6. Position main heading at approximately 2" and center it. Check side headings again.

7. Save as **73e-d1**.

DRILL 2 — CREATE NAME BADGE LABELS

1. Use the same procedures and data source to create Name Badge labels.

2. In Step 5 of 107c (p. 420), *Change document layout*, under Label Options, choose **5895-Name Badge**, and click **OK**.

3. In Step 6 under *Select recipients*, click **Use an existing list**, click **Browse**, and then select **Review Labels** from the drive on which you stored it.

4. Click **Next: Arrange your labels**.

5. Click **More Items** and use the following fields: Nickname, First Name, Last Name, and Company Name.

6. Format the first label block as follows: Select the first label, click **Center** and **Bold**. Then select **Nickname** and change font size to 36 point. Select the first and last names and company name and change font to 18 point.

7. Update all labels and preview.

8. Save as **107c-drill2 Name Badge** and print on plain paper.

DRILL 3 — CREATE FILE FOLDER LABELS

1. Use the same procedures and data source (**Review Labels**) to create file folder labels containing first and last name.

2. Use Label Option **5866-File Folder** labels.

3. When you select the recipients from the **Review Labels** data source, click the heading over Last Name so that the labels will be sorted in alphabetical order.

4. Save as **107c-drill3 Folder Labels** and print on plain paper.

APPLICATIONS

107d-d1
Address Labels

1. Prepare labels for all participants in a Customer Service training program.

2. Use the information below to prepare a data source for address labels. The same data source will be used for name badges, file folder labels, and e-mail addresses; therefore, include all of the information in the data source when you prepare it.

3. Name the data source **Customer Service**.

4. Select an address label of your choice from the Avery Standard list.

5. Save as **107d-d1** and print on plain paper.

Customer Service Seminar Participants

Mr. Alfred Carter
ATA Supplies, Inc.
2155 Mack Ave.
Los Angeles, CA 90155-2074
Al
alfred.carter@atasupplies.com

Ms. Pamela Cox
Ashcraft, Inc.
8265 Oregon Ave.
Arvada, CO 80002-3749
Pam
pamela.cox@ashcraft.com

Mr. Edward Nix
LeVan, Inc.
2986 Sky Way
Seattle, WA 05671-4342
Ed
edward.nix@levan.com

Ms. Janice Hill
SDG, Inc.
9170 Glacier Dr.
Selden, NY 11784-3579
Jan
janice.hill@sdg.com

(continued on next page)

Forms Design, Management, and Control

In 2003, a survey of the forms used by Hess and Glenn, Inc. indicated that 74 percent of all forms were paper based, and only 26 percent were in electronic format. Forms were produced both internally and externally. However, the majority of the forms were created internally. The following table shows the source of the forms used at that time.

5.5" leader tab   6.0" right tab

Employee—Paper	26%
Company—Paper	35%
Vendor—Paper	9%
External—Paper	4%
Company—Electronic	17%
Employee—Electronic	9%

The bulk of the paper-based forms were created either by individual employees to simplify their work or as standard forms used throughout the company. These forms were targeted for conversion to electronic format.

Existing System

No centralized forms management or control system existed at the time of the 2003 study. The responsibility for managing each form rested with the individual who created it. The cost, quality, and effectiveness of forms that were in use varied widely. Many forms were poorly designed and were ineffective. An analysis of the forms indicated that a significant number of them could be put online. Taking this action would reduce the cost and increase the effectiveness of all forms used by Hess and Glenn, Inc.

New System

A new system was recommended to the Executive Committee. The Executive Committee approved the recommendation and authorized the consultant to develop the implementation plan. The office manager was made responsible for the design, management, and control of all forms. Three components comprised the system.

Forms Analysis and Design

A checklist was created to evaluate each form. Because of the large inventory of forms, it was determined that the stock of forms should be used until the supply was depleted. However, before a form was reprinted, it would be analyzed for effectiveness. New forms could be designed by departments and submitted for review, or they could be designed by a forms designer on the office manager's staff.

Conversion from Paper to Electronic Forms

The primary goal of the program was to convert as many of the paper-based forms as possible to electronic forms. Forms that were used by or at the request of external customers were exempt from the mandate to convert paper forms to electronic forms. Forms that were filled in using pen or pencil would be considered on a case-by-case basis.

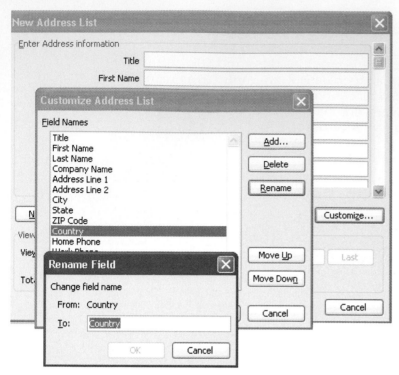

6. Under Select recipients, click **Type a New list** and then click **Create**. The New Address List box displays.

7. Click **Customize** to edit the default field names provided. For Drill 1, select **Country** and click **Rename**. Key **Nickname**.

8. Select each of the following fields and click the **Delete** button: **Address Line 2**, **Home Phone**, **Work Phone**, and **E-mail address**.

9. Key the variables for each record.

10. Click **Close** after keying all the records. The Save Address List dialog box displays. Enter the filename (**Review Labels**) in the File name box and click **Save**. (First select the correct drive to store the file; if you do not, it will be stored to the folder **My Data Sources** in the **My Documents** Folder.) Click **OK**; then **Next**.

11. Under Arrange your labels, click **Address block** (click **More items** if you prefer to select items individually).

12. Under Replicate labels, click **Update all labels** to replicate the address block merge field on each label across the page. Click **Next**.

13. From Preview your labels, click the arrows to preview labels; then click **Next**.

14. From Complete the merge, click **Edit individual labels**. Click **All**; then **OK**.

15. Resave the main document.

DRILL 1   CREATE LABELS

1. Create address labels for the records shown below.

2. Save the address list as **Review Labels**.

3. Save the labels as **107c-drill1 address** and print on plain paper.

Review Labels

Title	First Name	Last Name	Company Name	Address Line 1	City	State	ZIP Code	Nickname
Mr.	Reginald	McWhorter	Circle R, Inc.	1896 Lawndale Ave.	Salt Lake City	UT	84110-9365	Reggie
Ms.	Julie	Hartwell	Thomas General Hospital	2765 Sheridan Rd.	Chicago	IL	60650-7169	Julie
Dr.	Margaret	Wilson	Weeks Medical Center	957 W. Lake Dr.	Milwaukee	WI	53221-2956	Peggy
Mr.	William	Bass	Marcus, Inc.	830 Birch Cir.	Clinton	MS	39056-2864	Bill
Ms.	Rebecca	McGee	Circle R, Inc.	1896 Lawndale Ave.	Salt Lake City	UT	84110-9365	Becky
Mr.	Charles	Kapp	Marcus, Inc.	830 Birch Cir.	Clinton	MS	39056-2864	Chuck
Dr.	Henry	Wise	Weeks Medical Center	957 W. Lake Dr.	Milwaukee	WI	53221-2956	Hank
Ms.	Marjorie	Keene	Thomas General Hospital	2765 Sheridan Rd.	Chicago	IL	60650-7169	Margie

74a
Warmup
Key each line twice.

alphabet	1	Jack won five or six pan pizzas after the racquetball game today.
fig/sym	2	My $5,406 of stock (102 shares at $53/share) is now worth $7,489.
adjacent reaches	3	Klaus and Opal were going to try hard to prepare the guide today.
easy	4	Alan, a neighbor, may fix a clam or lamb dish for us at the lake.

| 1 | 2 | 3 | 4 | 5 | 6 | 7 | 8 | 9 | 10 | 11 | 12 | 13 |

DOCUMENT DESIGN

74b

Unbound Reports

Reports generally include the report body, title page, and often a table of contents. Follow the information and models shown to format these pages.

Body of the Report

Margins: Use default side margins, top margin, and bottom margin in an unbound report. In a leftbound report, set the left margin at 1.5, allowing $^1/_4$" for binding.

Page numbers: Create a header to number pages at the top right. Suppress the Number pages so that the number prints at the top right. Suppress the page number so that it does not print on the first page of the report. Use either the Page Number or the Header command to position the page number $^1/_2$" from the edge of the page.

Preliminary pages include the Title Page and Table of Contents. These pages are numbered with Roman numerals at the bottom center. The page number should be suppressed, however, on the Title Page.

Headings: Headings should reflect a hierarchy, with main headings being most important. To create this hierarchy, follow these guidelines:

Main heading (Level 1 heading): Strike ENTER to position the main heading about 2" from the top edge of the paper. Center-align in all caps, bold, and 14 point.

Side headings (Level 2 heading): Key at the left margin in bold. Capitalize all main words. Use Keep with next when headings appear close to the bottom of the page to keep the side headings with at least two lines of the paragraph. If Styles are applied, use Heading 2.

Paragraph headings (Level 3 heading): Indent paragraph headings 0.5" and bold. Capitalize the first word and follow the heading with a period.

Styles: Headings may also be formatted with styles. Although various styles may be applied, as a general rule, format the main heading using either the Title Style or Heading 1 (capitalize only the main words and center it), side headings (Heading 1), and paragraph headings (Heading 2). All headings, including paragraph headings, must be freestanding (on separate lines) when styles are applied.

Spacing: Single-space business reports and block paragraphs. Double-space educational reports and indent paragraphs 0.5".

Single lines: Avoid single lines at the top or bottom of a page (called widow/orphan lines).

LESSON 107 | Name Badges and Labels

SKILLBUILDING

107a
Warmup
Key each line twice SS.

alphabet 1 Paxton quoted Jay in an amazing article this week before leaving.
symbols 2 Take the 15% discount on the invoice (#4973280); then add 6% tax.
double letters 3 Bobby Lott feels that the meeting at noon will be cancelled soon.
fluency 4 Did Leigh visit the Land of Enchantment or a neighbor in Orlando?

| 1 | 2 | 3 | 4 | 5 | 6 | 7 | 8 | 9 | 10 | 11 | 12 | 13 |

DOCUMENT DESIGN

107b

Labels

Label options exist for a variety of purposes, such as address labels, name badges, file folders, CD-ROM labels, and many others. Many of these labels are useful in managing meetings effectively. Because all of these labels can be created from the same data source, it is important to capture all of the data that is needed in the data source. In this lesson, you will use the same data source to prepare address labels, name badges, and file folder labels.

Name badges for meetings and conferences are printed in large type so that they can be read easily. The tone for the conference is usually set by the way the name is printed on the badge. If a meeting is designed to be informal and interactive, the name badge usually features the individual's first name or nickname with the full name below it. A more formal meeting would include the full name. Rarely is a courtesy title (Ms., Mr., Mrs., or Dr.) used on a name badge. Professional titles and company or organization information may be included.

FUNCTION REVIEW

107c

Merge Labels

To create labels:

1. Open a new document and save with an appropriate filename. (For Drill 1, save as **107c-drill1 address**.)
2. Choose **Tools**, then **Letters and Mailings**, and then **Mail Merge Wizard**. Follow the steps of the Mail Merge Wizard to create labels. Click **Next** to move to the next step.
3. Under Select document type, select **Labels**. Click **Next**.
4. Under Select starting document, click **Change document layout**.
5. Under Change document layout, click **Label Options**. Choose **5922-address** from the Avery Standard Product number in the Label Options dialog box. Click **OK**.

(continued on next page)

References

A references page or bibliography includes a complete listing of references cited in the report. Position the title References or Bibliography approximately 2" from the top of the page. If styles are used, format the title using the Title style or use Heading 1 style and center-align it. List references alphabetically by author surname. Use hanging indent format to position the first line at the left margin and indent all other lines 0.5". Double-space between entries. Number the references page sequentially with the body of the report.

Title Page

The title page of a report includes a concise title of the report, name and title of the individual or the organization for whom the report was prepared, name and title of the individual preparing the report, and the date.

Center each line; leave approximately 8 lines between parts. Center the page vertically. Use the same side margins as the report. A page number is not printed on the title page.

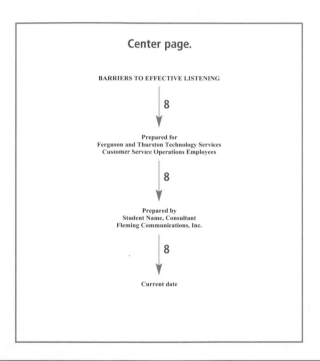

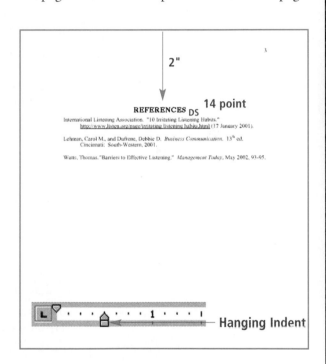

APPLICATIONS

74c-d1
Multipage Unbound
Report with References
Page

1. Key the model unbound report on pp. 287–288.

2. Insert a page number at top right; suppress the page number on the first page.

3. Use the information in the data file **references** to create a separate references page at the end of the report; format appropriately.

4. Switch to Print Layout View to verify page numbers and ensure that side headings are not alone at the bottom of the page.

5. Save the report as **74c-d1** and print.

74c-d2
Title Page

1. Prepare a title page for the report in **74c-d1** and save it as **74c-d2**.

2. Use the information shown above in the illustration, add the title in 14-point font, and insert the current date. Use bold for all text on the title page.

106c-d2
Revise Itinerary

1. Open **106c-d1** and save it as **106c-d2**.

2. Several plans have changed. Make the following modifications to Ms. Zachary's agenda.

   a. Brad Matthews cannot attend the 12:30 luncheon; he will meet with Ms. Zachary at the Mile High Hotel in Conference Room A at 2:30. June Wiley and Joseph Todd will be with him.

   b. Change the tour of the Azure Manufacturing Plant to 4:00.

   c. An earlier return flight was booked, Flight 482; depart at 2:45 and arrive at 5:40.

   d. Resave and print.

106c-d3
Itinerary

1. Use the same format as **106c-d1** and the following information to prepare an itinerary for Travelle Gortman who is attending and making a presentation at the Technology Summit in Washington, D.C. on June 1–3.

   a. Leave Mobile on Wednesday, June 1, on Freedom Flight 1475 at 7:00 a.m. and arrive in Atlanta at 7:35. Leave Atlanta on Freedom Flight 290 at 8:45 a.m. and arrive at Ronald Reagan Washington National Airport at 9:53; met by Executive Conference Service at baggage claim.

   b. Reservation on concierge level of the Hampton Hotel, 2300 Pennsylvania Ave., NW (Confirmation #527918).

   c. Conference (preregistration confirmation #S-963248); see conference program for schedule.

   d. Dinner on June 1 at 8:30 p.m. at Crystal's in Georgetown; reservations in your name for six (Anne Moore, Lee Roswell, Andy Cox, Leslie Kline, and Takisha Penn).

   e. Presentation at 10:00 a.m. on Thursday, June 2, in Ballroom A on the third floor of the Hampton Hotel; lunch with the Technology Summit Executive Committee at 12:30 in the Terrace Room.

   f. Depart at 6:30 p.m. for performance at Kennedy Center followed by dinner at Marbelle Estate with Larry Newman, president of the Technology Summit.

   g. Washington, D.C. to Mobile. Depart at 1:00 on Friday, June 3, for Ronald Reagan Washington National Airport (Executive Conference Service provides transportation) for return on Freedom Flight 861 at 2:45 p.m. and arrive in Atlanta at 3:51. Leave Atlanta on Freedom Flight 1683 at 4:45 p.m. and arrive in Mobile at 5:28.

2. Save as **106c-d3** and print.

2.1"

Main heading **BARRIERS TO EFFECTIVE LISTENING** 14 point

1.25"

In the initial phase of study of customer service operations, Fleming Communications, Inc., determined that listening is the communication task that our customer representatives spend almost 50 percent of their time doing. This report is the first in a series of reports. The purpose of this report is to explain a major barrier to effective listening and to present poor listening habits.

1.25"

Side heading **Issues in Listening**

Contrary to common belief, listening is not an easy task. Two issues to consider are the rate that listeners can process words and barriers to listening.

Paragraph heading **Rate.** Studies show that listeners can recognize words at a rate of 500 words per minute while speakers speak from 100 to 150 words per minute. A very important question to consider is at what rate does the mind process these words? With the mind processing information at over 1,000 words per minute, the listener is challenged to listen actively (Lehman and Dufrene, 1999).

Listening barriers. Listeners are also confronted with various other barriers to effective listening. These might include assumptions already made about the topic, about the speaker, about what the speaker will say, or about the specific setting. All of these assumptions will lead the listener to tune out what the speaker is actually saying. Another barrier to listening may be simply fatigue--the listener is too tired or perhaps too hungry or too busy to listen. Distractions often influence the listener's

1"

ITINERARY FOR SUSAN C. ZACHARY

May 6-8, 200-

14 point

Monday, May 6	**Dallas to Denver**
9:25 a.m.	Leave Dallas Fort Worth International Airport on Skyway Flight 498 and arrive at Denver International Airport at 10:28 a.m.; Bronco Rental Car (Confirmation #492084); Mile High Hotel, (Confirmation #360457) 3961 E. Louisiana Ave. (20 minutes).
12:30 p.m.	Luncheon meeting with Robert Jarworzky, Leigh Moreau, and Brad Matthews at Cherry Creek Eatery at 4827 Cherry Creek S. Dr.
3:00 p.m.	Tour of the Azure Manufacturing Plant; followed by meeting with the Quality Assurance team. Transportation: picked up at hotel by Dave S. Roane. Dinner arranged by Azure. Return to hotel by 10:00 p.m.
Tuesday, May 7	**Lakewood**
8:30 a.m.	Drive to Lakewood (map in Lakewood file).
9:30 a.m.	Full-day meeting with Lakewood Pharmaceuticals.
6:00 p.m.	Dinner with Christopher Davis, President of Lakewood Pharmaceuticals and Karen Davis. Return to hotel by 9:30 p.m.
Wednesday, May 8	**Denver**
9:30 a.m.	Meeting with the Gentry Group at the Mile High Hotel, Conference Center Board Room.
12:00 noon	Lunch for the Gentry Group in Skyview Room.
3:55 p.m.	Leave Denver International Airport on Skyway Flight 639; arrive Dallas/Fort Worth at 6:25 p.m.

ability to be an active listener. These annoyances may be loud noises near the speaker or a room that is too cold or too warm (Watts, 2002).

Poor Listening Habits

The poor listening habits presented here by Lehman and Dufrene (1999) and the International Listening Association (2001) are quite common among listeners. Being aware of the most common poor listening habits will aid in overcoming them.

SS each item.

DS between items.

Indent to paragraph point.

1. Pretending to listen is easy to do. By nodding, saying yes, and looking directly at the speaker, listeners can fake listening.

2. On the other hand, not looking at the speaker also results in poor listening as facial expressions and gestures are not communicated to the listener.

3. A listener's commitment to recording detailed notes often results in poor listening or overlistening.

4. Judgments by the listener about the speaker or the topic result in poor listening.

5. Rushing the speaker causes the speaker to think the listener's time is being wasted.

6. Interrupting the speaker is rude and does not enhance listening.

7. Showing interest in something other than the conversation and allowing any distractions to obtain the listener's attention result in poor listening.

Summary

Understanding that listening is not easy is a first step in becoming a better listener. Identifying individual habits that do not enhance effective listening is the next step. The first session of the Listening Skills Training Program will focus on the poor listening habits listed here and others.

LESSON 106 | Itineraries

SKILLBUILDING

106a
Warmup
Key each line twice SS.

alphabet	1	Rex Patey quickly moved to a new zone just before the group came.
figures	2	Vi paid $19.50 for Seats 7 and 8; Pat paid $26 for Seats 3 and 4.
1st/2nd fingers	3	Guy tried to come to my rescue before going to work this morning.
easy	4	Jay and I may go with eight girls to fish on the docks by a lake.

| 1 | 2 | 3 | 4 | 5 | 6 | 7 | 8 | 9 | 10 | 11 | 12 | 13 |

DOCUMENT DESIGN

106b

Itinerary

An **itinerary** is a detailed schedule prepared for individuals who are traveling or who are working away from their offices. Normally when people are working in their offices, they have a variety of information available to them. When they are out of the office, a comprehensive itinerary provides a quick summary of all the logistical information needed to function effectively. Itineraries for international travel typically require more information than for domestic travel. Types of information normally included in an itinerary include:

- Dates and times of meetings and events
- Transportation information—airline flight numbers and times, ticket information, passport or visa requirements, rental car or ground transportation
- Hotel information—name and address, confirmation number, special requests made
- Restaurant information—name and address, reservation information
- Meetings or appointments—individual and company names, times, addresses, transportation information if needed
- Leisure time activities and information

Most organizations use a list-type format so that the information is easy to read. Fragments are generally used rather than complete sentences. Position the heading for short itineraries about 2" from the top of the page and 1" to 1.5" for long itineraries. Set a hanging indent about 1.5" for the descriptive information. The itinerary shown on the next page illustrates a typical itinerary for a domestic business trip.

APPLICATIONS

106c-d1
Itinerary

1. Key the itinerary on the next page.
2. Position the heading at about 1.5" and format it in bold, 14-point type.
3. Use a default left tab of 1.5" and set a hanging indent at 1.5" for the second column.
4. Save as **106c-d1** and print.

75a
Warmup
Key each line twice.

alphabet	1	Chris Zweig quickly examined the job analysis forms we developed.
fig/sym	2	The trip cost $545.68 (1,859 miles at $.32 + $136.70 for a room).
double letter	3	Ann called a committee meeting at noon to discuss several issues.
easy	4	Claudia and my neighbor got fishbowls by the docks on the island.

| 1 | 2 | 3 | 4 | 5 | 6 | 7 | 8 | 9 | 10 | 11 | 12 | 13 |

75b
Leader Tabs

1. In the Tabs dialog box, set a left tab at 0.5", a leader tab at 5.5", and a right tab at 6.0".
2. Key the table of contents at the bottom of this page. Save as **75b**.

75c

Table of Contents

A **table of contents** contains a list of the headings in a document along with the page number on which each heading appears. The table of contents is created after the document has been completed. In a report, the table of contents is placed at the beginning of a document and is considered one of the preliminary pages. The table of contents (and other preliminary pages) is numbered with lowercase Roman numerals positioned at the bottom center of the page.

To create a table of contents, set three tabs: 0.5" left tab, 5.5" leader tab, and 6.0" right tab. Key the side headings at the left margin. Press TAB to indent the paragraph headings at the first tab. Press TAB again to display the dot leaders; then press TAB to move to the right tab to key page numbers.

Position heading at about 2.1".

Bold, 14-point font ⟶ **TABLE OF CONTENTS**   default margin

DS

Organization	1
.5" ⟶ Audience Analysis..	1
left tab Clear Purpose...	2
Organizational Pattern..	3

DS

Delivery..	4
Gestures...	4
Posture...	5

Number preliminary pages with ⟶ ii   5.5"   6.0"
lowercase Roman numerals.   leader tab right tab

1. Key the following information to prepare minutes; then add the remaining part of the document from **minutes** in the data files.

2. Use the same format as **105c-d1**.

3. Number pages as a right-aligned header; do not show page number on the first page.

4. Preview to make sure that headings are not left alone at the bottom of the page.

5. Save as **105c-d2** and print.

Palmetto Children's Home / Meeting of Board of Directors / May 20, 200-

The Board of Directors of Palmetto Children's Home met on May 20, 200- at 8:00 in the Board Room. Mary Ott called the meeting to order and welcomed all participants.

Board members present were Allen Brown, Jeff Green, Steve Islam, Fred Jones, Jake Lee, Carol Marks, Mary Ott, Keith Price, Ann Ray, and Julie Wills. Staff members present were Nate Lipscomb, Wayne Simmons, Suzanne Reed, and Jack Washburn.

Mission Statement Review
Jake Lee reported that the Executive Committee reviewed the mission statement and recommended no changes in it. The Executive Committee also recommended that the mission statement be read at the beginning of each board meeting to ensure that all actions were focused on accomplishing the mission of the Palmetto Children's Home.

Development Update
Julie Wills reported on development activities since the last meeting. She provided an updated list of the major gift prospects and asked each board member to review the list and provide her with information about any of the prospects they knew. She reviewed the solicitation plan that was included in the meeting materials and on behalf of the Development Committee moved the acceptance of the plan. The motion was approved unanimously.

Financial Report
Jeff Green presented the actual revenues and expenditures year-to-date and compared them to the current budget. Revenues and expenditures were on target, and no budget revisions were recommended. He then reviewed the quarterly financial statements. The financial report was presented for information and no action was required until the audit report is presented.

Jeff Green then provided an update on the $6,000,000 proposed bond issue and moved on behalf of the Finance Committee that the transaction be finalized. The motion was approved unanimously.

Insert **minutes** here.

1. Key the unbound report that follows with DS. Pay particular attention to the content that gives guides for formatting reports.

2. Key the main heading; position at about 2.1", and format appropriately. Key the side headings at the left margin and bold.

3. Indent the paragraph headings as shown. Bold and capitalize only the first word. Follow paragraph headings with a period.

4. Number the pages at the top right; suppress the page number on the first page.

5. Preview the document before printing to see that the page numbers display on the second and succeeding pages. If any headings are left alone at the bottom of the page, use the **Keep with next** function to position the heading with the paragraph that follows.

6. Save the document as **75d-d1**; print.

FORMATTING GUIDES FOR REPORTS

Business reports are used internally and externally. Managers often delegate the preparation of internal reports to subordinates; therefore, most reports go up to higher ranks in the organization. External reports often are used to secure business or to report on business that has been conducted for a client. Since reports can have a significant impact on an organization's business and on an individual's upward career mobility, they are usually prepared with care. Two important factors to be considered in formatting reports are placement and headings.

Placement

Effective report design requires many decisions about each of the factors just listed. A few basic guides can be applied to assist in making good formatting decisions.

Spacing. Reports may be formatted using either single or double spacing. Commercially prepared reports are generally single-spaced using many typesetting features. The desktop publishing capabilities of word processing software enable employees to prepare reports similar to those prepared professionally. Therefore, the trend is to single-space reports, to use full justification, and to incorporate desktop publishing features in the report.

Margins. Reports may be formatted with a default or 1" top, side, and bottom margins. An inch of extra space is provided in the top margin (2") for the first page of the report and for major sections that begin a new page. Extra space is required for binding. Most reports are bound at the left (1.5" left margin); a few are bound at the top (1.5" top margin).

Position the main heading at about 1" to 2", depending upon the length of the document.

CENTRAL UNIVERSITY MASTER PLAN FOR RESEARCH FACILITIES
Planning and Data Analysis Meeting Minutes
February 15, 200-

14 point

The Central University Master Plan for Research Facilities team met on February 15, 200- in the Plaza Board Room.

Team members present were Shirley Marshall, Team Leader; Chuck Taylor, President, Taylor Properties; Scott Johnson, Architect; Jim Hendley, Vice President for Research; Toni Hess, Provost; Andy Maxwell, Chief Financial Officer; and Joyce Martin, Chief Executive Officer, Foundations.

Work Session

Shirley Marshall opened the meeting and indicated that all team members were present. The team devoted the first half hour of the meeting to a working session designed to review a series of concepts relating to the design of the Phase I building. Scott Johnson charted the pros and cons on each concept presented and will finalize the analysis that will guide the conceptual design of the Phase I building.

Project Goals and Process Review

Shirley Marshall reminded the team that the primary goal of this project was to complete the preliminary design work that Central University could use to develop state-of-the-art research laboratory and office facilities on the property designated as the research block. The team agreed that the highest and best use of the research block was for three separate buildings connected by an open plaza. All parking was moved from the research block to the block across the street on the east side. A 1,000-car parking deck was proposed for that site. All information collected to date has been processed and incorporated in the initial site plan options.

Site Plan Options

Chuck Taylor summarized the data collected and analyzed in the site evaluation. The topography of the site presents design challenges because there is a 50-foot difference in the highest and lowest points on the block. Slides detailing the four options were presented for the conceptual design of the team. The team selected the horseshoe terrace as the preferred option, but recommended some modifications in the conceptual design.

Architectural Image Concepts

A series of architectural image concepts for the first building were critiqued. The feedback provided on the concepts will be used in preparing the building design to be presented at the next meeting.

After a general discussion of the progress on the project, the meeting was adjourned at 3:55 p.m.

Pagination. The way a report is paginated depends on the binding and the preference of the writer. Usually, leftbound and unbound reports are paginated at the top right margin, and topbound reports are paginated at the center bottom margin. However, other positions are acceptable. Arabic numerals (1, 2, 3) are used for the body of the report and the appendix; lowercase Roman numerals (i, ii, iii) are used for preliminary pages. The body of the report starts with page 1, but it is not numbered.

Headings

Topical headings or captions introduce the material that follows and provide structure in a report. Position, capitalization, font size, and attributes, such as bold and italic, indicate levels of importance. Headings also set segments of copy apart and make the copy easier to read. The spacing before and after headings depends on the font and attributes used.

75d-d2
Table of Contents

1. Key the table of contents for the report prepared in **75d-d1**. Refer to the illustration on page 289 to assist you.
2. Key the main heading at the center; format bold, 14-point font.
3. In the Tabs dialog box, set a left tab at 0.5" to indent for the paragraph heading, a leader tab at 5.5" for the dot leaders, and a right tab at 6.0" for the page number.
4. Key the side headings at the left margin. Press TAB and key the paragraph headings indented ¹/₂" from the left margin. After keying the heading, press TAB to display the dot leaders; press TAB again to move to the right tab. Key the page number. DS between the side headings to show the report division.
5. Save as **75d-d2** and print.

75d-d3
Title Page

1. Prepare a title page for the report in **75d-d1** and save it as **75d-d3**.
2. Use the following information: key the title in 14-point font and insert the current date. Use bold for all text on the title page.
3. Print; then assemble the report in the following order: title page, table of contents, and report.

Prepared for
Phoenix Technology, Inc.

Prepared by
Student Name, Information Manager
Phoenix Technology, Inc.

75d-d4
Table of Contents

1. Prepare a table of contents for **74c-d1**, the report prepared in Lesson 74.
2. Save as **75d-d4** and print.

105a
Warmup
Key each line twice SS.

alphabet	1	Gayle just told them about five quick trips to Arizona next week.
figures	2	The system provides 168 majors to 39,475 students on 20 campuses.
direct reaches	3	Ned used their sled on cold days and my kite on warm summer days.
fluency	4	Sidney may go with us to the lake to fish with worms on the dock.

| 1 | 2 | 3 | 4 | 5 | 6 | 7 | 8 | 9 | 10 | 11 | 12 | 13 |

DOCUMENT DESIGN

105b

Minutes

Minutes provide a record of what occurred in a meeting. Two significantly different types of minutes may be prepared. Verbatim minutes provide a complete record of everything said in a meeting. Usually verbatim minutes are prepared only for very formal meetings or for meetings that have legal implications. Most organizations prefer to use minutes that capture the essential or very important information that needs to be recorded for future use. These minutes are often referred to as action minutes because they capture the decisions that are made and the actions that take place—such as assigning responsibilities to particular individuals and specifying deadlines for the responsibilities to be completed.

Typically minutes contain the following types of information:

1. Date, time, and place of the meeting
2. Name of the presiding officer or meeting leader
3. Names (may also include titles) of attendees
4. Meeting objectives
5. Summary of decisions made
6. Summary of action items
7. Handouts and meeting materials are often attached to the minutes so they become part of the record.

Minutes are formatted in basic report style. Shortened versions of agenda items are often used as headings in the minutes. Review the minutes illustrated on the next page; then review the agenda that you prepared in **104e-d1**. Note that the minutes summarize the actions that took place in the meeting. Note also that this meeting was a working and planning type meeting rather than one in which formal action was taken and recorded.

APPLICATIONS

105c-d1
Minutes

1. Key the minutes illustrated on the next page. Position the heading at about 1.5"; bold and single-space it.
2. Single-space the minutes with 6-point space after paragraphs.
3. Bold all headings.
4. Save as **105c-d1** and print.

76a
Warmup
Key each line twice SS.

alphabet	1	Jim Winnifred, the proud quarterback, got criticized excessively.
fig/sym	2	Pat paid $85.90 each ($171.80) for 2 tickets in Row #34 on May 6.
double letters	3	Will the committee have access to all the books at noon tomorrow?
easy	4	Jake, their neighbor, paid for the right to fish on the big dock.

| 1 | 2 | 3 | 4 | 5 | 6 | 7 | 8 | 9 | 10 | 11 | 12 | 13 |

76b
Technique Builder
Key each line twice SS (slowly, then faster); DS between 2-line groups.

8/2	5	Row 2; Show 8; Page 82; Seat 28; Line 8228; Part 2822; Level 2882
1/7	6	1 second; 7 hours; 17 months; 717 seconds; 717 minutes; 1771 days
3/5	7	bake 3; take 5; give 53; grade 35; skip 535; call 5335; join 3535
4/6	8	Test 4; Pack 6; Troop 64; team 66; Tract 464; Ext. 664; memo 4466
9/0	9	0 errors; 9 cats; 0 dogs; 90 cows; 99 hooks; 990 words; 9009 laws
All	10	Call Ext. 3819 and ask Inspector 521 to explain Rules 50 and 467.

| 1 | 2 | 3 | 4 | 5 | 6 | 7 | 8 | 9 | 10 | 11 | 12 | 13 |

76c
Review Styles

1. Open **75d-d1** and save as **76c**.
2. Apply the **Heading 1** style to the main and side headings. Center the main heading and make it initial caps. Press ENTER one time after the main heading.
3. Edit the paragraph headings to display on a separate line; delete the period. Capitalize all important words, and apply the **Heading 2** style.
4. Preview the document to ensure no headings are left alone at the bottom of the page.
5. Print.

76d

Report Formatted with Styles

Reports are often formatted using predefined styles or by creating a custom style. Study the illustration on page 283. Only the first page is shown as an example. Note the main heading and the second-level heading are formatted with the Heading 1 style. When styles are applied, main headings are easier to read in initial caps rather than all capital letters. When a third-level heading (or a paragraph heading) is required, key the third-level heading on a separate line, capitalize in initial caps, and apply the Heading 2 style, as shown in the illustration.

The spacing before and after the headings is automatically determined by the style. Be cautious not to insert an additional ENTER before or after the heading.

Position the main heading 1" to 2", depending upon length of document.

CENTRAL UNIVERSITY MASTER PLAN FOR RESEARCH FACILITIES

Planning and Data Analysis Meeting Agenda

14 point

Left Tab 1"   **February 15, 200-**   Right Leader Tab 6"

DS

2:00 – 2:30   Work Session—Design Options . . . . Team

DS

2:30 – 2:50   Project Goals and Process Review. . . . . Shirley Marshall

Develop State-of-the Art Research Laboratories and
Offices
Develop Concept for "Highest and Best Use" for
Research Block
Create an Architectural Image for the Project
Process to Date

Left Tab 1.25"   Needs Assessment
Data Collection
Site Evaluation
Best Practices for Research Laboratories

2:50 – 3:20   Site Plan Options . . . . Chuck Taylor

Site Evaluation Conclusions
Options for Buildings on Block
Central Courtyard
Dense Linear Design
Horseshoe Terrace
Perimeter Buildings with Central Parking

3:20 – 3:50   Architectural Image Concepts . . . . Scott Johnson

3:50 – 4:00   General Discussion . . . . Team

76e-d1
Unbound Report with Styles

1. Open **nutrition** from the data files. Format the unbound report SS.

2. Position the main heading at approximately 2".

3. Apply the **Heading 1** style to the main heading and to the two level-two headings. Center the main heading. Apply the **Heading 2** style to the three level-three headings (shown in italics in the data file).

4. Number the pages at the top right; suppress the page number on the first page.

5. Key the paragraph below at the end of the document.

6. Save the document as **76e-d1** and print.

Food Preparation   Heading 2

Foods should be prepared in a manner that does not add fat to the food. Baking, steaming, poaching, roasting, and cooking in a microwave are the best ways to prepare foods.

76e-d2
Table of Contents

1. Prepare a table of contents for **76e-d1**.

2. Save as **76e-d2** and print.

76e-d3
Title Page

1. Prepare a title page for the report in **76e-d1** and save it as **76c-d3**. Format in Arial 14 point.

2. Assume the report is prepared by you for your instructor (include title and full name).

3. Print; then assemble the report in the following order: title page, table of contents, and report.

76e-d4
Edit Report

> Change Case: Select the text to be changed. Choose **Format, Change Case**, and then the desired option.

1. Open the report keyed in **75d-d1**. Save as **76e-d4**.

2. Follow the directions below to change to a single-spaced report with styles.

   a. Select the entire report. Change to SS.

   b. Delete the paragraph indent since SS reports are formatted with block paragraphs.

   c. Apply **Heading 1** style to the main heading; press ENTER once after the main heading. Change the format to initial caps (Title Case).

   d. Apply **Heading 1** style to the side headings.

   e. Edit the paragraph headings to display on a separate line and delete the period. Apply **Heading 2** style.

3. Save.

Agendas

Generally an **agenda** has four components:

1. Heading providing information about the meeting

2. List of the topics to be discussed at a meeting

3. Name of the person or group responsible for leading the discussion of each topic

4. Amount of time allocated for the topic

Attachments may be used to provide additional information about selected topics. The attachment number may be indicated in parentheses next to the agenda item (*See attachment 1*) or may just be attached without comment. Some organizations also like to include the primary objective of the meeting. Both the format and the level of detail vary depending on the organization. If an agenda is short, typically the heading will be positioned at about 2", and it will be double-spaced. If the agenda is long, it may be preferable to position the heading at about 1" or 1.5", and single-space it to fit the agenda on one page. An Agenda Wizard is also available in *Microsoft Word* to assist in the development of an agenda.

Review the agenda illustrated on the next page. This type of agenda was used in a client meeting by an architectural firm planning the development of research laboratories on an entire city block of property.

APPLICATIONS

104e-d1
Agenda

1. Key the agenda shown on the next page. Position the heading at approximately 2"; bold and double-space the heading.

2. Use an en dash for times (**Insert menu**, **Symbol**, **Special Characters**). *Hint:* Use copy and paste to insert the en dash the second through the fifth times.

3. Set left tabs at 1" and 1.25" and set a right tab with style 2 leader at 6".

4. Use spacing illustrated on the next page.

5. Save as **104e-d1** and print.

104e-d2
Save Agenda as Web Page

1. Open **104e-d1** and save it as a Web page.

2. Name the file **104e-d2** and save it in the **Web Page** folder you created.

3. Preview the Web page using your browser.

104e-d3
Agenda
(Challenge)

1. Open **104e-d1** and save it as **104e-d3**.

2. Add the following line as the first line of the agenda:

   12:30–2:00 Lunch and Presentation . . . . Team

3. Set decimal tabs at .3" and .75", left tabs at 1.25" and 1.5", and a right tab with style 2 leader at 6". You will need to tab before each time to make the times align correctly.

4. Resave and print.

Unbound Report with Footnotes

77a
Warmup
Key each line twice SS.

1 Oak Road; Ninth Blvd; Union Avenue; Main Court; High Circle
shift 2 Wade and Jeff; Randy and Paul; Carl and Nan; Teresa and Jane
3 Mr. and Mrs. Brian Nunn's grandson is Andrew Michael Quincy.

4 Keep your fingers curved.
5 Keep your eyes on the copy.
ENTER 6 Use quick and snappy keystrokes.
7 Strike Enter without pausing.

77b
Timed Writing
Key a 3' and a 5' writing.

all letters/figures

	gwam	3'	5'

Now and then the operation of some company deserves a closer look by investors. For example, Zerotech Limited, the food, oil, and chemical company, says in its monthly letter that it will be raising its second-quarter dividend to 85 cents a share, up from 79 3/4 cents a share, and that a dividend will be paid July 12.

This fine old area firm is erecting an enviable history of dividend payment, but its last hike in outlays came back in 1987, when it said a share could go above 65 cents. Zerotech has, however, never failed to pay a dividend since it was founded in 1937. The recent increase extends the annual amount paid to $5.40 a share.

In this monthly letter, the firm also cited its earnings for the second quarter and for the first half of this year. The net revenue for the second quarter was a record $1.9 billion, up 24.2 percent from a typical period just a year ago. Zerotech has its main company offices at 9987 Nicholas Drive in Albany.

gwam	3'	5'
4	2	41
8	5	44
13	8	46
17	10	49
21	13	51
25	15	54
30	18	56
34	21	59
38	23	61
42	25	64
43	26	65
47	28	67
52	31	70
56	34	72
61	36	75
64	38	77

3' | 1 | 2 | 3 | 4
5' | 1 | 2 | 3

Save a Word Document as a Web Page

To distribute a *Word* document on the World Wide Web, you must first convert the document to HTML format by saving it as a Web page document. *Word* automatically creates the HTML codes for the desired format. To view the new Web document as it will appear online, choose Web Layout View. After correcting any formatting problems, you may then preview the new Web document in your default Web browser.

To save a *Word* document as a Web page:

1. On the File menu, click **Save as Web Page.**

2. Select the drive and folder where you wish to save the file. (*Hint:* Save Web files in a folder created for that purpose. Storing these files in one location simplifies your work when you are ready to post the files to the Web.)

3. In the File name box, key the filename or accept the name provided. *Word* automatically adds the file extension .htm at the end of the document.

4. Click **Save.** (Click **Continue** if *Word* warns that the document has formatting not supported by the Web browser.)

help keywords

Create a Web page from an existing Microsoft Word *document*

About ways to view a Word *document*

Preview a document as a Web page

To view a document in Web Layout view:

1. On the View menu, click **Web Layout.** (*Shortcut:* Click the **Web Layout View** button on the status bar.)

2. Make any necessary formatting revisions (e.g., reposition graphics).

To preview the file in your browser:

On the File menu, click **Web Page Preview.** The file opens in your default Web browser. If the browser is not open, *Word* automatically opens it.

(*Note:* Web documents do not always display the same in all browsers. Using *Internet Explorer,* a *Microsoft*-compatible browser, will reduce these formatting differences.)

DRILL 1   SAVE AS WEB PAGE

1. Create a folder named *Web Page.* You will save the *Word* document used in this drill in this folder.

2. Open **orgchart** from the data files.

3. Save this *Word* document as a Web page to the *Web Page* folder created in Step 1. Name the file **104c-drill1**.

4. View the document in your browser.

(*Note:* The file **104c-drill1** and a folder **104c-drill1_files** are created when you save a document as a Web page.)

---

help keywords
insert footnote

Footnotes

References cited in a report are often indicated within the text by a superscript number (... story.[1]) and a corresponding footnote with full information at the bottom of the same page where the reference was cited.

Word automatically numbers footnotes sequentially with Arabic numerals (1, 2, 3), positions them at the left margin, and applies 10-point type. After keying footnotes, select them and apply 12-point type to be consistent with the report text. Indent the first line of a footnote 0.5" from the left margin. Footnotes are automatically SS; however, DS between footnotes.

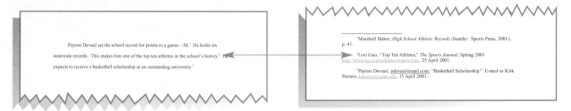

To insert and edit footnotes:

1. Switch to Normal view and position the insertion point where you want to insert the footnote reference.

2. On the menu, click **Insert**, **Reference**, and then **Footnote**. The Footnote and Endnote dialog box displays.

3. Be sure Footnotes is selected and Bottom of page (the default location) is displayed. Then click **Insert**.

4. The reference number and the insertion point appear in the Footnote Pane.

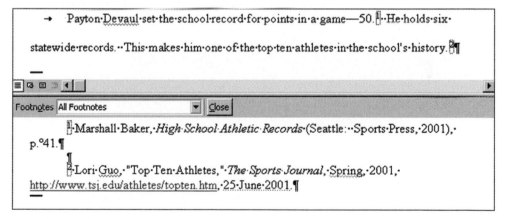

5. Move the insertion point before the reference number, and press TAB to indent it. Then move the insertion point beyond the number and key the footnote. Click **Close** to return to the document text. (*Note:* If you are in Print Layout View, click anywhere above the footnote divider line to return to the document.)

6. To edit a footnote, double-click the reference number in the text. Edit the footnote text in the Footnote Pane.

7. To delete a footnote, select the reference number in the text and press DELETE.

TIP

To insert a nonbreaking space, click **Insert**, **Symbol**, **Special Characters, Nonbreaking Space**.

Meeting Management

- Build keyboarding skill.
- Format agendas.
- Format minutes.
- Format itineraries.
- Prepare labels and name badges.

LESSON 104   Skillbuilding and Agendas

SKILLBUILDING

104a
Warmup
Key each line twice SS.

alphabet 1 Jeff and Gwen quickly analyzed the complex problem and solved it.
figures 2 Of the 20,473 square feet of office space, 16,598 is on Floor 16.
adjacent reaches 3 I saw her at an airport at a tropical resort leaving on a cruise.
easy 4 Andy and Blanche may make a map for a neighbor to go to the city.

| 1 | 2 | 3 | 4 | 5 | 6 | 7 | 8 | 9 | 10 | 11 | 12 | 13 |

104b
Timed Writing
Take two 3-minute timed writings.

gwam 3'

For many years, readers who had chosen a particular book had   4
just one question to answer. Do you want to purchase a hardcover   8
or a paperback book? It was assumed that books would be purchased   13
from a retail outlet, such as a bookstore. Currently, books are   17
being marketed and sold online. The book itself, however, is still   22
printed on paper.   23

With the technology that is on the market today, a third   27
alternative, the electronic or the so-called e-book, is emerging.   31
E-books are sold in digitized form. The book must be read from the   36
web site on a computer or on a special device designed for reading   40
e-books.   41

3'   1   2   3   4

1. Key the paragraph in Drill 2 DS, and add the three footnotes. Insert a nonbreaking space to keep p. and the number on the same line in footnote 1 (**Insert, Symbol, Special Characters**).

2. Format footnotes in 12 point and DS between them.

3. Include all three sources on a separate references page in proper reference format. Select the title *References* and apply the **Heading 1** style and center.

4. Save as **77c-drill1** and print.

DRILL 2 DELETE FOOTNOTES AND UPDATE REFERENCES PAGE

1. Open **77c-drill1**. Delete the second footnote. Update the references page.

2. Save as **77c-drill2** and print.

Payton Devaul set the school record for points in a game—50.[1] He holds six statewide records. This makes him one of the top ten athletes in the school's history.[2] He expects to receive a basketball scholarship at an outstanding university.[3]

Footnotes

Book —————— [1]Marshall Baker, *High School Athletic Records.* (Seattle: Sports Press, 2001), p. 41.

Online Journal —————— [2]Lori Guo, "Top Ten Athletes," *The Sports Journal*, Spring 2001, http://www.tsj.edu/athletes/topten.htm, 25 June 2001.

E-mail —————— [3]Payton Devaul, pdevaul@mail.com. "Basketball Scholarship." E-mail to Kirk Stennis, kstennis@umt.edu, 15 April 2001.

References

Baker, Marshall. *High School Athletic Records.* Seattle: Sports Press, 2001.

Devaul, Payton. pdevaul@mail.com. "Basketball Scholarship."
    E-mail to Kirk Stennis, kstennis@umt.edu. 15 April 2001.

Guo, Lori. "Top Ten Athletes." *The Sports Journal*, (Spring 2001).
    http://www.tsj.edu/athletes/topten.htm (25 June 2001).

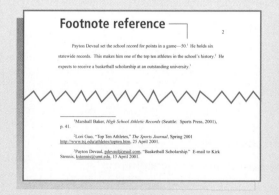

Report with footnote

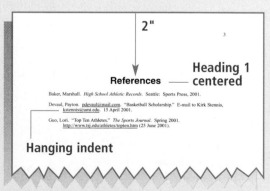

References page

«AddressBlock»

«GreetingLine»

For over fifty years, the Las Cruces community has enjoyed the magnificent concerts offered by the Las Cruces Symphony Association. Offering six concerts per year, including an outdoor concert and a special concert for children, the Association has drawn large audiences throughout the state and surrounding area.

All of this is made possible through the generosity of Las Cruces Symphony Association members who contributed more than $100,000 last year. Our plans for this season are even more ambitious, and we need your support in making these efforts possible. Please review the enclosed brochure detailing our "Plan for 2002" and consider becoming a supporter at one of the levels outlined below.

Membership Levels			
Patron	Over $5,000	Friend	$500 to $999
Benefactor	$2,500 to $4,999	Member	$50 to $499
Donor	$1,000 to $2,499	Contributor	Up to $50

Your membership in the Las Cruces Symphony Association is tax-deductible and can be mailed to the Las Cruces Symphony Association, P.O. Box 8390, Las Cruces, NM 88001. Join with other supporters of the fine arts in Las Cruces and contribute to the lives of the Las Cruces community and beyond.

Sincerely | Hung-Yueh Weng | xx | Enclosure

Document 2
Edit Data Source

1. **Ck16-d1merge** should be open.
2. Add the following record:

   Mr. and Mrs. Juan Rodriquez
   93 Maple Dr.
   Las Cruces, NM 88012

3. Change Dr. and Mrs. Sijansky's address to **P.O. Box 96396, ZIP 88001**.
4. Save the changes.
5. Sort by Last Name in ascending order.
6. Merge the data source and the main document and print the merged letters.
7. Save the merged letters as **Ck16-d2**.

Document 3
Mailing Envelopes

1. Prepare envelopes for the records stored in the data source **Ck16-d1data**.
2. Sort by Last Name in ascending order. Save as **Ck16-d3**.
3. Arrange each envelope with the appropriate letter. Be sure to keep in Last Name order.

77d-d1
Report with Footnotes

TIP

To increase the indent, click the **Increase Indent** button.

TIP

When e-mail or Internet addresses appear in a printed report, remove the hyperlink (right-click the hyperlink; then click **Remove Hyperlink**).

1. Key the unbound, educational report that follows with DS.
2. Indent the footnotes and change the font to 12 point.
3. Position the main heading at approximately 2". Format the headings appropriately.
4. Align the bullets with the beginning of the paragraph. (Click the **Increase Indent** button on the Formatting toolbar.)
5. Number the pages at the top right; suppress the page number on the first page.
6. Prepare the references page. Position the title at approximately 2"; apply Heading 1 style and center it. Key the references in alphabetical order; format as a hanging indent. Remove the hyperlinks.
7. Preview the document to see that page numbers display correctly and that no headings are left alone at the bottom of a page. If any headings appear at the bottom of a page, use **Keep with next** to keep the heading with the paragraph that follows.
8. Save the report as **77d-d1** and print.

Avoid Computer-Related Injuries

In the business environment, repetitive stress injuries (RSI), cumulative trauma disorder (CTD), and carpal tunnel syndrome (CTS) have mushroomed to afflict everyone from secretaries to executives with hurting muscles, tendons, and nerves. The Bureau of Labor Statistics reports that 70 percent of all occupational illnesses reported in the United States will be cases of repetitive stress injuries. Medical expenses and lost work for U.S. businesses are totaling $20 billion.[1]

The center of keyboard repetitive stress injuries is hand-arm alignment. Misalignment causes muscles to become overworked, causing stress and fatigue in the hands, arms, neck, and shoulders. Also, with the rapid rise of mouse-driven software and the large number of people surfing the Internet via a mouse, new ergonomic issues related to the use and the location of the mouse must be studied. To avoid computer-related injuries, all computer users can benefit from understanding basic guidelines for proper positioning at the computer and effective workstation design.

Position Yourself Properly

Preventing tired wrists and hands is really a matter of taking charge of your posture and computer work environment. Awkward posture while keying and failure to change your keying or sitting position can add to wear and tear on your wrists and hands.

Hand position. Keep your wrists and hands straight. When you work with straight wrists and fingers, the nerves, muscles, and tendons stay relaxed and comfortable. Therefore, they are less likely to develop the strains and pains that are often associated with keying.

Insert file **injuries**; format like the rest of the report.

Module 16: Checkpoint

Read the text in column A and match the correct term in column B. Enter the correct letter in the blank provided to the left of column A.

____ 1. Contains the text and graphics that remain the same for each version of the merged document.

____ 2. Inserted as placeholders at the place where the merge names, addresses, and other data will appear in a form letter.

____ 3. To access the Mail Merge Wizard, select _____ from the Tools menu.

____ 4. All the variables for one individual are called a _____.

____ 5. A file that contains the names, addresses, and other variables to be merged with the main document is the _____.

____ 6. The _____ button on the Mail Merge toolbar is used to edit the data source.

____ 7. The _____ button on the Mail Merge toolbar is used to complete the merge so the merged letters appear as a new document.

____ 8. Records sorted as A to Z or 1, 2, etc., are sorted in _____ order.

____ 9. _____ allows the user to select a specific set of records to merge.

____ 10. The _____ is the standard business envelope.

A. #8 landscape
B. #10 landscape
C. Ascending
D. Compare and Merge Documents
E. Customize
F. Data source
G. Descending
H. Filter
I. Letters and Mailings
J. Mail Merge Recipients
K. Main document
L. Merge fields
M. Merge to New Document
N. Merge to Printer
O. Record
P. Sort

Performance Assessment

Document 1
Mail Merge

1. Save a new document as **Ck16-d1merge**.
2. Create the data source. Save as **Ck16-d1data**.

Field names	Record 1	Record 2	Record 3
Title	Dr. and Mrs.	Mr. and Mrs.	Ms.
First Name	Hayden	Cory	Ruth
Last Name	Sijansky	Mandeville	Ikenberry
Address Line 1	1112 Woodview Dr.	135 N. Densbrook Ln.	P.O. Box 35329
City	Las Cruces	Las Cruces	Las Cruces
State	NM	NM	NM
ZIP Code	88012	88003	88012
Salutation	Dr. and Mrs. Sijansky	Mr. and Mrs. Mandeville	Ms. Ikenberry

3. Key the main document and insert the merge fields in it. Use open punctuation. Save the changes. The date should update automatically. Do not close this document; you will make changes indicated in Document 2.

6. Do you tilt your neck backward to see the computer screen? (No)

7. Do you take two 5-minute breaks and one 15-minute break in the morning and afternoon? (Yes)

8. Do you vary your activities to break the repetitive motion? (Yes)

9. Do you drink plenty of water to lubricate your joints? (Yes)

For each of your responses that do not match the desired response, please accept the challenge today to correct the undesired practice and avoid computer-related stress injuries.

Footnote text:

[1]"Repetitive Strain Injuries—The Hidden Cost of Computing," http://www.webreference.com/rsi.html, (8 March 2001).

[2]Jonathan Lee, *Comfortable Computing for Your Hands and Wrists* (Liberty Insurance Company, 2001), p. 53.

[3]Mason E. Gentry, "Workplace Ergonomics," *Computing*, March 2001, p. 46.

References text:

Lee, Jonathan. *Comfortable Computing for Your Hands and Wrists.* Liberty Insurance Company, 2001.

Gentry, Mason E. "Workplace Ergonomics." *Computing.* March 2001.

"Repetitive Strain Injuries—The Hidden Cost of Computing." http://www.webreference.com/rsi.html (8 March 2001).

> When e-mail or Internet addresses appear in a printed report, remove the hyperlink (right-click the hyperlink; then click **Remove Hyperlink**).

77d-d2
Table of Contents

1. Prepare a table of contents for **77d-d1**. List **References** as a side heading in the table of contents.

2. Save as **77d-d2** and print.

77d-d3
Title Page

1. Prepare a title page for the report in **77d-d1** and save it as **77d-d3**. Assume the report is prepared for your course (include course number and title) and is prepared by you.

2. Save and print; then assemble the report in the following order: title page, table of contents, and report.

77d-d4
Edit Report with Styles

1. Open **77d-d1** and save as **77d-d4**. Reformat the report using styles.

2. Change the main headings to initial caps and to Heading 1 style. (*Note:* When styles are applied, titles are easier to read in initial caps.)

3. Change side headings to Heading 1 style.

4. Change paragraph headings to side headings and apply **Heading 2** style. Delete the period after the heading, position the text at the left margin, and capitalize the main words in each heading.

5. Save and print.

103c-d2
Sort and Filter Mail Merge Document

Prepare form letters for your patients who are 45 days delinquent on their payments.

1. Save a new document as **103c-d2merge**.
2. Prepare the form letter below as the main document. Use block letter style, open punctuation. Send a copy of this letter to **Justin Langberg**.
3. Choose the file **103c-d2data** as the data source.
4. Sort the data source by ZIP Code in ascending order. Filter to select those patients past due 45 days.
5. Merge the main document and the data source. Save the merged letters as **103c-d2**.

«AddressBlock»

«GreetingLine»

Your unpaid balance of $«Unpaid_Balance» is now past due. We have requested payment from you on «No_Contacts_Made» occasions; however, we have received neither payment nor an explanation as to why payment has not been made.

Although we have no desire to cancel your credit privileges, we are forced to disallow any increase to your balance until payment of the past-due amount is paid. Future dental services for you and your family can be provided on a cash basis only.

Please call me at (305) 555-0135 and make arrangements for paying your overdue amount. If we do not hear from you regarding a revised payment schedule, please pay $«Minimum_Payment», a minimum payment. This payment must be received by March 20.

Sincerely | Paul Vanzandt | Office Manager | xx

103c-d3
Mailing Labels

Prepare cards for the individuals who have ordered bakery goods from your organization.

1. Save a new document as **103c-d3cards**. Use the file **103c-d3data** as the data source.
2. Prepare the note card below (**Avery 3259**) as the main document. Include the fields shown. Format the card attractively. Sort by Delivery date in ascending order.
3. Merge the main document and the data source. Save the merged cards as **103c-d3**.

«Name»

«Delivery_Location»
«Delivery_Date»

«Order_Item_1»
«Order_Item_2»

We appreciate your bakery order and wish you a happy holiday.

(662) 555-0090

Leftbound Report with Endnotes

78a
Warmup
Key each line twice SS.
Concentrate on keying the
reach correctly.

i	1	sit in said did dirk city did fin its lit iris wit hit ilk simmer
e	2	gem ewe men eke ever me le hen cede key led fen eye be pen leader
i/e	3	pie lei piece feign mein feint neigh lie reign die veil vein diem
i/e	4	Either Marie or Liem tried to receive eight pieces of cookie pie.
w	5	new jaw awe win we was awe away hew saw flaw law wan pew wit wavy
o	6	to onto rot job coho sox box oboe wok roe out oil dot tote oriole
w/o	7	ow wows how won worn now woe wool mow row work cow woke flows low
w/o	8	Women won't want to work now; we are worn out after woeful worry.
s	9	sans is ants sons has sun spas his six bus asps skis its spy sobs
l	10	el let la alp lot lilt led elk lab old lily fly lip ilk loll milk
s/l	11	also slow else sly false slaw sells slag sails sly sled slip slam
s/l	12	Slater tells us Elsie is also slightly slow to slip off to sleep.

| 1 | 2 | 3 | 4 | 5 | 6 | 7 | 8 | 9 | 10 | 11 | 12 | 13 |

78b

help keywords
endnote

Endnotes

An **endnote** consists of two linked parts—the endnote reference in the text and the corresponding endnote with full information at the end of the report. Create endnotes in Normal view; an endnote pane displays for keying the endnote text.

Word automatically numbers endnotes with small Roman numerals (i, ii, iii), positions them at the end of the document, and applies 10-point type. After keying endnotes, select them and apply 12-point type to be consistent with the report text.

To insert and edit endnotes:

1. Switch to Normal view and position the insertion point where you want to insert the endnote reference.

2. On the menu, click **Insert**, **Reference**, **Footnote**. The Footnote and Endnote dialog box displays.

3. Select **Endnotes**. The default location for endnotes is after the last line of document text.

4. Change the Number format to Arabic numerals (1, 2, 3). Click **Insert**.

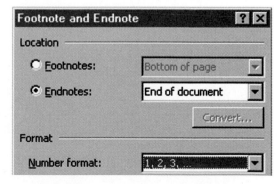

103c-d1
Mail Merge and Edit Data Source

Prepare the main document and data source for a form letter to participants of a summer workshop. You will need to edit your data source after you create it.

1. Save a new document as **103c-d1merge**.
2. Create the data source. Save as **103c-d1data**.

Field names	Record 1	Record 2	Record 3
Title	Mr.	Ms.	Ms.
First Name	Phillip	Anele	Anna
Last Name	Lancaster	Nyiri	Skelton
Company Name	Fulton High School	Curtis Middle School	Curtis Middle School
Address Line 1	35 Wallace Cir.	16060 Aspen Rd.	1355 Palomino Dr.
City	Norfolk	Richmond	Richmond
State	VA	VA	VA
ZIP Code	23501	27173	27173
Date	June 15–16	June 23–24	June 23–24
Room	204	205	205

3. Move Ms. Skelton to the **June 15–16** workshop. Change Mr. Lancaster's address to **89 Castle Rd.**
4. Key the main document (mixed punctuation style) and insert the merge fields in it. Add notations as needed. Save the changes. Be sure the date updates automatically.

Date

«AddressBlock»

Dear «First_Name»:

I am delighted that you will be attending the Principles and Applications of Web Design Workshop on «Date» at Braswell Community College. Please arrive at Room «Room» of the Harper-Kock Union Building at 8 a.m. for registration and a brief orientation.

As the workshop title indicates, the objectives include learning principles of web design and applying these principles in realistic exercises. The first day is filled with outstanding assignments highlighting important principles of web design. During the second day, you will team with one of your colleagues to plan and design impressive web pages for «Company_Name». Do take time before coming to the workshop to locate materials from your office that you will need to create these web pages.

Directions to Hathorn Hall, the residence hall designated for summer workshop participants, are enclosed. You may check in at Hathorn from 8 a.m. to 10 p.m. Housing payment can be made at the residence hall.

«First_Name», should you have any questions about the workshop, please call me at 555-0234. I look forward to your being a part of our workshop series.

Sincerely | Jane D. Gunter | Workshop Coordinator

5. Merge the data source and the main document and print. Save as **103c-d1**.

5. The Endnote Pane displays with the reference number and the insertion point in the Endnote Pane.

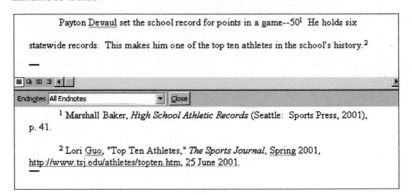

Payton Devaul set the school record for points in a game--50[1] He holds six

statewide records. This makes him one of the top ten athletes in the school's history.[2]

Endnotes All Endnotes   Close

[1] Marshall Baker, *High School Athletic Records* (Seattle: Sports Press, 2001), p. 41.

[2] Lori Guo, "Top Ten Athletes," *The Sports Journal*, Spring 2001, http://www.tsj.edu/athletes/topten.htm, 25 June 2001.

6. Position the insertion point before the reference number, and press TAB to indent it. Then move the insertion point beyond the number and key the endnote.

7. DS between endnotes and remember to change the font to 12 point.

8. To edit an endnote, double-click on the reference number in the text. To delete an endnote, select the reference number in the text and press DELETE.

Word inserts a line between the report text and the endnotes. Because endnotes will appear on a separate Notes page, remove the line.

To delete the divider line: Click the down arrow to the right of the Endnotes box at the top of the Endnote Pane, and then choose **Endnote Separator**. Select the line, press DELETE, and click **Close**.

DRILL 1   ENDNOTES

1. Open **endnotes** from the data files. Save it as **78b-drill1**.

2. Insert as endnotes the three footnotes shown in Lesson 77 Drill 1, p. 294.

3. Select the endnotes and format them in 12 point.

4. Save and print.

---

help keywords
page numbers, specify

Change Page Number Value

Occasionally it may be necessary to start numbering pages at a number other than the default of 1.

To change the starting number value:

1. Select **Page Numbers** from the Insert menu. Select the desired position for the page numbers.

2. Click the **Format** button. Click **Start at,** enter the page number, and click **OK**.

DRILL 2   CHANGE PAGE NUMBERS

1. Open **78b-drill1** and prepare the references page for this document.

2. Copy all text on the references page and paste it to a new document.

3. Position the main heading at 2", apply **Heading 1** style, and center it.

4. Insert page numbers at top right; change the value to 3. Save as **78b-drill2**.

Note: The references page could not be keyed after the Notes page because the endnote feature does not allow a hard page break at the end of the endnotes.

SKILLBUILDING

103a
Warmup
Key each line twice SS.

alphabet 1 Our unexpected freezing weather quickly killed Jo's mauve shrubs.
figures 2 Paula has moved from 8195 East 26 Street to 1730 West 148 Street.
double letters 3 Betty fooled Annabell by hitting a ball across the narrow valley.
easy 4 I fish for a quantity of smelt and may wish for aid to land them.

| 1 | 2 | 3 | 4 | 5 | 6 | 7 | 8 | 9 | 10 | 11 | 12 | 13 |

103b
Timed Writings
Key one 3' and one 5' writing at your control rate.

 all letters

gwam 3' 5'

Most people today have become very health conscious. Some   4 2 52
individuals worry about the bad effects of a diet that contains   8 5 55
far too much fat and a life style that does not include very much   13 8 57
exercise. However, many of those people never get past the stage   17 10 60
of worrying. Others just try to find a quick solution to the   21 13 63
problem. They try zany diets and easy exercise programs. The   25 15 65
real solution is to get in the habit of eating correctly and doing   30 18 68
exercise on a regular basis. The results are well worth the effort.   34 21 70

The combination of exercising on a regular basis and eating   38 23 73
properly produces much better results than either of these activi-   43 26 76
ties can produce by itself. An effective diet includes food from   47 28 78
all of the major food groups. Eating food that has a very high   51 31 81
fiber content and a very low fat content can help to prevent a   56 33 83
number of diseases. Not eating a meal to save a few calories is   60 36 86
not a very good idea. A good exercise program has several important   65 39 89
characteristics. Each session lasts approximately twenty minutes   69 41 91
and occurs at least three times a week. Also, the activity should   73 44 94
be fast enough to increase your heart rate. Walking at a fast pace   78 47 97
is one of the best and one of the most desirable activities that   82 49 99
you can do.   83 50 100

| 3' | 1 | | 2 | | 3 | | 4 | |
| 5' | | 1 | | 2 | | 3 | |

APPLICATIONS

103c
Assessment

On the signal to begin, key the documents in sequence. Correct errors. When time has been called, proofread all documents again and correct any errors you may have overlooked. Reprint if necessary.

Notes Page

When endnotes are used to cite references, the endnotes are placed on a separate page titled *Notes* at the end of the document.

To create the notes page:

1. After all endnotes are keyed, delete the endnote divider line.

2. Insert a page break below the last line of the report to position the endnotes on a separate page.

3. Position the insertion point at approximately 2"; key **Notes**; apply **Heading 1** style and center it; press ENTER.

4. Endnotes should be single-spaced with a double space between them. Remember to change the font to 12 point.

Note: You will still need to create a separate references page to include a complete listing of references.

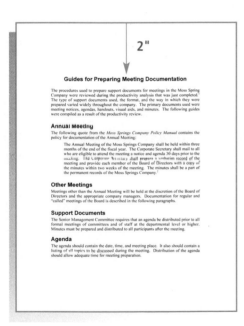

First Page

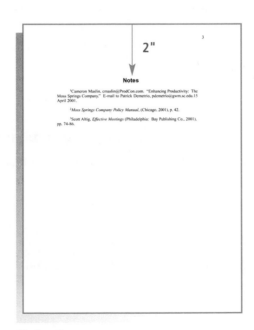

Notes Page

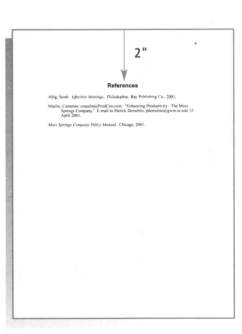

References Page

DRILL 3   NOTES PAGE

1. Open **78b-drill1**, save it as **78c-drill3**, and create the notes page.

2. Delete the divider line between the report text and the endnotes.

3. Follow Steps 2–4 in section 78c.

4. Save the document again and print.

The Holland Eye Center invites you to attend a special seminar sponsored for our patients who are potential candidates for laser vision correction. This seminar held at our clinic on «Date» at 7 p.m. will feature a panel of doctors and patients and a live laser vision correction procedure. A question/answer period will also provide an opportunity to have all your questions answered by these laser vision correction experts. You'll also have an opportunity to enter your name in a drawing for a complimentary laser vision correction procedure to be presented at the close of the seminar.

Would you like to join the millions of people who have chosen laser vision correction and be free of the daily hassles of glasses and contact lenses? Get started today by completing the enclosed reservation card indicating you will attend the seminar on «Date» and learn for yourself the details of laser vision correction.

Sincerely | Edward S. Vickery, M.D. | xx | Enclosure

4. Sort by ZIP Code in ascending order. Merge the data source and the main document and print. Save the merged document as **102c-d1**.

102c-d2
Edit Data Source

Several changes require you to edit the data source for the patients invited to the seminar on laser vision correction. Follow the directions below to make the edits and to print only those records with changes.

1. Open **102c-d1merge**. Edit the data source as follows:
   - Invite Dr. Jantz to the February 25 seminar.
   - Ms. Wiseman's new address is **235 N. Fifth St., Omak, WA 98841**.

2. Add two new records for the February 25 seminar.

   Mrs. Darlene Chism   Mr. James Lee
   830 Yorkville St.   332 Matilda Rd.
   Tonasket, WA 98855   Omak, WA 98841

3. Filter to select records of patients invited to the February 25 seminar. Merge to a new document; save the merged letters as **102c-d2**.

102c-d3
Envelopes

Prepare envelopes for all the patients invited to the laser vision correction seminar. (*Reminder*: Clear the filter used in **102c-d2** above.)

1. Prepare envelopes for the records stored in the data source **102c-d1data**.

2. Sort by ZIP Code in ascending order. Save the merged envelopes as **102c-d3**.

102c-d4
Name Badges

All the patients you invited to the laser vision correction seminar have agreed to attend the seminar. Prepare name badges for their use at the seminar.

1. Prepare name badges (**Avery 5095**) for the records stored in the data source **102c-d1data**. Include the first name and last name fields on the name badge. Sort by last name in ascending order. Format attractively (e.g., font, size, alignment, etc.).

2. Save the merged labels as **102c-d4**.

78d-d1
Leftbound Business
Report with Endnotes

1. Review the model on page 1 on the previous page. Notice that paragraphs are not indented. You're going to revise this rough draft and apply styles to the headings. Format the report as a leftbound report, single-spaced, and full justification. (*Remember*: 1.5" left margin for leftbound reports.)

2. The report includes three notations for endnotes. Indent the endnotes and change them to 12 point.

3. Apply **Heading 1** style to all side headings. Change all paragraph headings to side headings and apply **Heading 2** style. Remember to delete the period and place the heading on a separate line; capitalize all important words.

4. Insert page numbers at the top right; suppress the page number on the first page.

5. Prepare the notes page. Position the title at approximately 2", apply **Heading 1** style, and center it.

6. Preview the document to see that page numbers display correctly and to ensure that no headings are left alone at the bottom of a page. (Compare your document to the three illustrations on the previous page.)

7. Save as **78d-d1** and print.

Apply Heading 1 and center → Guides For Preparing Meeting Documentation

The procedures used to prepare support documents for meetings in the Moss Springs Company were review*ed* during the productivity analysis that was completed. ① The type of support documents used, *the format,* and the way in which they were prepared varied widely through out the company. The primary document*s* used were meeting notices, agendas, handouts, visualaids, and minutes. The following guides were compiled *as a result* on the basis of the productivity review.

Heading 1 **Annual Meeting**

The following quote from the Moss Spring*'s* Company Policy Manual *italic* contains the policy for the documentation of the Annual Meeting:

The annual Meeting of the Moss Springs Company shall be held within ③ *sp* months of the end of the fiscal year. The Corporate Secretary shall mail to all

Indent and SS who are eligible to attend the meeting a notice and agenda *30* thirty days prior to the meeting. The Corporate Secretary shall prepare a verbatim record of the meeting and provide each member of the Board of Directors with a copy

MERGE LABELS

1. Follow the directions provided on the previous page to prepare address labels for the data source file **learn-data**.

2. Save the merged address labels as **102b-drill3**. (*Reminder*: Resave the main document **learn-labels** after all steps of the Mail Merge Wizard have been completed.)

DRILL 4 **MERGE LABELS**

1. Prepare file folder labels (**5066-File Folder**) for the records stored in data source **99d-d1data**. Open a new document and save it as **102b-drill4 Labels**. From the More items list, select the following merge fields and arrange as shown below:

   Last Name First Name Title
   Company Name

2. Sort by Last Name in ascending order. (*Note*: If desired, edit the merged labels to include uppercase according to standard record management procedures.)

3. Save the merged labels as **102b-drill4**.

APPLICATIONS

102c-d1
Mail Merge

The Holland Eye Center is hosting two seminars to inform their patients about laser vision correction. Prepare the form letters for the records shown below.

1. Save a new document as **102c-d1merge**.

2. Create the data source. Save as **102c-d1data**.

Field names	Record 1	Record 2	Record 3
Title	Mr.	Dr.	Ms.
First Name	Angelo	Karen	Mary
Last Name	Seay	Jantz	Wiseman
Address Line 1	P.O. Box 88	137 Sonoma Dr.	539 Swoope Ave.
City	Tonasket	Omak	Tonasket
State	WA	WA	WA
ZIP Code	98855	98841	98855
Date	January 31	January 31	February 25

3. Key the main document and insert the merge fields in it. Use open punctuation. Save the changes. (*Reminder*: The date should update automatically.)

«AddressBlock»

«GreetingLine»

Do you ever imagine being able to see the alarm clock when you wake up? Do you ever imagine no more hassles of daily contact lens maintenance? Perhaps you may have imagined playing your favorite sport with complete peripheral vision—no fogging or slipping glasses. Millions of people across the world have chosen laser vision correction as an alternative to glasses and contact lenses. They now are enjoying these freedoms that you have only imagined.

(continued on the next page)

of the minutes within two weeks of the meeting. The minutes shall be a part of the permanent records of the Moss Springs Company. ②

Heading 1 style Other Meetings

Meetings ~~other than the annual meeting~~ will be held at the discretion of the Board of Directors and the appropriate company managers. Documentation for regular and "called" meetings of the Board ~~as~~ *is* described in the following paragraphs.

Heading 1 style Support Documents *Management*

The Senior Committee required that an agenda be distributed prior to all formal meetings of committees and of staff at the departmental level or higher. Minutes must be prepare*d* and distributed to all participants after the meeting.

Minutes

The Administrative Manager developed the following procedures to *to* implement the policy on maintaining ~~appropriate~~ minutes. The Senior Management Committee ~~met and~~ approved these procedures for immediate implementation.

Agenda

The agenda should contain the date, time, and place of the meeting. It also should contain a listing of all topic*s* to be discussed during the meeting. Distribution of the agenda should allow adequate time for ~~participants to prepare for the~~ *stet* meeting.

Verbatim Minutes. The Annual Meeting will be recorded, and a **Heading 2 style** verbatim transcript of the meeting will be prepared by the Corporate Secretary. Verbatim minutes are costly, ~~and~~ will be used only for the Annual *therefore, they* Meeting.

Remember to delete period and place heading on separate line. Capitalize all important words in heading 2.

Action minutes. Action minutes, consisting of identifying information, *and* a brief summary of decisions made, and of key views expressed, will be used for most meetings. ③ The emphasis should be on decisions, assignment of responsibility, and action planned for the future.

1. Follow the directions provided on the previous page to prepare envelopes for the data source file **learn-data**.

2. Save the merged envelopes as **102b-drill1**. (*Reminder*: Resave the main document **learn-envelope** after all steps of the Mail Merge Wizard have been completed.)

1. Prepare envelopes for the records stored in data source **99d-d1data**. Open a new document and save as **102b-drill2 Envelope**. From the More items list, select the following merge fields and arrange as shown here:

Title First Name Last Name
Company Name
Address Line 1
City, State ZIP Code

2. Sort by ZIP Code in ascending order.

3. Save the merged envelopes as **102b-drill2**.

Merge Labels

help keywords
*Create and print labels
for a mass mailing*

Labels designed for printers are available in all sizes and for many purposes, including file folder labels, mailing labels, name badges, and business cards. The data source is often used for merging letters, registration forms, envelopes, and numerous types of labels. Merging labels is very similar to merging envelopes.

To create labels:

1. Open a new document and save with an appropriate filename. (For Drill 3, save it as **learn-labels**.)

2. Choose **Tools**, then **Letters and Mailings**, and then **Mail Merge Wizard**. Follow the steps of the Mail Merge Wizard. Click **Next** to move to the next step.

3. Under *Select document type*, select **Labels**. Click **Next**.

4. Under *Select starting document*, click **Change document layout**.

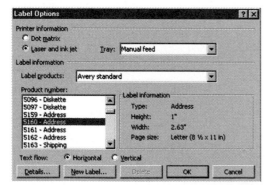

5. Under *Change document layout*, click **Label options**. Choose **5160-Address** from the Product number in the Label Options dialog box. Click **OK**.

6. Under *Select recipients*, click **Use an existing list**. Under *Use an existing list*, click **Browse**. From the appropriate disk drive, select **learn-data**, the data source created in Lesson 99. The Mail Merge Recipients dialog box displays the records. Click **OK**; then **Next**.

7. Under *Arrange your labels*, click **Address block**. (To select the merge fields individually for the address block, click **More items** and select each desired merge field.)

8. Under *Replicate labels*, click **Update all labels** to replicate the address block merge field on each label on the page. Click **Next**.

9. From *Preview your labels*, click the navigation buttons to preview envelopes if needed. (If changes in the data source are needed, click **Edit recipient list**.) Click **Next**.

10. From *Complete the merge*, click **Edit individual labels**. Click **All**; then **OK**. The merged labels will appear on the screen.

11. Resave the main document.

Use this information to prepare the Notes page.

[1]Cameron Maslin. cmaslin@ProdCon.com, "Enhancing Productivity: The Moss Springs Company." E-mail to Patrick Demetrio, pdemetrio@gwm.sc.edu. 15 April 2001.

[2]*Moss Springs Company Policy Manual.* (Chicago, 2001), p. 42.

[3]Scott Altig. *Effective Meetings.* (Philadelphia: Bay Publishing Co., 2001), pp. 74-86.

78d-d2
References Page

1. Prepare the references page for **78d-d1**. Position the title at approximately 2"; apply **Heading 1** style and center it.
2. Key the references that follow in alphabetical order; format with a hanging indent. Remove the hyperlinks.

Maslin, Cameron. cmaslin@ProdCon.com. "Enhancing Productivity: The Moss Springs Company." E-mail to Patrick Demetrio, pdemetrio@gwm.sc.edu (15 April 2001).

Moss Springs Company Policy Manual. Chicago, 2001.

Altig, Scott. *Effective Meetings.* Philadelphia: Bay Publishing Co., 2001.

3. Insert a page number at the top right on the references page; change the value to the appropriate starting number. All pages will now be numbered.
4. Save the document as **78d-d2** and print.

78d-d3
Table of Contents

1. Prepare a table of contents for **78d-d1**. List Notes and References as the last two side headings in the table of contents.
2. Save as **78d-d3** and print.

78d-d4
Title Page

1. Prepare a title page for the report in **78d-d1** and save it as **78d-d4**. Format in Arial 14 point.
2. Assume the report is prepared for Moss Springs Company and is prepared by you, Project Director.
3. Save; print; then assemble the report in the following order: title page, table of contents, report, notes, and references.

102a
Warmup
Key each line twice SS.

alphabet	1	Zan saw Jeffrey exit the park very quickly with a mean black dog.
figures	2	The stock price has increased 24.50 points to 189.75 in 36 weeks.
double letters	3	Pattie and Tripp meet at the swimming pool after football drills.
easy	4	Did the firm or their neighbor own the auto with signal problems?

| 1 | 2 | 3 | 4 | 5 | 6 | 7 | 8 | 9 | 10 | 11 | 12 | 13 |

NEW FUNCTIONS

102b

help keywords
*Create and print
envelopes for a
mass mailing*

Merge Envelopes

Envelopes can be merged from the data source. When printing envelopes, you will need to know the type of envelope feeder your printer uses. In this lesson, you will create #10 landscape envelopes (standard business envelopes).

To create envelopes:

1. Open a new document and save it with an appropriate name. (For Drill 1, save it as **learn-envelope**.)

2. Choose **Tools**, then **Letters and Mailings**, and then **Mail Merge Wizard**. Follow the six steps of the Mail Merge Wizard Task Pane explained below. Click **Next** to move to the next step.

3. Under *Select document type*, select **Envelopes**. Click **Next**.

4. Under *Select starting document*, click **Change document layout**.

5. Under *Change document layout*, click **Envelope options**. The Envelope Options dialog box displays. The Size 10 envelope is the default. Click **OK**; then **Next**.

6. Under *Select recipients*, click **Use an existing list**. Under *Use an existing list*, click **Browse**. From the appropriate disk drive, select **learn-data**, the data source created in Lesson 99. The Mail Merge Recipients dialog box displays the records. Click **OK**. Click **Next**.

7. In the envelope document at the left of the screen, position the insertion point in the letter address area.

8. Under *Arrange your envelope*, click **Postal bar code**. Click **OK** to accept the default merge fields for ZIP Code and Address 1.

9. Position the insertion point under the postal bar code. Click **Address block**. (If you prefer to select the merge fields individually for the address block, click **More items** and select each desired merge field.) Click **OK**; then **Next**.

10. From *Preview your envelopes*, click on the navigation buttons to preview envelopes. Click **Edit recipient list** to edit data source. Click **Next**.

11. From *Complete the merge*, click **Edit individual envelopes**. Click **All**; then **OK**. Merged envelopes will appear as a new document with a page break between each.

12. Save the document again (for Drill 1, save it as **learn-envelope**).

SKILLBUILDING

79a
Warmup
Key each line twice SS. Work at a controlled rate.

1st/2nd fingers

1 dirt nut fun drum try buy been curt very hunt bunt rent cent jump
2 We think Julio may give Ruth a ring Sunday if she will accept it.
3 My name is Geoffrey, but I very much prefer Jeff on this nametag.

3rd/4th fingers

4 was pill look zoom loop west low loose quiz walk saw wax box zeal
5 Paul Velasquez was at a popular plaza quilt shop when he saw Sal.
6 Sal was at a Palawan zoo; he was also at Wuxi Plaza for six days.

| 1 | 2 | 3 | 4 | 5 | 6 | 7 | 8 | 9 | 10 | 11 | 12 | 13 |

79b
Technique Builder
Key each line once; fingers curved and relaxed; wrists low.

third row

7 query were pure wipe wept you tort twirp report rip tire weep tip
8 Perry required two types of paper, a protractor, and four rulers.

3rd/home

9 we tattle wayward pepper rattle eloped require your yellow queasy
10 Patty wrote poetry, took art, and worked two jobs this past year.

1st/3rd

11 minimum box zip zinc bomb ripen corner mine cure woven zoo winner
12 Merv and Robert were to turn a valve to terminate the water flow.

| 1 | 2 | 3 | 4 | 5 | 6 | 7 | 8 | 9 | 10 | 11 | 12 | 13 |

79c
Timed Writing
Key a 3' and a 5' writing.

gwam 3' | 5'

	3'	5'
As you read copy for keyboarding, try to read at least a word	4	2 44
or, better still, a word group ahead of your actual keyboarding	8	5 46
point. In this way, you will be able to recognize the keystroking	13	8 49
pattern needed as you learn to keyboard balanced-hand, one-hand,	17	10 51
or combination word sequences. The adjustments you make in your	22	13 54
speed will result in the variable rhythm pattern needed for expert	26	16 57
keyboarding. It is easy to read copy correctly for keyboarding	30	18 59
if you concentrate on the copy.	32	19 60
When you first try to read copy properly for keyboarding, you	36	22 63
may make more errors, but as you learn to concentrate on the copy	41	25 66
being read and begin to anticipate the keystroking pattern needed,	45	27 68
your errors will go down and your keyboarding speed will grow. If	50	30 71
you want to increase your keyboarding speed and reduce your errors,	54	33 74
you must make the effort to improve during each and every practice	59	35 76
session. If you will work to refine your techniques and to give a	63	38 79
specific purpose to all your practice activities, you can make the	68	41 82
improvement.	69	41 82

3' | 1 | 2 | 3 | 4 |
5' | 1 | 2 | 3 |

DRILL 5 FILTER DATA RECORDS

1. With **learn-merge** open, filter as follows:
   Field: **State**
   Comparison Phrase: **Equal to**
   Compare to: Illinois (**IL**)

2. Merge to a new document; save as **101b-drill5**.

DRILL 6 FILTER DATA RECORDS

1. With **learn-merge** open, clear filters used in Drill 5.

2. Filter to select records of speakers who live in Chicago and are scheduled to speak at 8:30 a.m.

(*Hint:* Because both conditions must be met, select **and**; then key the requirements for the second condition.)

3. Merge to a new document; save as **101b-drill6**.

APPLICATIONS

101c-d1
Edit Data Source and Merge Letters

1. Open **99d-d1merge**. Edit data source as follows:
   - Mr. Bouchillon now works for **Prestage Technology Company**.
   - Ms. Vang's new address is **983 Old Cedar Pl.**; ZIP Code is **39704-0983**.

2. Add two new records. Print the selected records.

   Ms. Brenda Andres
   Gifts and More
   1456 W. 18 St.
   Starkville, MS 39759-1456
   Oktibbeha County

   Mr. Juan Seuffer
   Kubly and Ross Associates
   356 Airline Rd.
   West Point, MS 39773-0356
   Clay County

3. Add **Representative** as a new field.

4. Edit the records with the following data:

Record	Representative
Quarrels	Beth Stevens
Bouchillon	Kelly Cancienne
Vang	Patrick Konscak
Andres	Wade Sanford
Seuffer	Jennifer Fleming

5. Edit the main document to include the word *Representative* as the writer's title.

6. Sort by Last Name in ascending order and merge to a new document.

7. Save the merged document as **101c-d1**; print the merged letters. (*Reminder:* Save the main document, **99d-d1merge**.)

101c-d2
Filter Data Source

1. With **99d-d1merge** open, filter the data source to select records in Oktibbeha County.

2. Merge to a new document; save as **101c-d2**.

Sections

Often long documents such as reports are formatted in **sections** so that different formats may be applied on the same page or on different pages using section breaks. Normally, the preliminary pages of a report are numbered at the bottom center with lowercase Roman numerals. The pages in the body of a report are numbered in the upper right with Arabic numerals. Page numbers are usually inserted as headers or footers. For convenience, you will want to save the report as one file and not two or more.

To use different page number formats within the same document, you must format the preliminary pages as one section and the remainder of the report as another section. *Word* continues to use the same format for headers and footers in a new section as it did in the previous section until you first break the link or connection between the sections.

Section 1

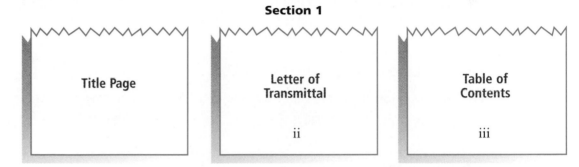

Title Page	Letter of Transmittal	Table of Contents
	ii	iii

Section 2
(Break link before changing page format)

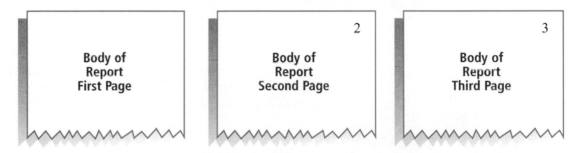

Body of Report First Page	Body of Report Second Page 2	Body of Report Third Page 3

To enter a section break:

1. Select **Break** from the Insert menu.

2. Click the type of Section break desired, and then click **OK**.

   Next page: Begins a new page at the point the section break is entered.

   Continuous: Begins a new section on the same page.

   Even page: Begins a new section on the next even-numbered page.

   Odd page: Begins a new section on the next odd-numbered page.

To sort records by multiple fields:

1. Open the main document; click the **Mail Merge Recipients** button.
2. Click the arrow next to any column name, and then click **Advanced**.
3. From the Filter and Sort dialog box, select the **Sort Records** tab.
4. Click the down arrow by Sort by and select the first field to be sorted in the multiple sort.

   Click the arrow by Then by and select the second field, and so forth. Click **OK**.

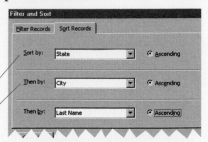

DRILL 2   SORT IN ASCENDING ORDER

1. With **learn-merge** open, sort by ZIP Code in ascending order and merge to a new document.

2. Save the merged document as **101b-drill2**. Close **learn-merge** without saving.

DRILL 3   SORT IN DESCENDING ORDER

1. With **learn-merge** open, sort by ZIP Code in descending order.

2. Merge to a new document; save as **101b-drill3**. Close **learn-merge** without saving.

DRILL 4   MULTIPLE SORT

1. With **learn-merge** open, sort in ascending order first by State, then by City, and then by Last Name.

2. Merge to a new document; save as **101b-drill4**. Close **learn-merge** without saving.

Filter Records

help keywords
Select recipients to include in mail merge

Filtering records before merging the main document and the data source allows you to select a specific set of records to merge. For example, you can create a target mailing to individuals in a specific state or ZIP Code area.

To filter data records:

1. Open the main document; click the **Mail Merge Recipients** button on the Mail Merge toolbar.
2. Click the arrow next to any column name, and then click **Advanced**.

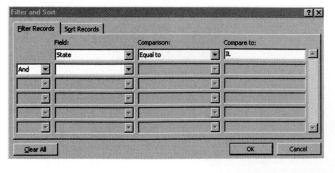

3. From the Filter and Sort dialog box, select the **Filter Records** tab.
4. Choose the appropriate data field (e.g., *State*); click a comparison phrase (e.g., *Equal to*); and key the text or data you will use for the comparison (e.g., *IL*). Click **OK**. (*Note*: Click down arrow for comparison and note the comparison phrases.)
5. Note the records displaying in the Mail Merge Recipients dialog box to determine if you have filtered correctly. Click **OK**.

To merge, click the **Merge to New Document** button on the Mail Merge toolbar.

(*Reminder*: Click the **Clear All** button in the Filter and Sort dialog box to remove filters before using the main document again to ensure all records will merge.)

In Normal View, section breaks appear as a dotted line with the type of break indicated. *Word* displays the current section number on the status bar.

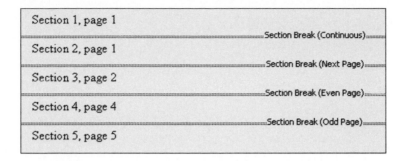

1. Open **sections** from the data files. Save as **79d-drill1**.

2. Insert a next page break after *Current date* on the title page.

3. Insert a next page section break after the table of contents.

4. Check that the table of contents and the first page of the report begin at approximately 2".

5. Save. Keep this document open for the next drill.

Insert Page Numbers and Break Link Between Sections

After learning to insert section breaks, you are ready to learn to insert page numbers with appropriate format in Section 1, break the link between Sections 1 and 2, and then insert the appropriate page format for Section 2.

To insert page numbers on preliminary pages:

1. Position the insertion point at the beginning of Section 1. Note that the status bar at the bottom left of the screen indicates *Sec 1*.

2. Click **Insert, Page Numbers**. For the position, choose **Bottom of page (Footer)** and for alignment, choose **Center**. Click **Show on first page** to deselect this option. Then click the **Format** button.

3. From the Format dialog box, choose lowercase Roman numerals for the number format (**i, ii, iii**). For Start at, key **1**. *Note:* You will not actually number the title page, but it still is considered p. 1. Click **OK** twice.

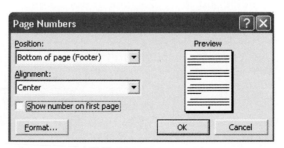
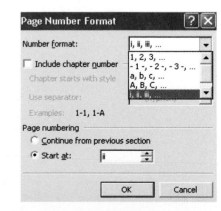

Changes to fields are made by editing the data source. Once the change is made, all of the records are revised.

To edit fields:

1. Click the **Customize** button on the Address List dialog box.

2. Edit as follows:
   a. *Add new field:* Click the **Add** button; key the field name. Use the move buttons to position correctly. (*Reminder:* Be sure to update the main document by inserting the new merge field.)
   b. *Delete field:* Select the field to be deleted. Click the **Delete** button.
   c. *Rename field:* Select the field to be renamed. Click the **Rename** button. Key new name.

3. Save your main document to update your data source.

DRILL 1   **EDIT RECORDS AND FIELDS**

1. Open **learn-merge**.

2. Add **Fax Number** as a new field after the ZIP Code field.

3. Update the records with the following fax numbers:

   Ms. Hershbarger (708) 555-0881
   Dr. Hodnett (414) 555-0094
   Mr. Zuber (708) 555-0692

4. Change Ms. Hershbarger's address to **206 Fourth Ave., Chicago, IL 60650-0206**.

5. Save edited records' main document and close it.

Sort Data Records

help keywords
Sort items in the list

Sorting records determines the order in which the records are merged. You might sort records in ZIP Code order, Last Name order, or City order. Occasionally, a multiple sort is needed to sort first by one field and then a second field, and so forth. For example, merged name badges or registration letters might be sorted first by state, then by city, and then by last name. Records are sorted either in **ascending order** (A to Z *or* 1, 2, etc.) or **descending order** (Z to A *or* 100, 99, etc.).

To sort records by one field:

1. Open the main document; click the **Mail Merge Recipients** button.

2. Click the column heading of the field to be sorted to display the data in ascending order. Click again to display data in descending order. Click **OK**.

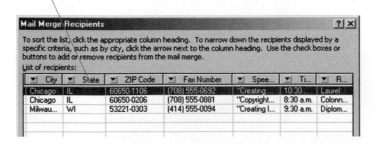

To merge, click the **Merge to New Document** button on the Mail Merge toolbar.

---

4. Scroll to the bottom of the table of contents and check the page number in Section 1.

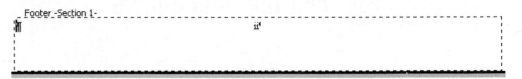

To break the link in Section 2:

5. Position the insertion point at the beginning of Section 2. Display the Header/Footer toolbar (**View**, **Header/Footer**). Click the **Same as Previous** button to break the link for the header. (Section 1 did not have a header; in Section 2 you want to add a header.)

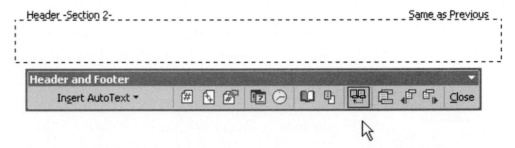

6. Click the **Switch between Header and Footer** button to go to the footer, and click the **Same as Previous** button to break the link for the footer. Delete the page number that appears in the Footer box. (Section 1 had a footer with a centered lowercase Roman numeral; Section 2 will not have a footer.)

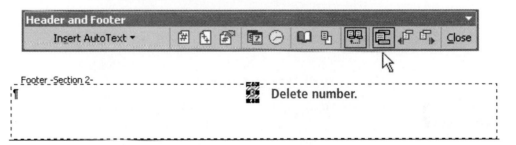

To insert page numbers in Section 2:

7. Switch back to the header. Click **Insert**, **Page Numbers**. Top of Page (Header) is already selected for you because you are still in the Header. For alignment, select **Right**. Do not show number on the first page.

8. Click the **Format** button. Choose the Arabic numeral (**1, 2, 3**). Start the page number at 1.

9. Close the Header/Footer toolbar.

10. Check the page numbers in Section 2. No number should appear on p. 1; a page number should display at the top right of the remaining pages.

101a
Warmup
Key each line twice SS.

alphabet	1	Jacky was given a bronze plaque for the extra work he did for me.
fig/sym	2	Order 12 pairs of #43 skis at $75.59 each for a total of $919.08.
3rd/4th fingers	3	Zane, Sally, and Max quit polo to swim six laps and work puzzles.
easy	4	Claudia and I do handiwork at both the downtown and lake chapels.

| 1 | 2 | 3 | 4 | 5 | 6 | 7 | 8 | 9 | 10 | 11 | 12 | 13 |

101b

> **TIP**
>
> An alternate way to display the toolbar is to use **Tools, Letters and Mailings**, and **Show Mail Merge toolbar**.

Mail Merge Toolbar

After all the steps of the Mail Merge Wizard are completed, you may want to edit your data source. To do this, you may reopen the Mail Merge Wizard (**Tools, Letters and Mailings**, and **Mail Merge Wizard**) or use the Mail Merge toolbar.

The Mail Merge toolbar is accessed from the View menu (**Toolbars, Mail Merge**). Use the Insert Address Block, the Insert Greeting Line, and Insert Merge Fields buttons to create the placeholders for the merge fields in the main document. The Mail Merge Recipients button is used to edit the data source while the Merge to New Document button is used to complete the merge.

Mail Merge Recipients
Insert Address Block
Insert Greeting Line
Insert Merge Fields

Merge to New Document

help keywords
About mail merge data sources

Edit Data Source

Sometimes you will need to edit the data source (list of variables) by changing individual records or revising the fields for all records.

To edit records:

1. From the main document, click **Mail Merge Recipients** on the Mail Merge toolbar.

2. Click **Edit**. The Address List dialog box displays.

   a. Use the navigation buttons to move from record to record, or click **Find Entry** to locate a record quickly.

   b. Make the desired changes.

   c. Click **Delete Entry** to delete a record.

   d. Click **New Entry** to add a new record.

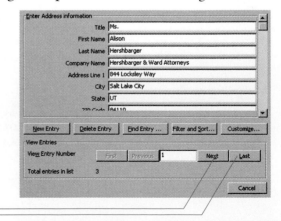

Navigation buttons

1. Open **79d-drill1** and save as **79d-drill2**.

2. Position insertion point in Section 1. Insert lowercase Roman numeral page numbers centered at the bottom of the page. Deselect **Show number on first page**.

3. Check page numbers in Section 1.

4. Position insertion point in Section 2. Display the Header/Footer toolbar, and break the links between both the header and the footer. Delete the page number in the footer.

5. Switch back to the header of Section 2. Insert Arabic numeral page numbers at the top right. Deselect **Show number on first page**, and click the **Format** button to start the numbers at 1.

6. Check page numbers in Section 2.

7. Switch back to header. Now that the link has been broken for both the header and footer, you can insert page numbers from the menu bar. Click **Insert**, **Page Numbers**, and **Right Alignment**. Do not show number on the first page.

8. Save and print the report.

APPLICATIONS

79e-d1
Report with Side Headings

1. Open **forms**. Save as **79e-d1**.

2. Key the remainder of the report. Check that side headings are not left alone at the bottom of the page.

3. Save and print. Keep this document open for use in the next application.

Forms Inventory

A perpetual forms inventory system was designed and maintained online for all company-wide forms. Employees were encouraged to add their individual or departmental forms to the inventory system so that they could be shared with others.

Goal of the System

The goal of the system was to convert 70 to 75 percent of the forms to an electronic format within a three-year time period. This goal was considered to be ambitious because a wide range of computers were used in the various departments, and some departments did not have access to the central network. During this same time frame, the company planned to upgrade computers and make the network available to all employees except warehouse and delivery personnel.

Follow-Up Study

This phase of the study was authorized to determine the effectiveness of the program that was implemented. The following chart shows the progress made since the program was instituted.

Results

Currently, 80 percent of all forms are in electronic format, and 20 percent are paper-based. The four forms that are currently purchased from vendors are being redesigned so that they can be made available electronically. The remaining paper-based forms are used primarily by warehouse and delivery personnel. However, the technology committee has recommended providing these employees with handheld computers to perform their work. As soon as this recommendation is implemented, the forms they use can be converted to electronic format.

100c-d1
Mail Merge

Prepare the main document and data source for a form letter to new members of the Jefferson City Chamber of Commerce.

1. Save a new document as **100c-d1merge**.

2. Create the data source. Save as **100c-d1data**.

Field names	Record 1	Record 2	Record 3
Title	Mr.	Ms.	Dr.
First Name	Dennis	Catherine	Stephanie
Last Name	Lamar	Bradberry	Wade
Company Name	Lamar Office Products, Inc.	ITC, Inc.	Jefferson City Medical Clinic
Address Line 1	P.O. Box 983	100 Jones Rd.	P.O. Box 3832
City	Jefferson City	Jefferson City	Jefferson City
State	MO	MO	MO
ZIP Code	65101	65111	65101

3. Key the main document (open punctuation style) and insert the merge fields in it. Add notations as needed. Save the changes. Be sure the date updates automatically.

Thank you for your continued support of the Jefferson City Chamber of Commerce. Your generous contributions made 2003 a great year for the Jefferson City Chamber. The enclosed *Annual Report* outlines just a few of our accomplishments.

A new membership decal and plaque for your business are enclosed. Please display those proudly on your car and in a prominent place in your business. We encourage you to promote the Chamber to fellow business colleagues and friends.

<<Title>> <<Last Name>>, again, we thank you for your support and invite you to join us the first Friday of each month at the Chamber Business Hour. Because we rotate locations among business members, be sure to watch the monthly newsletter for the specific location.

Sincerely | Your Name, Director | Jefferson City Chamber of Commerce | Enclosures

4. Merge the data source and the main document and print. Save as **100c-d1**.

100c-d2
Mail Merge

1. Consider the various form letters that are often used by businesses or organizations. Decide upon one effective use of form letters.

2. Save a new document as **100c-d2merge**.

3. Create the data source. Save as **100c-d2data**.

4. Key the main document and insert the merge fields in the main document.

5. Merge the data source and the main document and print. Save as **100c-d2**.

The new system has resulted in a 20 percent cost savings over the previous system. In addition, more than 80 percent of the employees indicated that the new system improved their efficiency and effectiveness.

79e-d2
Title Page

1. Open **79e-d1** and save as **79e-d2**.

2. At the top of the document, create a title page as the first page of the report. Assume the report is prepared for Hess and Glenn, Inc. and prepared by you as Consultant. Use the current date. Do not center vertically; position the main heading so title page is centered on the page.

3. Save. Keep this document open for use in the next application.

79e-d3
Table of Contents

1. Open **79e-d2** and save as **79e-d3**.

2. As the second page of the report, create a table of contents. Begin main heading at about 2".

3. Set tabs as follows: leader tab 5.5" and right tab 6.0".

4. Position insertion point at the end of the table of contents. Insert a next page section break. (*Note:* If you had already entered a hard page break so the report would print on the next page, delete the page break to avoid a blank page.)

5. In Section 1, insert lowercase Roman numeral page numbers centered at the bottom of the page. Do not show page number on the first page.

6. Position insertion point in Section 2. Display the Header/Footer toolbar and break the links between both the header and the footer. Delete the page number in the footer.

7. Switch back to the header and insert Arabic numeral page numbers at the top right. Do not print a page number on the first page.

8. Check that page numbers are positioned correctly and that the main heading is positioned at about 2". Save and print. Check the table of contents with the printed report.

79e-d4
(Challenge)
Generate Automatic Table of Contents

1. Open **79e-d1** and save as **79e-d4**.

2. Apply **Heading 1** style to the main and side headings. Center the main headings and make them initial caps.

3. Position insertion point at the top of the document. Click **Insert, Reference, Index and Tables**. Choose the **Table of Contents** tab. Accept the defaults by clicking **OK**. The table of contents is automatically generated.

4. Open **79e-d2**. Copy the title page. Go to **79e-d4** and paste as the first page.

5. Insert a section break at the end of the table of contents. Insert page numbers for Section 1. Break the link between the two sections. Insert page numbers for Section 2.

6. Save and print the report. Check the table of contents page numbers with the printed report.

SKILLBUILDING

100a
Warmup
Key each line twice SS.

alphabet	1	Dubuque's next track meet will have prizes given by forty judges.
fig/sym	2	Interest in 2000 climbed $346 (as the rates rose from 7% to 20%).
double letters	3	Ann and Buzz will carry my bookkeeping supplies to Judd's office.
easy	4	The auditor may laugh, but the penalty for chaotic work is rigid.

| 1 | 2 | 3 | 4 | 5 | 6 | 7 | 8 | 9 | 10 | 11 | 12 | 13 |

100b
Timed Writings
1. Key three 1' writings on each ¶.
2. Key one 5' writing or two 3' writings.

  all letters

gwam 3' | 5'

What do you think about when you hear individuals being — 4 | 2 50
called student athletes? Many people think only of the very — 8 | 5 52
visible football or basketball players who attract a lot of — 12 | 7 55
attention and often get special treatment on campus. Few people — 16 | 10 57
think about the large numbers of young men and women who put in — 20 | 12 60
long hours working and training to be the very best they can be — 25 | 15 62
in a wide variety of sports. These students may never receive — 29 | 17 65
any type of recognition in the news media, and they do not — 33 | 20 67
attract large crowds to watch them perform. They frequently — 37 | 22 70
excel in both academic and athletic performance. — 40 | 24 72

What does a student athlete in one of the less visible — 44 | 26 74
sports with very little opportunity to become a professional — 48 | 29 76
athlete gain from the significant investment of time and ef- — 52 | 31 79
fort in a sport? To be successful in a sport, a student must — 56 | 34 81
be organized, be an effective time manager, and have self- — 60 | 36 83
confidence. An athlete learns that teamwork, ethical conduct, — 64 | 38 86
and hard work are a major part of success in any type of en- — 68 | 41 88
deavor. The skills do not apply just to sports; they also apply — 72 | 43 91
to jobs and to life. Most important of all, these individuals — 77 | 46 93
are doing what they really enjoy doing. — 79 | 47 95

3' | 1 | 2 | 3 | 4 |
5' | 1 | 2 | 3 |

SKILLBUILDING

80a
Warmup
Key each line twice SS.

adjacent keys

1 Jamie quickly apologized for submitting the complex reviews late.
2 Where were Mario, Guy, and Luis going after the water polo class?

fig/sym

3 Jay paid Invoice #2846 ($3,017.35) and Invoice #7925 ($8,409.16).
4 I caught 20 halibut (69.5# average) and 37 trout (4.81# average).

| 1 | 2 | 3 | 4 | 5 | 6 | 7 | 8 | 9 | 10 | 11 | 12 | 13 |

80b
Timed Writing
Key a 3' and a 5' writing.

gwam 3' 5'

Just what does it mean to be young and when is a person young? `4 | 3 | 49`
To be young is perhaps a feeling or disposition, a particular manner `9 | 5 | 51`
of looking at things and responding to them. To be young is never `13 | 8 | 54`
a chronological period or time of life, although it might be a young `18 | 11 | 57`
person examining some material with fascination and pleasure or `22 | 13 | 59`
the composer Verdi in his eighties writing his best opera. To be `26 | 16 | 62`
young might be a person "hanging ten" on a surfboard or swinging `31 | 18 | 64`
to a musical composition. To be young might be Einstein in his `35 | 21 | 67`
seventies still working with his field theory, sailing his boat, `39 | 24 | 70`
or playing his cherished fiddle. `41 | 25 | 71`

To be young is never the monopoly of youth. It flourishes `45 | 27 | 73`
everywhere visionaries have stimulated our thinking or amazed us. `50 | 30 | 76`
To be young in nature is quite desirable whether you are a young `54 | 32 | 78`
person, a middle-aged person, or a chronologically old person. To `59 | 35 | 81`
be young should be respected whether the beard is soft and curly `63 | 38 | 84`
or firm and gray. To be young has no color; it seems often trans- `67 | 40 | 86`
lucent with its own imaginative light. There is no generation `71 | 43 | 89`
space between the young of any age because they see things as they `76 | 46 | 92`
ought to be. `77 | 46 | 92`

3' | 1 | 2 | 3 | 4 |
5' | 1 | 2 | 3 |

3. Key the main document and insert the merge fields in the main document. Use open punctuation. Save the changes. (*Reminder:* The date should update automatically.)

Date

«AddressBlock»

«GreetingLine»

Thank you for submitting your proposal for enacting a more culturally diverse employment program for city workers to the American Studies Association.

The American Studies Association continually strives to work with city governments in three area counties to provide work environments that value diversity. The goal, of course, is to employ persons who reflect differences in age, lifestyle, and interests. Different people solve problems differently, and that leads to better decisions.

You may be contacted, «Title» «Last_Name», to represent «County» County on the special Council for Managing Diversity that is being established in our three-county region. Again, thank you for letting us know what you are doing to ensure diversity at «Company_Name».

Sincerely | Hunter Nyiri, Director | xx

4. Merge the data source and the main document and print. Save as **99d-d1**.

99d-d2
Mail Merge

1. Decide on a form letter that would be useful to you personally or to your class. Secure the names and addresses of the recipients of the form letter.
2. Save a new document as **99d-d2merge**.
3. Create the data source. Save as **99d-d2data**.
4. Key the main document and insert the merge fields in the main document.
5. Merge the data source and the main document and print. Save as **99d-d2**.

On the signal to begin, key the documents in sequence. When time has been called, proofread the documents again and correct any errors you may have overlooked. Reprint if necessary.

80c-d1
Leftbound Report with References Page

1. Open **business** from the data files. Format as a leftbound report with references page. Apply styles and other features as indicated on the copy below and on the following pages.
2. Single-space the report. Insert page numbers at top right. Do not show page number on first page.
3. Use Heading 1 style centered for titles, Heading 1 style for level-one headings, and Heading 2 style for level-two headings (paragraph).
4. Insert footnotes where shown. Create the references page.
5. Save the document as **80c-d1** and print.

(title) Conducting Business on the Internet

This study was conducted to determine the desirability of enhancing the current Web site to increase Internet advertising and to begin conducting business over the Internet. Several factors were considered:

(Bullet each factor and delete commas) Internet advertising by competitors, Level of business conducted by competitors, Site development strategies, Estimated cost of enhancing the Web site

(Level 1 heading) Competitive Internet Usage

Of the 1,000 randomly selected firms in the industry that were surveyed, 520 (52 percent) responded. Firms were asked to indicate if Internet advertising was one of their top five marketing strategies in each of three years (1998, 2000, and 2002). They were also asked to indicate if they conducted at least 15 percent of their business over the Internet.

Analysis of the data shows that firms in the industry have increased their usage of the Internet as one of their top five marketing strategies from 1998 to 2000. However, the growth in the percentage of firms in the industry that conduct at least 15 percent of their business on the Internet has not been as rapid.

6. Click **Save** on the Standard toolbar to update the changes you have made to the file **learn-merge**.

7. Click **Next: Preview your letters**.

Step 5: Preview your letters

1. Click on the navigation buttons to preview each of your letters. (*Tip:* Should you need to edit one of the letters, click **Edit recipient list** and make the necessary changes to the data source file.)

2. Click **Next: Complete the merge**.

Step 6: Complete the merge

1. Click **Edit individual letters**. Click **All**; then **OK**. The merge letters will appear on the screen as a new document with a page break between each.

2. Save the merged file as **99c-drill1** and print.

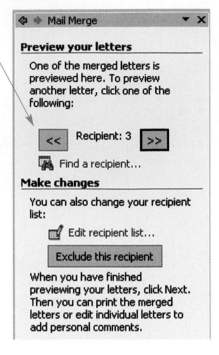

APPLICATIONS

99d-d1
Mail Merge

1. Save a new document as **99d-d1merge**.
2. Create the data source. Save as **99d-d1data**.

Field names	Record 1	Record 2	Record 3
Title	Mrs.	Mr.	Ms.
First Name	Jessica	Allen	Paje
Last Name	Quarrels	Bouchillon	Vang
Company Name	Hendrix Plastics	Magnolia Chemicals	Faulkner Florists
Address Line 1	5689 Old Vinton Rd.	538 Hill St.	885 N. Third St.
City	Starkville	Columbus	West Point
State	MS	MS	MS
ZIP Code	39759-5689	39701-0538	39773-0885
County	Oktibbeha	Lowndes	Clay

Firms using the Internet as one of their top five marketing strategies reported mixed results. Most of the firms indicated that the results over the past two years far exceeded the results of the earlier years. Many firms were still experimenting with alternatives for using the Internet. Most of them were using the equivalent of reprints of catalogs and other promotional materials.

(Level 1 heading) Site Development Strategies

Firms in the industry generally had developed their own Web site. Advertising experts interviewed believe that site development is critical to the success of cyberspace advertising and that the poor results some firms reported might be attributed to poorly developed Web pages. Benchmarking companies in a range of industries produces better results than using only the industry of a company.

(Insert footnote 1)

Three types of strategies for developing a Web site predominate: in-house development, the use of traditional full-service advertising agencies, and the use of the new cyberagencies that specialize in interactive marketing.

(Level 2 heading) In-House Development

The obvious advantage of in-house development is lower costs. The primary disadvantage is that most organizations have limited expertise in developing effective Web sites. A review of the literature indicates that about 45 percent of all Web sites currently in use were developed by company employees.

(Insert footnote 2)

(Level 2 heading) Traditional Full-Service Agencies

The key advantage of using the traditional advertising agency that handles other advertising for a company is that the Internet advertising can be an integral part of the company's total advertising plan. The primary disadvantage is that the traditional agency is not likely to have much expertise in cyberadvertising. About 25 percent of the Web sites in use were developed by traditional advertising agencies.

(Level 1 heading) Cyberagencies

These agencies specialize in interactive advertising on the Internet. The advantage they have over traditional agencies is the level of expertise in this new field. The disadvantages are lack of knowledge about the company and making interactive advertising an integral part of the company's total advertising.

Experts point out that cyberadvertising will be effective only when it is integrated into the mainstream advertising media such as radio, television, and print media. A joint venture of traditional and cyberagencies may offer the greatest promise for using the Internet effectively.

4. Click **Greeting line** in the far right pane of the Mail Merge box (or click the **Insert Greeting Line** button on the Mail Merge toolbar). The Greeting Line dialog box displays. Business letters may use open or mixed punctuation (mixed punctuation includes a colon after the salutation and comma after the complimentary closing). This letter applies mixed punctuation; therefore, click the down arrow to the right of the comma. Select the colon and click **OK**. Press ENTER two times and continue keying the letter until you reach the merge field code for Speech.

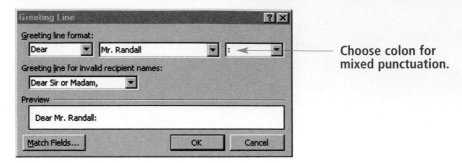

Choose colon for mixed punctuation.

5. Insert the merge field for Speech:
   a. Click **More Items** from the right pane (or click the **Insert Merge Fields** button on the Mail Merge toolbar).
   b. Select **Speech**, click **Insert**, and then click **Close**. (*Tip:* When necessary, strike the Space Bar to insert a blank space between fields. Insert punctuation as necessary between fields or at the end of a field.)
   c. Continue keying the letter. Insert the merge fields for Time and Room at the appropriate places.

(Date Code) (Enter 4 times)

«AddressBlock» (Enter 2 times)

«GreetingLine» (Enter 2 times)

Thank you for agreeing to present your paper titled «Speech» at the International Conference on Technology to be held at the Omni Hotel in San Francisco on May 12. Your presentation is scheduled for «Time» in the «Room». You may expect approximately 100 participants.

You are also invited to be our special guest at the annual awards luncheon on Friday at 11:45 a.m. in the Grand Ballroom. Your conference registration materials and a luncheon ticket will be held for you at the hotel registration desk. If you need assistance when you arrive at the hotel, please call conference headquarters at Extension 7532.

«Title» «Last_Name», we look forward to your presentation and to your outstanding contribution to our program.

Sincerely yours, (Enter 4 times) | Ms. Jacqueline VonKohn

Program Coordinator | xx

(Level 1 heading) Web Site Development Costs

The projected costs of developing a Web site that is capable of handling a reasonably high volume of transaction type business and the associated advertising materials are expensive. The estimated cost of an in-house development team is $110,000; traditional agency, $225,000; and cyberagency, $275,000.

(Level 1 heading) Recommendations

Pat's Place must enhance its Internet marketing. A number of strategies will be presented to the Executive Committee for accomplishing this objective. Considerable Web site work must be done before Pat's Place will be able to conduct a significant amount of business over the Internet. A team is developing a strategy to enhance the Web site and ways to increase the amount of business conducted on the site.

Footnote text:

1. Mark Levinson, "Benchmarking Internet Advertising," *The Small Business Journal* (March 2001), p. 49.

2. Mary Stackhouse, *Web Site Development* (Chicago: Seiver, Inc., 2002), pp. 86–92.

80c-d2
Title Page

1. Prepare a title page for the report in **80c-d1** and save it as **80c-d2**. Format in Arial 14 point.
2. Assume the report is prepared for **Meredith Ravennel** by you as Project Director.
3. Save. Do not close the document; you will use it in the next application.

80c-d3
Table of Contents

1. The document **80c-d2** should be open. Save as **80c-d3**.
2. As the second page, prepare a table of contents for **80c-d1**.
3. Number these preliminary pages appropriately. Do not print a page number on the title page.
4. Save; print and then assemble the report in the correct order.

80c-d4
(Challenge)
Section Breaks

1. Open **80c-d3**. Save as **80c-d4**.
2. Position insertion point at the end of the document. Insert the file **80c-d1**. You have inserted the title page and table of contents as the preliminary pages.
3. Insert section breaks appropriately and number pages appropriately.
4. Save and print. Assemble in correct order.

4. Key the variables for Record 1. Click **New Entry** to begin a new record; key variables for Record 2. Repeat for Record 3.

To move within the New Address List dialog box:

SHIFT + TAB   Move to the previous field.

TAB   Move to the next field.

ENTER *after last field*   Move to new record.

Field names	Record 1	Record 2	Record 3
Title	Ms.	Dr.	Mr.
First Name	Alison	Lisa	Joseph
Last Name	Hershbarger	Hodnett	Zuber
Company Name	Hershbarger & Ward Attorneys	Columbia Hospital	First Bank of Chicago
Address Line 1	844 Locksley Way	303 Park Circle Rd.	1106 Whispering Pines Rd.
City	Salt Lake City	Milwaukee	Chicago
State	UT	WI	IL
ZIP Code	84110-0844	53221-0303	60650-1106
Speech	"Copyright Issues in the Digital Age"	"Creating Interactive Presentations"	"Creating a Web Presence for Your Organization"
Time	8:30 a.m.	9:30 a.m.	10:30 a.m.
Room	Colonnade Room	Diplomat Room	Laurel Suite

5. Click **Close** after keying all of the records. The Save Address List dialog box displays. Enter a filename (**learn-data**) in the File name box and click **Save**. (*Note*: By default, data files are saved to the folder My Data Sources under the My Documents folder.) In the Save in box, choose the appropriate folder for saving this file.

6. The Mail Merge Recipients dialog box shows the variables in table format. Click **OK** (or click **Edit** to view the data in the New Address List dialog box).

7. Click **Next: Write your letter** from the Mail Merge Task Pane.

Step 4: Write your letter

1. Begin keying the main document on approximately line 2.1". Insert the date as a field (**Insert menu, Date and Time**; click the **Update automatically box**). Press ENTER four times.

2. Click **Address block** from the right pane (or click the **Insert Address Block** button on the Mail Merge toolbar). The Insert Address Block dialog box displays. Click **OK** to accept the default settings for recipient's name, company name, and postal address.

3. Press ENTER two times.

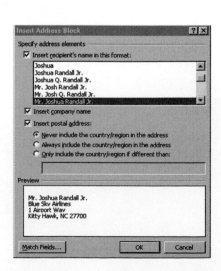

Module 12: Checkpoint

Objective Assessment
Answer the questions below to see if you have mastered the content of this module.

1. _____ are references at the bottom of a page; _____ are references at the end of the document.

2. To enter a section break, click _____ on the Insert menu.

3. To change page number format, select Page Numbers on the _____ menu.

4. To change to a different format for numbers in Section 2 of a document, you must first _____ _____ between sections.

5. A(n) _____ is a list of topics in a document and the page numbers on which they appear.

Performance Assessment

Document 1
Report

1. Open **Multimedia Artists** from the data files.
2. Insert page numbers at top right. Do not print on the first page.
3. Apply **Heading 1** style to the main and side headings.
4. Check that side headings are not alone at the bottom of the page.
5. Save as **Checkpoint12-d1**; print.

Document 2
Title Page

1. Create a title page for **Checkpoint12-d1**. Assume you are preparing for your instructor by you. Use the current date.
2. Save as **Checkpoint12-d2**. Do not close; you will use it in the next document.

   Option: You may create the title page in the same file as the report (**Checkpoint12-d1**).

Document 3
Table of Contents

1. The document **Checkpoint12-d2** should be open. Save as **Checkpoint12-d3**.
2. Create a table of contents. Set a leader tab at 5.5" and a right tab at 6.0".
3. Save and print. Assemble the report in the correct order.
4. Number the preliminary pages using lowercase Roman numerals at the bottom center. Do not print number on the first page.

   Option: You may create the table of contents in the same file with the title page and the report. You will need to use section breaks to number pages correctly.

The Mail Merge Wizard is a straightforward way to produce a merged document such as the form letter you will create.

To start the Mail Merge Wizard:

1. Open a new document and save it with a meaningful name.
2. Select **Tools**, then **Letters and Mailings**, and then **Mail Merge Wizard**. The Mail Merge pane displays at the right of the screen.

DRILL 1   MAIL MERGE WIZARD

1. Follow steps 1 and 2 above to start the Mail Merge Wizard. In step 1, save the blank document as **learn-merge**.

2. Follow the six steps of the Mail Merge Wizard explained below and on the next few pages. To move from one step to the next, click **Next** located at the bottom of the pane. This drill will lead you through the steps for using the Mail Merge Wizard.

Step 1: Select document type

1. Choose **Letters** (or the type of document you will use for the main document).
2. Click **Next: Starting document** to go to Step 2 of the Wizard.

Step 2: Select starting document

1. Click **Use the current document** to create a new form letter in the active window (or choose **Start from a template** to use a *Word* template, or choose **Start from existing document** to use a form letter you have already created).
2. Click **Next: Select recipients**. (*Note:* You may click **Previous: Select document type** to return to the previous step.)

Step 3: Select recipients

1. Click **Type a new list** because the data source does not yet exist. (Choose **Select from Outlook contacts** to use the Outlook address book, or choose **Use an existing list** to use a file that you created previously.)
2. Under *Type a new list*, click **Create**. The New Address List dialog box displays.
3. Click **Customize** to edit the default field names provided in the Wizard. The Customize Address List dialog box displays.

   a. To delete a field name, select the field and click **Delete**. Click **Yes** to confirm the deletion of each field. For this drill, delete **Address Line 2**, **Country**, **Home Phone**, **Work Phone**, and **E-mail address**.

   b. To add a field name, click **Add**. The Add Field dialog box displays. Add three fields: **Time**, **Room**, and **Speech**.

   c. To position the new fields correctly, select the field to be moved. Click **Move Up** or **Move Down** as appropriate. Move the field names so they are positioned as shown at the left.

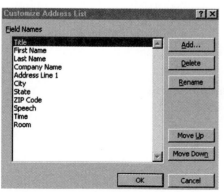

Table Mastery

- Review create tables.
- Edit and format tables.
- Perform calculations in tables.
- Landscape tables.
- Rotate text in tables.

LESSON 81 — Table Review

SKILLBUILDING

81a
Warmup
Key each line twice SS.

figures 1 The winning numbers for this week are 15, 27, 36, 48, 19, and 10.
2 Weekday show times are 12:30, 6:30, 7:15, 8:00, 9:45, and 10:15.
3 Take Highway 693 to Route 28 and exit 145th to get to 7th Avenue.
| 1 | 2 | 3 | 4 | 5 | 6 | 7 | 8 | 9 | 10 | 11 | 12 | 13 |

81b
Timed Writings
Key a 3' and a 5' writing.

gwam 3' | 5'

	3'	5'
A day planner can make your life easier by giving order to	4	2	38
chaos. It will organize the details of your week and notify you	8	5	40
when you should be somewhere. It will zealously remind you of	12	7	43
your duties and obligations. Just store the names and addresses	17	10	45
of your contacts, and it will quickly retrieve them for you.	21	12	48
You can enjoy life more when you are organized. You will	25	15	50
be able to remember all your usual classes, quizzes, projects,	29	17	53
and work responsibilities. You can also expect to know where you	33	20	55
need to go, arrive promptly, and not miss any important events.	37	22	58
Electronic planners are called "personal digital assistants"	42	25	60
or PDAs. A PDA can carry out all the functions of a day planner	46	28	63
and also let you send and receive e-mail. In addition, many PDAs	50	30	65
can share files with Word and Excel software; some allow you to	55	33	68
use the Internet. You can even use certain PDAs as telephones.	59	35	70

3' | 1 | 2 | 3 | 4 |
5' | 1 | 2 | 3 |

Mail Merge

Creating personal form letters, printing labels, and addressing envelopes to a large number of individuals are tasks done easily using the mail merge feature. **Mail merge** is creating a new (merged) document by combining information from two other documents—the main document and the data source.

The **main document** contains the text and graphics that remain the same for each version of the merged document. Within the main document, **merge fields** are inserted as placeholders in locations where you want to merge names, addresses, and other variable information that comes from the data source file.

The **data source** is a file that contains the names, addresses, and other variables to be merged with the main document. All the variables for one individual person are called a **record**. The separate variables for each record are called **fields**.

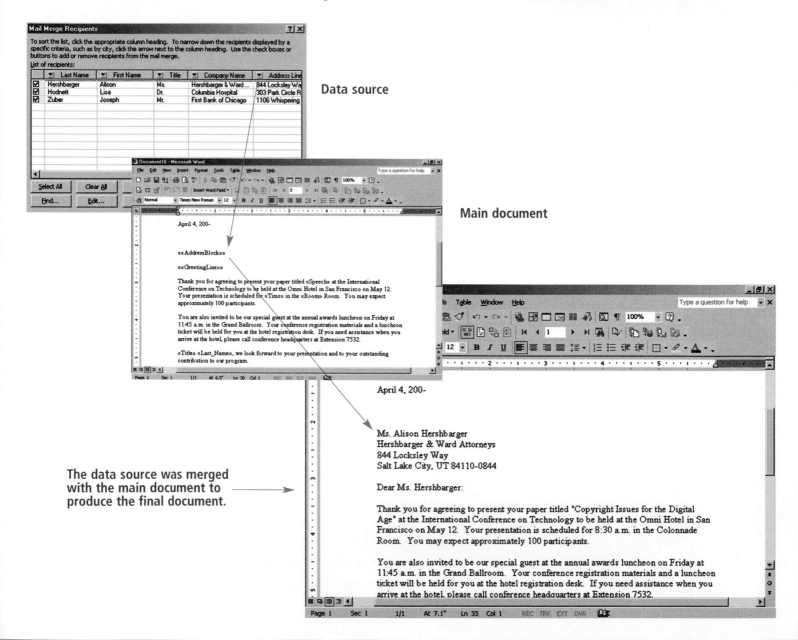

Data source

Main document

The data source was merged with the main document to produce the final document.

Table Format Guides

1. Leave an approximate 2" top margin or center the table vertically on the page.

2. Center, bold, use 12-point font, and key the main heading in all caps. Key the secondary heading a DS below the main heading in bold, centered, and 12-point font; capitalize main words. Center and bold all column headings.

3. Adjust the column widths attractively, and center the table horizontally.

4. Increase the row height to .3" and center the text vertically in the cell.

5. Align text within cells at the left. Align numbers at the right. Align decimal number of varying lengths at the decimal point.

6. When a table appears within a document, DS before and after the table.

To center the table horizontally, increase the row height and center the text vertically in the cell:

1. Select only the table; be careful not to select any ¶ markers outside the table.

2. Select **Table Properties** from the Table menu. Click the **Table** tab, and then select **Center Alignment**.

3. Click the **Row** tab. Key the desired height in the Specify Height box.

4. Click the **Cell** tab. Choose Center Alignment and click **OK**.

Tables and Borders Toolbar

The Tables and Borders toolbar allows you to add shading, borders, patterns, and color to your tables. Table AutoFormat, which allows you to apply a variety of preformatted styles to your tables, can also be accessed from the toolbar.

Shading. Select the cells or the row, click the down arrow, and choose a color or shade of gray. *Option*: Choose **Borders and Shading** on the Format menu. Click the **Shading** tab. Under Style, click the down arrow to change *Clear* to **15%**; then click **OK**.

AutoFormat. Click the table, click the **AutoFormat** button, and select a style.

DRILL 1

Key the table and shade row 1 15%. Key the text so that it fits on one line in each row. Save as **81c-drill1**.

DRILL 2

Open **81c-drill1**. Remove the shading and apply **AutoFormat List 8** style. Recenter table and text in cells. Save as **81c-drill2**.

Agent	Sales $	Office
Jacqueline C. Zahradnik	3,869,451	Lakeshore Boulevard
Katherine Ann Harrington	2,564.081	Lexington Heights
Michael T. Wang	1,975,392	Center City

Mass Mailings

- Merge form letters.
- Merge envelopes and labels.
- Edit the data source and sort and filter records.

LESSON 99 — Skillbuilding and Mail Merge

SKILLBUILDING

99a
Warmup
Key each line twice SS.

adjacent keys	1	Ty was going to see the trio perform at a junior college theater.
	2	My class was starting to talk about tilling the soil in Freeport.
fig/sym	3	My mileage is 28,475 on 2 front tires and 39,610 on 2 rear tires.
	4	Mark paid $230.49 plus 6% tax for 1.75# of pate & 1/8# of caviar.
fluency	5	The Orlando auditor did a formal audit of the firm on the island.
	6	Jane may work as a tutor for eight girls; Ty may also tutor them.

| 1 | 2 | 3 | 4 | 5 | 6 | 7 | 8 | 9 | 10 | 11 | 12 | 13 |

99b
Technique Builder
Key each line twice SS.

balanced hand	7	pens turn fur slam pay rifle worn pan duck ham lap slap burn girl
	8	Andy Clancy, a neighbor, may visit at the lake and at the island.
one hand	9	read ploy create kiln crate plum were pony cats jump severe hump
	10	Phillip, as you are aware, was a reader on deferred estate cases.
combination	11	did you we spent pony street busy jump held severe pant exert due
	12	Were profits better when we were on Main Street than Duck Street?

| 1 | 2 | 3 | 4 | 5 | 6 | 7 | 8 | 9 | 10 | 11 | 12 | 13 |

81d-d1
Table with Shading

1. Key the heading, **LAUREL CANYON ENTERPRISES**, and create the table shown below. Save as **81d-d1**.

2. Apply 20% shading to row 1. Center the column headings. Center column B and right-align columns C and D. Center the table vertically on the page.

Employee	I.D.	Hardware	Software
Alexander, J.	R492	$105,134,384	$1,868,553,280
Courtenay, W.	R856	79,364,091	1,384,219,500
Holsonback, E.	C845	27,386,427	1,098,237,260
Palombo, L.	K511	44,296,101	971,360,515
Rajeh, C.	M451	82,665,900	1,052,564,100
Talbert, S.	P053	82,091,433	985,201,500

81d-d2
AutoFormat

1. Place the title, **SOFTWARE TRAINING SCHEDULE**, on Line 2.1". Apply **Table List 4** format. Center columns B and C. Save as **81d-d2**.

Software	Date	Time	Room
Microsoft Word	02-18-04	9:00	Ballroom A
WordPerfect	02-18-04	10:30	Ballroom A
Microsoft Excel	02-18-04	1:00	Red Lion
Lotus	02-19-04	9:00	Diamond
Microsoft Access	02-19-04	1:30	Emerald
Oracle	02-20-04	9:00	Emerald
Windows 2000	02-19-04	10:30	Ballroom A
Windows Me	02-20-04	1:30	Diamond
Windows 2000 Server	02-20-04	3:00	Emerald

81d-d3
Table

The Grid 8 style bolds the last column and the last row. Deselect the checkboxes for Last row and Last column so they will not be placed in bold print.

1. Key the table and add the title **GOLDEN HANDSHAKE CANDIDATES**. Apply the **Table Grid 8** style. Center the table vertically. Save as **81d-d3**.

Employee	Department	Hire Date
Thayer, Jeffrey	Information Systems	8/21/75
Stevenson, Allison	Human Resources	7/27/72
Lew, Richard	Marketing	6/15/76
Gore, Rajah	Information Systems	8/16/76
Castillo, Maria	Human Resources	10/23/74
Husaan, Miram	Information Systems	12/2/72
Nelson, Barbara	Marketing	3/16/74
Wallace, Reggie	Human Resources	8/10/75

Module 15: Checkpoint

1. To wrap text around clip art, set the text wrapping style in the _____ dialog box.

2. To insert a picture that is available in your files, click **Picture** on the Insert menu and select _____.

3. Clip art size can be changed by holding the insertion point over the handle until the pointer turns to a _____ arrow and dragging a corner handle to increase or decrease it.

4. To wrap text around a graphic so that it is very close to the graphic, select _____ wrapping style.

5. AutoShapes, WordArt, and Rectangle can be accessed from the _____ toolbar.

6. A heading that spans two or more columns is called a masthead or a _____.

7. To balance columns so that they end at the same point on the page, insert a _____ break at the end of the text.

8. To force text to move to the next column, insert a _____ break.

9. To indicate that text is continued on the next page, insert a footer with the word _____ centered.

10. To indicate the end of a news release, key _____.

Performance Assessment

Document 1
Two-Column Newsletter

1. Open **cu news** from the data files.

2. Insert a continuous section break at the beginning of the body of the newsletter.

3. Format the document into two equal columns.

4. Check to see that the table is centered horizontally in the column.

5. Save the document as **Checkpoint15-d1**.

Document 2
Announcement

1. Format the document landscape with 1" margins on all sides.

2. Use keywords *buildings*, *house*, or *lake* to find appropriate clip art. Position it at top left margin with **Square** wrapping style and **left** alignment.

3. Use 36-point type and key to right of clip art: **Century Service Club / Picnic at the Lake House / 28 Lake Wateree Road**.

4. Center and key below clip art: **Club members and their immediate families / Saturday, June 10 from 12:30 to 6:30 p.m. / Make reservations by June 1 (555-0148) / Food and beverages provided / Bring lawn chairs or blankets**.

5. Save as **Checkpoint15-d2**.

Century Service Club
Picnic at the Lake House
28 Lake Wateree Road

Club members and their immediate families
Saturday, June 10 from 12:30 to 6:30 p.m.
Make reservations by June 1 (555-0148)
Food and beverages provided
Bring lawn chairs or blankets

LESSON 82

Reviewing Editing and Formatting Tables

NEW FUNCTIONS

82a

Decimal Tabs

Numbers containing decimals are often more attractive if they are aligned with a decimal tab. The decimal tab allows you to center the numbers in the column and still have them aligned at the decimal point. Notice how the numbers in column B are easier to read than those in column A.

Right-align on Toolbar	Decimal Tab
1.2	1.2
39.45	39.45
678.3	678.3

To set a decimal tab in a column:

1. Select the column or cells to be aligned (do not include the column heading).

2. Click the tab marker at the far left of the Horizontal Ruler, and change the tab type to a decimal tab.

3. Click the Horizontal Ruler to set the tab. Repeat the process with each column that requires a tab.

DRILL 1   SET DECIMAL TABS

1. Key the table above. Use left alignment when keying rows 2–4.

2. Select rows 2–4 in column A and click the **Align Right** button.

3. Select rows 2–4 in column B; set a decimal tab in the column so the numbers automatically align with the decimal point.

4. Save as **82a-drill1**.

DRILL 2   MERGE CELLS AND ADJUST ROW HEIGHT

1. Key the table. Right-align column B. Set a decimal tab in column C.

2. Merge row 1 and increase height to .5". Center the title vertically and horizontally in the row.

3. Save as **82a-drill2**.

INVESTMENT PORTFOLIO		
Company	**Units Sold**	**Increase/ Decrease**
Aztec Printing	55,275	+4.85
Palomar Clothing	120,890	−.59
Quest Supplies	8,321	−10.5
Robles Framing	986	−39.1

1. Open the News Release form **ppfe** from the data files and save as **98c-d3**.

2. Use the following information to key a one-page news release; double-space.

3. Resave, preview, and print.

Contact Person: Sherry Sinago

Current date

For Release: Immediately

CELEBRATION TO BENEFIT SCHOOLS

OKEMOS, MI—The Okemos Chapter of Parents' Partnership for Education will hold its annual Celebration of the Arts, Friday from 7:30 to 11 p.m. at the Talbert Hotel.

Participants will have an opportunity to enjoy an hors d'oeuvres buffet, see excellent musical and dramatic entertainment by students of Okemos Schools, view award-winning student artwork, and bid on artwork by locally and nationally known artists. An annual fundraising event for the Okemos Chapter of Parents' Partnership for Education, Celebration of the Arts serves several key purposes, according to organizers.

"The Celebration of the Arts provides an opportunity to showcase the superior quality of talent that is being nurtured in the Okemos Schools," said Chapter President Sherry Sinago. "It also provides an evening when people of the community can come together to socialize and share their support of the schools of Okemos. Also, this event enables our chapter to raise funds to carry out projects for the next school year," Sinago added.

The annual Celebration of the Arts is open to the public. Reservations may be made by calling 555-0134. Tickets will also be available at the door.

###

82b-d1
AutoFormat/Decimal Tab

1. Key the heading and create the table shown below.
2. Apply the **Table List 6** format.
3. Center column B; right-align columns C and D.
4. Center the table vertically and horizontally. Save as **82b-d1**.

LAUREL CANYON ENTERPRISES

Employee	I.D.	Hardware Sales	Software Sales
Alexander, J.	R492	$105,134,384	$1,868,553,280
Courtenay, W.	R856	79,364,091	977,219,500
Holson, E.	C845	9,987,120	81,003,367
Rajeh, C.	M451	82,665,900	1,052,564,100

82b-d2
Insert Rows

1. Open **82b-d1**. Save as **82b-d2**.
2. Insert additional rows and key the names and accompanying information below in correct alphabetical order. Save again and print.

Palombo, L.	K511	44,296,101	971,360,515
Talbert, S.	P053	82,091,433	985,201,500

> **TIP**
> A quick way to insert a row at the end of the table is to click the insertion point in the last cell and press TAB.

82b-d3
Delete Rows and Insert Column

1. Open **82b-d2**. Save as **82b-d3**.
2. Delete the rows that contain ID numbers **R856** and **M451**.
3. Insert a new column to the left of the Employee column and key the following information. Center the column.

> **TIP**
> To insert a column, select **Table**, **Insert**, and then choose **Columns to the Left** or **Columns to the Right**.

Team
Blue
Gold
Blue
Gold

4. Change the table to **Table List 3** format. Recenter the table and recenter the copy vertically in the cells.
5. Save again and print.

Pediatric News

PACIFIC NEWPORT MEDICAL GROUP

HEPATITIS B VACCINE

Hepatitis B is most commonly contracted in the teenage and adult years. It is highly recommended that all pre-teens and teenagers be vaccinated with the series of three Hepatitis B vaccines. The three shots are administered over a six-month period.

Hepatitis B can affect anyone—in fact, it is estimated that one in ten adults may acquire Hepatitis B at some time unless immunized. The most serious complications of Hepatitis B are a deterioration of liver function and development of liver cancer.

The vaccine is safe and has no side effects. We can administer the MMR or tetanus booster (if they are due) at the same time as the Hepatitis vaccine.

INSURANCE COVERAGE

All health insurance policies are required to cover your child's well child care visits as well as immunizations. Most insurance policies cover the cost of one well care visit each year.

PEDIATRIC ASTHMA

The number of cases of asthma in children under 18 years of age was reported as 2.7 million during this past year. At least one child with asthma was reported by 4.3 percent of households.

Similar to an overly sensitive car alarm, the cells that line the lungs of adults and children with asthma are often set off by the smallest disturbance. The trigger may be a bit of pollen, cat dander, dust, tobacco smoke, or some other pollutant. It may also be a draft of cold air, the common cold virus, or even the demands of exercise.

Many children do outgrow asthma, but that is not a reason to ignore treating it appropriately. If your child has problems with recurrent coughing, coughing with exercise, shortness of breath, nighttime coughing, or poorly controlled asthma, please discuss it with us. We have many treatment options to try to make your child as healthy as possible.

PHYSICAL EXAM FOR SCHOOL ENTRY

Call now to set up an appointment for a physical exam if your child will be entering kindergarten or first grade this year. We recommend vision and hearing screenings before school entry. There are a limited number of appointments allocated for physical exams each day, so call in advance to reserve your time.

1. Key the table as a 3-column, 8-row table. Save as **82b-d4**.

2. Increase the height of row 1 to .75". Center the headings vertically and horizontally in the row. Change the height of rows 2–7 to **.3**.

3. Merge cells A2 and A3; center *College* horizontally and vertically in the cell.

4. Center the table vertically and horizontally.

TIP

Split columns B and C by
selecting the column;
then click **Table**, click
Split Cells, and change
the number of columns
to 2.

OREGON STATE COLLEGE 2004–2005 Enrollments				
College	**Semester**		**Division**	
	Fall	**Spring**	**Upper**	**Lower**
Business	1,043	677	120	1,600
Computer Science	750	322	63	1,095
Agriculture	43	12	2	53
Arts and Literature	68	21	3	86
Allied Health	875	192	191	873

1. Key the table as a 3-column, 7-row table; split columns B and C. Save as **82b-d5**.

2. Adjust the height of row 1 to **.8"**. Center and bold the headings. Center the headings vertically and horizontally in the row.

3. Center-align columns B and C. Decimal-align columns D and E.

4. Change the height of rows 2–6 to **.3**.

5. Center the table vertically and horizontally.

OUTPATIENT PROSPECTIVE PAYMENT SYSTEM Unadjusted National Medicare Reimbursement				
Description	**Code**		**Insurance**	
	CPT	**APC**	**Medicare**	**Coinsurance**
Immobilization	77341	0303	71.08	69.28
Basic Dosimetry	77300	0304	388.52	498.26
Daily IMRT Treatment	60174	0302	7,625.19	8,662.14
Continuing Physics	77336	0311	270.48	253.26

1. Set margins for 1" on all sides; use landscape orientation; use 48-point font.

2. Insert **andy** from the data file.

3. Select the picture; use **Square** wrapping and **left** alignment; select **Picture** tab; crop the picture .8" from the bottom, left, and top; size the picture 4.5" wide.

4. Position the picture at the top left margin.

5. To the right of the picture, key and center: **Lost Pet Named / Andy / Honey-Colored / Cairn Terrier**.

6. Below the picture and information in #5, center: **North Hopkins Neighborhood / $100 Reward / Call Pat at 555-0189**.

7. Save as **98c-d1**, preview to make sure the announcement fits on one page, and print.

1. Use .75" margins on all sides of the newsletter shown on the next page.

2. Use WordArt for banner; select the style in the fifth row of the fifth column. Put a double line below the banner using a color similar to the color of the WordArt.

3. Key **PACIFIC NEWPORT MEDICAL GROUP**; format using bold and same text color as the double line. Follow with a single line.

4. Insert a continuous section break about .5" below the single line and key the newsletter shown on the next page using two equal columns.

5. Format all headings using bold, ALL CAPS, and the same text color.

6. Insert clip art appropriate for pediatric medicine. Format clip art using a **Tight** wrapping style, **center** alignment, and size it about 2.5" wide. Position it near the center of the page.

7. Save as **98c-d2**, preview to make sure the newsletter fits on one page, and print.

LESSON 83 | Calculations in Tables

SKILLBUILDING

83a
Warmup
Key each line twice SS.

1 it to the us me you so go now we my he two in can her by of do no
2 it is | it is the | is it | is it you | he can | can he | he can go | can he go
3 who is | who is it | is it you | you can go | can you go | you can go to it

4 car mail two you may just can lake ask sail sign his form her who
5 who can sail | you can sail | you may sign | can you sign | sign his form
6 sign the form | mail the form | sign and mail | sign and mail that form

7 it was | was it so | if she can go to | can he go to the | can she go to the
8 she can | she may not | she may not go | can you go to the | so we may go
9 sign the | sign the form | they may sign that | they may sign that form

NEW FUNCTIONS

83b

help keywords
*Perform calculations;
repeat last action*

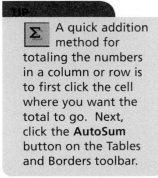

TIP

Σ A quick addition method for totaling the numbers in a column or row is to first click the cell where you want the total to go. Next, click the **AutoSum** button on the Tables and Borders toolbar.

Formulas

Microsoft *Word* has the ability to perform basic mathematical calculations, such as addition, subtraction, multiplication, and division when numbers are keyed in a table. *Word* also can recalculate an answer when the numbers in a table change. While *Word* is excellent for working with basic formulas, more complex calculations are better performed in a spreadsheet, such as *Excel*.

Using the SUM Function

SUM is the default formula or function that displays in the Formula dialog box. Columns or rows of numbers can be quickly added by clicking OK or pressing ENTER.

Formulas can be repeated by placing the insertion point in the next cell to be calculated and choosing Repeat Formula from the Edit menu.

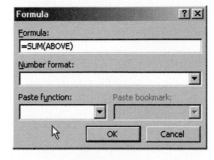

To total a column or row of numbers:

1. Position the insertion point in the empty cell that is to contain the answer.
2. Select **Formula** from the Table menu. *=SUM(ABOVE)* displays in the Formula box.
3. Click **OK** if you wish to add a column of numbers.
4. Change the word *ABOVE* to *LEFT* if you are adding numbers in a row; then click **OK**.

SKILLBUILDING

98a
Warmup
Key each line twice SS.

alphabet 1 Mickey bought six lavender azaleas and quite a few nice junipers.
fig/sym 2 We gave a 15% discount on 3 invoices (#28574, #6973, and #12095).
3rd & 4th fingers 3 Pam was quick to zap Dex about a poor sample that was on display.
easy 4 Jan and six girls may go to the lake to sit on the dock and fish.

| 1 | 2 | 3 | 4 | 5 | 6 | 7 | 8 | 9 | 10 | 11 | 12 | 13 |

98b
Timed Writing
Take one 3' and one 5' writing.
Work for control.

 all letters

	gwam	3'	5'

Something that you can never escape is your attitude. · 4 · 2 · 44

It will be with you forever. However, you decide whether your · 8 · 5 · 47

attitude is an asset or a liability for you. Your attitude · 12 · 7 · 49

reflects the way you feel about the world you abide in and · 16 · 9 · 52

everything that is a part of that world. It reflects the way you · 20 · 12 · 54

feel about yourself, about your environment, and about other peo- · 25 · 15 · 57

ple who are a part of your environment. Oftentimes, people with · 29 · 17 · 59

a positive attitude are people who are extremely successful. · 33 · 20 · 62

At times we all have experiences that cause us to be · 36 · 22 · 64

negative. The difference between a positive and a negative per- · 41 · 24 · 66

son is that the positive person rebounds very quickly from a bad · 45 · 27 · 69

experience; the negative person does not. The positive person is · 49 · 30 · 72

a person who usually looks on the bright side of things and · 53 · 32 · 74

recognizes the world as a place of promise, hope, joy, excite- · 58 · 35 · 77

ment, and purpose. A negative person generally has just the · 62 · 37 · 79

opposite view of the world. Remember, others want to be around · 66 · 40 · 82

those who are positive but tend to avoid those who are negative. · 70 · 42 · 84

3' | 1 | 2 | 3 | 4 |
5' | 1 | 2 | 3 |

APPLICATIONS

98c
Assessment

On the signal to begin, key the documents in sequence. Correct errors. When time has been called, proofread all documents again and correct any errors you may have overlooked. Reprint if necessary.

1. Open **Data83b-drill1**, compare it to the illustration at the right, and make changes as instructed. **Save as 83b-drill1**.

2. Position the insertion point in the last cell and press TAB to add a row at the bottom. Key **TOTAL** in cell A8.

3. Use the SUM function to insert the total for column C in cell C8.

4. Use the SUM function to insert the total for column D in cell D8. Save again. Continue with Drill 2.

LAUREL CANYON ENTERPRISES

Employee	I.D.	Hardware	Software
Alexander, J.	R492	$105,134,384	$1,868,553,280
Courtenay, W.	R856	79,364,091	1,384,219,500
Holsonback, E.	C845	27,386,427	1,098,237,260
Palombo, L.	K511	44,296,101	971,360,515
Rajeh, C.	M451	82,665,900	1,052,564,100
Talbert, S.	P053	82,091,433	985,201,500
TOTAL			

1. Insert a column to the right of the table.

2. Key **Total per Employee** in cell E1, and then adjust the column to accommodate the header on one line.

3. Add the numbers in columns C and D, and place the total for each row in column E.

4. If =SUM(ABOVE) displays in the formula box, delete the word *ABOVE* and replace it with *LEFT*.

5. Save as **83b-drill2**.

Writing Formulas

help keywords
Formulas in tables; repeat a formula

You can write your own formulas directing *Word* to add, subtract, multiply, divide, or average numbers in a table. A formula always begins with an equal sign. It then includes identification of the cells and the math symbol. For example, =B2-C2 means "column B, row 2 minus column C, row 2."

To write a formula:

1. Place the insertion point in the cell that is to contain the calculation.

2. Choose **Formula** from the Table menu. The Formula dialog box displays.

3. Delete the **SUM** formula.

4. Enter the formula in the Formula text box, beginning with =.

5. Click **OK**. Repeat steps 1–4 for each formula.

> **Formula**
>
> Formula:
>
> =B2-C2

The following symbols can be used in formulas. (Do not key the D2 and F2 as shown in the example column; your cursor will already be in that cell.)

Operation	Symbol	Example
Addition	+	D2=B2+C2
Subtraction	- (hyphen)	D2=B2-C2
Multiplication	*	D2=B2*C2
Division	/	D2=B2/C2
Average	Place parentheses ( ) around the part of the calculation to be performed first.	F2=(B2+C2+D2+E2)/4

97c-d3

Two-Page News Release

1. Prepare the following news release on the Suarez news release form (**97c-d1**).

2. For the release date, use one week from today.

3. Add a footer with *–more–* positioned at the center.

4. On the second page, add the header **Suarez Scholarship Program/page number**. Click **Page Setup** and click **Different First Page**.

5. Key the text double-spaced.

6. At the end of the text, double-space and key **###.** Click the footer on the second page and remove *–more–* .

7. Save as **97c-d3**, preview, and print.

Suarez Corporation announced that the Suarez family has established the Suarez Scholars Foundation with a $25 million endowment and will begin the Suarez Scholars program immediately. The foundation will give 30 scholarships each year to outstanding graduating seniors from high schools throughout the ten-state region in which the company operates. Seniors from Alabama, Arkansas, Florida, Georgia, Kentucky, Louisiana, Mississippi, North Carolina, South Carolina, and Tennessee are eligible to apply to become a Suarez Scholar.

The 10 top students will be designated as Suarez All South Scholars and the remaining 20 students will be designated as Suarez Scholars. Suarez All South Scholars receive $7,500 per year for four years for a total scholarship value of $30,000. Suarez Scholars receive $2,500 a year for four years for a total scholarship value of $10,000.

Criteria for determining scholarship winners include academic achievement (rank in class, grade point average, and scores on standardized tests), leadership, and community service. Students who have overcome adversity to excel may be given additional consideration. A computer program selects the semifinalists and a panel of business and educational leaders from the ten states select the 30 finalists.

The Suarez All South Selection Panel—a group of leaders selected from across the region—will interview the 30 finalists in Memphis and select the ten Suarez All South Scholars. The remaining 20 finalists are named Suarez Scholars. An exciting program is planned for the three-day visit to Memphis to ensure that the event is a memorable one for all Suarez Scholars.

Recalculate

When a change is made to a number that was part of a calculation, *Word* can automatically recalculate the answer. To recalculate an answer, click on the number in the cell that contains the formula. Press F9; the new answer will display in the cell.

Number Format

You can specify the format in which your answer is to be displayed. To do so, select one of the choices listed in the Number format drop list found in the Formula box. For example, if you are calculating money amounts, you can choose to have the answer display with two decimal places, with or without a dollar sign, and with or without commas.

DRILL 3 CALCULATE AND FORMAT

1. Open **Data83b-drill3**, compare it to the illustration below, and make necessary changes.

2. Calculate Net Profits by subtracting Expenses from Income. Display the answer in $#,##0.00 format.

3. Change the height of row 1 to approximately 1". Center the headings in row 1 vertically and horizontally.

4. Change the height in rows 2–6 to .3 and center text vertically. Center the column headers horizontally.

5. Center column A. Decimal-align columns B, C, and D. Apply 15% shading to cells D2–D6.

6. Save as **83b-drill3**. Keep it open for Drill 4.

E-COMMERCE.COM

Income Summary

Year	Income	Expenses	Net Profits
2000	$129,050.00	$151,000.00	
2001	375,000.00	225,000.00	
2002	410,000.00	250,500.00	
2003	560,000.00	316,000.00	

DRILL 4 RECALCULATE IN A TABLE

1. Open **83b-drill3**, if necessary. Change the number in cell B3 to **165,000.00**.

2. Recalculate the answer in D3 by placing the insertion point in D3 and pressing F9.

3. Save as **83b-drill4**.

Paste Function

help keywords
Perform calculations

As you learned earlier, the default formula that displays in the Formula dialog box is SUM(ABOVE). Other functions are also available for use, such as AVERAGE, MIN, MAX, COUNT, etc. Click on the **Paste** function drop list arrow to display a complete list of available functions.

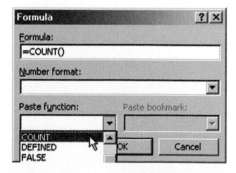

97c-d1
Formatting

1. Prepare the news release form shown below. Be sure to check update automatically in the date field. Add a top border below the telephone information line.

2. Save as a **document template** named **97c-d1**.

97c-d2
One-Page News Release

1. Open **97c-d1** and save as a *Word* document named **97c-d2**.

2. Prepare the following news release; double-space the text.

3. Resave, preview, and print.

July 2, 200-

For Release: Immediately

SUAREZ MOVES HEADQUARTERS

MEMPHIS, TN—The Suarez Corporation announced today that it is consolidating its statewide offices and moving its headquarters to Memphis. The company has leased space in the Davenport Building until its Churchill Tower can be built.

Suarez employs 785 people. Of the 785 employees, 300 are expected to transfer to Memphis. During the next 15 months, Suarez expects to hire 500 employees in sales, administrative support, accounting, engineering, architectural, and management areas.

Suarez develops projects throughout the South. Its primary focus is commercial real estate development. Suarez has already developed 3 shopping centers in the Hammond area and 25 in the state.

###

To paste a function:

1. Place the cursor in the cell where the calculation should be made.
2. Select **Formula** from the Table menu.
3. Delete the **SUM(ABOVE)**, but not the equal sign.
4. Click the **Paste** function drop list arrow.
5. Choose the new function, and then key between the parentheses the cell references (A1, D3, E4) or the direction (LEFT, RIGHT, etc) to which the function [formula] should apply. Click **OK**.

> *Note*: If the same formula is to be applied repeatedly, use the Repeat Formula command on the Edit menu.

DRILL 5   **PASTE FUNCTION**

1. Open **Data83b-drill5** and place the cursor in cell E1.
2. Click **Formula** on the Table.
3. Delete **SUM(LEFT)** from the Formula box. (Do not delete the equal sign.)
4. Click the **Paste** function drop list arrow.
5. Choose **COUNT** to total the number of cells that contain information.
6. Key **LEFT** between the parentheses ( ). Click **OK**.
7. Repeat for each row in column E. Save as **83b-drill5**.

APPLICATIONS

83c-d1
Format and Total

1. Key the following table and apply **Table Column 5** format. Center and bold the headings.
2. Decimal-align columns B through D.
3. In row 7, total the expenses for each month. Center vertically on the page. Save as **83c-d1**. Print.
4. Insert a column to the right of the table. Key **Monthly Average** in cell E1. Adjust width of columns so that all column heads fit on one line.
5. Calculate the average for each expense and place the answers in column E. The average answers should contain a dollar sign and two decimal places. Save as **83c-d2**.

83c-d2
Average Calculation

EXPENSES FOR JAMES STEWARD

First Quarter, 200-

Expense	January	February	March
Rent	$800.00	$800.00	$800.00
Food	270.50	255.25	290.00
Transportation	92.00	120.00	675.00
Clothing	90.75	95.50	80.25
Miscellaneous	50.00	75.00	83.00

LESSON 97   News Releases

SKILLBUILDING

97a
Warmup
Key each line twice SS.

alphabet	1	Jack Voxall was amazed by the quiet response of the big audience.
fig/sym	2	Our #3865 clocks will cost K & B $12.97 each (less 40% discount).
shift	3	In May, Lynn, Sonia, and Jason left for Italy, Spain, and Turkey.
easy	4	It is the duty of a civic auditor to aid a city to make a profit.

| 1 | 2 | 3 | 4 | 5 | 6 | 7 | 8 | 9 | 10 | 11 | 12 | 13 |

DOCUMENT DESIGN

97b

News Release

A news release conveys information an organization wishes to publish. Organizations prepare news releases to send to newspapers, radio stations, television stations, and other media outlets. News releases that make preparing the story easy save news writers time and are more likely to get published provided the information contained in the release is newsworthy. Often space limits prevent news media from publishing all of the information provided. Therefore, a good news release states the most important information first and the least important information last so that it can be cut or shortened from the end.

Most organizations prepare news releases on letterhead or on specially prepared forms for news releases. The form includes contact information in case the writer wishes to verify information and the date the news can be released. It also includes a short subject line that could serve as a heading. Double-space the text. Use ### or -30- to indicate the end.

Two-Page News Release

If a news release is two pages long, add a footer with the word *more* centered to indicate that the release continues on the next page. On the second page, add a header (often called a *slug line*) with a very short heading and a slash plus the page number.

SUAREZ CORPORATION
1986 Briarwood Circle
Memphis, TN 38116-1986

(901) 555-0132   Barbara.Hatten@suarez.com   (901) 555-0148 Fax

NEWS RELEASE   **Contact Person:** Barbara Hatten

November 20, 2003

For Release: (one week from today)

Suarez Corporation announced that the Suarez family has established the Suarez Scholars Foundation with a $25 million endowment and will begin the Suarez Scholars program immediately. The foundation will give 30 scholarships each year to outstanding graduating seniors from high schools throughout the ten-state region in which the company operates. Seniors from Alabama, Arkansas, Florida, Georgia, Kentucky, Louisiana, North Carolina, South Carolina, and Tennessee are eligible to apply to become a Suarez Scholar.

The 10 top students will be designated as Suarez All South Scholars and the remaining 20 students will be designated as Suarez Scholars. Suarez All South Scholars receive $7,500 per year for four years for a total scholarship value of $30,000. Suarez Scholars receive $2,500 a year for four years for a total scholarship value of $10,000.

Suarez Scholarship Program/2

The Suarez All South Selection Panel—a group of leaders selected from across the region—will interview the 30 finalists in Memphis and select the 10 Suarez All South Scholars. The remaining 20 finalists are named Suarez Scholars. An exciting program is planned for the three-day visit to Memphis to ensure that the event is a memorable one for all Suarez Scholars.

###

83c-d3
Paste MAX Function

The MAX ( ) function displays the largest value in a list of numbers. To figure the MAXIMUM, key **=MAX(LEFT)** in the Formula: field or use the **Paste** function within the Formula dialog box.

1. Key the table below. Center it vertically and horizontally on the page.
2. Adjust the height of row 1 to 1". Center the headings vertically and horizontally in row 1.
3. Center columns B–F.
4. Calculate the average for each test and place in row 7. Display the answer as a whole number (Number Format, 0).
5. Use the MAX function to find the maximum score for each student. Place answers in column F.
6. Save as **83c-d3**. Print.

COMPUTER INFORMATION SYSTEMS Spring, 200-					
Student	**Test 1**	**Test 2**	**Test 3**	**Test 4**	**Maximum Score**
Appleton, J.	81	74	83	86	
Carey, R.	87	92	93	91	
Palembo, T.	72	69	70	71	
Stover, A.	91	95	97	96	
Average per Test	83	83	86	86	

83c-d4
Calculate Net Profits in Table

1. Key the table below. Adjust the height of row 1 to approximately 1". Center headings vertically and horizontally in row 1.
2. Insert totals for each column in row 7.
3. Insert Net Profits in column D (Gross Revenue – Expenses).
4. Right-align columns B–D.
5. Save as **83c-d4**. Print.

COMTEK INCORPORATED Western Region			
Quarter	**Gross Revenue**	**Expenses**	**Net Profits**
First	980,000	375,000	
Second	877,000	320,000	
Third	795,000	310,000	
Fourth	991,000	420,000	
Total			

Healthy Heart Trails

The county, the Coastal University Foundation, and the Healthy Heart Foundation announced today a joint venture to build and interconnect a series of walking and bike trails throughout the coastal area.

Healthy Heart Study

Last week the Healthy Heart Foundation released the findings of a significant study showing that exercise, diet, and not smoking are the major controllable factors that lead to a healthy heart. Factors such as heredity cannot be controlled. The study included both males and females aged 25 to 65.

Individuals over 45 are more likely to have heart problems, but the number of young people experiencing heart problems is increasing. Scientists believe that the increasing number of heart problems experienced by younger adults stems from a combination of diet, smoking, and leading a sedentary lifestyle.

Just Take a Walk

The study showed that women especially benefited from just taking a walk. Those who walked an average of two to three hours a week were more than 30 percent less likely to have heart problems than those who did no exercise. Those who walked briskly for five or more hours a week were more than 40 percent less likely to have heart problems.

Make Exercising Fun

The key to a successful exercise program is to enjoy it. Most people who find exercise boring or painful do not continue the program long enough to accomplish the desired benefits. Interesting walking routes take the boredom out of the exercise.

The Bike Trail

The proposed bike trail will feature over 100 miles of packed surface, coquina, and boardwalk bike paths along the coast for those who enjoy biking. The bike trail is designed so that riders can take short loops (1 to 10 miles) or go on extended rides for the entire trail.

Walking Trails

A leading nature trails designer has been retained to design environmentally sensitive trails that are both interesting and educational. The initial Healthy Heart Trails project features six trails ranging from one to five miles long. Each trail features a different type of educational node—ranging from endangered species such as red cockaded woodpeckers and loggerhead turtle nests to sustainability exhibits and pond restoration projects to enhance the habitat for waterfowl.

Healthy Heart Trails Project			
Project Component	Primary Sponsor	Estimated Time	Estimated Cost
Trail design and layout	Coastal University Foundation	4–6 weeks	$ 22,500
Highway work at trail head	County	6–8 weeks	30,000
Parking lot at entrance	Coastal University Foundation	3–4 weeks	26,000
Visitor's center	Healthy Heart Foundation	6–8 months	100,000
Walking trails	Coastal Univ./Healthy Heart	6–8 months	80,000
Bike trail	County	2 years	400,000
Total Project	All	2 years	$658,500

Changing Page and Text Orientation

84a
Warmup
Key each line twice SS.

left hand

1	readers secrets dessert degrade cataracts abstracts basted create
2	barge adage beverages scarce assist trait area tea fast are dress
3	waves fatal taste zest craze star tear drawers garage grade trees

right hand

4	union poplin hookup hominy minimum onion link plump pool pink lip
5	million opinion pupil imply jolly knoll lymph yolk upon no nil on
6	nymph him hop hip ink mommy joy pin ply nip oil in poll oh pip my

both hands

7	work yams worn tutor vile slang shrug clams bogus slept me trains
8	blend sighs sign forks amend angle aisle visitor window if posted
9	tuck yield fowl cork duels roams tyrant clan soap rifle so jumped

| 1 | 2 | 3 | 4 | 5 | 6 | 7 | 8 | 9 | 10 | 11 | 12 | 13 |

84b
Timed Writings
Key a 3' and a 5' writing.

gwam 3' | 5'

	3'	5'
Have you ever heard the saying "dress for success"? If you	4	2	43
are going to a job interview, this is good advice to follow. Men	8	5	46
should wear a good quality business suit, or at least a blazer.	13	8	48
They should include a clean shirt, preferably white, and a nice	17	10	51
tie. Clean dark shoes and dark socks will complete the outfit.	21	13	53
Women should maintain a conservative look. A dark business suit	26	15	56
with a medium-length skirt is most appropriate. A blouse in a	30	18	58
modest color will help project a professional appearance.	34	20	61
Women's heels should be no more than two inches high. Both	38	23	63
men and women should be sure that their hair is clean and neatly	42	25	66
styled. Nails should be cut short and well groomed. Nail polish,	46	28	68
if worn, should be clear or a pastel color; no black or flashy	51	30	71
colors should be used. Little or no perfume is preferred, because	55	33	74
some interviewers may be sensitive to fragrances. Jewelry should	60	36	76
be kept to a minimum. Remember to devote extra effort to prepare	64	38	79
for your interview; your future job may depend on it.	67	40	81

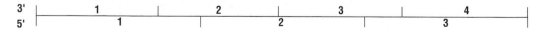

3' | 1 | 2 | 3 | 4 |
5' | 1 | 2 | 3 |

LESSON 96 — Newsletter with Graphics

SKILLBUILDING

96a
Warmup
Key each line twice SS.

alphabet 1 Joyce Wexford left my squad after giving back the disputed prize.
figures 2 Reply to items 4, 5, and 6 on page 39 and 1, 7, and 8 on page 20.
double letters 3 A committee supplied food and coffee for the Mississippi meeting.
easy 4 In Dubuque, they may work the field for the profit paid for corn.

| 1 | 2 | 3 | 4 | 5 | 6 | 7 | 8 | 9 | 10 | 11 | 12 | 13 |

96b
Timed Writings
Key two 3' timed writings.

	gwam	1'	3'

What do you like to do on a lazy, sunny weekend afternoon in 12 | 4
spring or summer? Some people may prefer a quiet afternoon of 25 | 8
watching television, while other people may want to wash the car 38 | 13
or work in their gardens. Many others, however, agree that the 51 | 17
very best way to enjoy a spring or summer afternoon is to attend 64 | 21
a college or professional baseball game. In fact, that choice is 77 | 26
so popular that the game is often said to be our national sport. 90 | 30
Many people even hope for extra innings to extend the fun. Over 103 | 34
the years, most baseball fans have shown excellent sportsmanship. 116 | 39
However, today many people are concerned that the bad behavior of 130 | 43
a few individuals may spoil the game for others. 139 | 46

1' | 1 | 2 | 3 | 4 | 5 | 6 | 7 | 8 | 9 | 10 | 11 | 12 | 13 |
3' | 1 | 2 | 3 | 4 |

APPLICATIONS

96c-d1
Newsletter with Graphics

TIP
#5 Keywords: medicine or heart
#6 Keyword: bicycle
#7 Keywords: trails, backpacker, or nature

1. Key the following newsletter using three equal-sized columns with a line between.
2. Set left and right margins at 0.5".
3. Use WordArt of your choice and color for the banner heading; about two lines below the banner, insert a continuous section break.
4. Use Heading 3 for all headings.
5. In the Heart Health Study section, insert from clip art an image symbolic of a heart and/or medicine.
6. In the Bike Trail section, insert from clip art a bicycle or bicycle rider.
7. In the Walking Trails section, insert from clip art a bird watcher, backpacker, or someone walking in a natural area.
8. Adjust text and clip art above the table so that all text fits on one page.
9. At the end of the text, insert a next page section break.
10. On the second page, change to 1" left and right margins and one column; apply to this section only.
11. Format the table. Select an appropriate AutoFormat style.
12. Save as **96c-d1** and print.

Landscape Orientation

Most documents are printed on standard 8.5" × 11" paper in portrait orientation. To print a wide document on a standard sheet of paper, you must choose landscape orientation. **Landscape** orientation positions the document horizontally on the paper (11" × 8.5").

To change the paper to landscape orientation:

1. From the File menu, choose **Page Setup**. Click the **Margins** tab.

2. Click the **Landscape** button in the Orientation section. Notice that the illustration in the Preview box changes from portrait to landscape. Click **OK**.

Change Text Orientation

Text is traditionally displayed horizontally in a cell. At times, you may wish to display the text vertically in the cell. You can rotate text in a cell by using the Change Text Direction button in the Tables and Borders toolbar or by selecting Text Direction in the Format menu.

To Change Text Orientation:

Click the table cell that contains the text you want to change.

1. On the Format menu, click **Text Direction**.

2. Click the desired orientation.

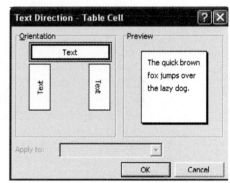

CHANGE PAGE ORIENTATION AND TEXT DIRECTION

1. Open **83c-d3**. Change the page to landscape orientation.

2. Delete row 1. Insert a column to the left of the table. Merge the rows in the new column.

3. Key **CIS TEST SCORES** in the new column; apply 15% shading.

4. Rotate the text in the cell as shown. Center the text vertically and horizontally in the cell. Adjust column width.

5. Rotate heads in columns C–F.

6. Save as **84c-drill1**. Print.

CIS TEST SCORES	Student	Test 1	Test 2	Test 3	Test 4	Maximum Score
	Appleton, J.	81	74	83	86	86
	Carey, R.	87	92	93	91	93
	Palembo, T.	72	69	70	71	72
	Stover, A.	91	95	97	96	97
	Average per Test	83	83	86	86	

This typeface, Times, is a serif typeface.

This typeface, Arial, is a sans serif typeface.

𝔗𝔥𝔦𝔰 𝔱𝔶𝔭𝔢𝔣𝔞𝔠𝔢, 𝔒𝔩𝔡 𝔈𝔫𝔤𝔩𝔦𝔰𝔥 𝔗𝔢𝔵𝔱 𝔐𝔗, 𝔦𝔰 𝔞 𝔡𝔦𝔰𝔭𝔩𝔞𝔶 𝔱𝔶𝔭𝔢𝔣𝔞𝔠𝔢.

The units of measure for type size are picas and points. An inch is roughly 6 picas, and a pica contains 12 points or 72 points per inch. A good rule of thumb in creating styles is to use 10- to 12-point type for the body and 14- to 18-point type for headings. Larger type sizes may be used for banners.

Vertical distance between lines of type (the height of a line) is called *leading*. Leading is set automatically, but it can be adjusted. A rule of thumb is to use 2 points more than the type size for small type.

Color   **second-level heading**

Color helps convey vivid images and adds a new dimension to document design. Using color consistently gives a feeling of comfort and helps the reader locate information quickly. Color helps to link elements of a document. Special care needs to be used in selecting colors. The color that displays on a computer screen may look quite different when printed or projected. Often color is a part of a logo, and an exact match is critical.

The color scheme of a document should be simple. A good rule of thumb is to use a maximum of four colors in a document. Graphs with multiple bars or pie segments may require more than four colors and would be an exception. Consistency in the use of color is extremely important.

Tables and Graphic Elements   **second-level heading**

Tables and graphic elements should be used when they simplify and clarify information. Limit the use of graphics to those that contribute to the content of a document. A picture often gets the message across quickly and effectively. Too many graphic elements can be distracting and confusing, however. Another important consideration is matching the graphic elements with the tone of a document. A formal document must be matched with a sophisticated but simple graphic. Limited use of WordArt can be effective for informal documents such as employee newsletters. Effective design of all graphic elements is important.

Insert the file Document Design here.

95b-d2
Reformat Document

1. Open **95b-d1** and save it as **95b-d2**.

2. Reformat the document using three equal-size columns with .25" spacing between columns.

3. Resave, preview, and print.

84d-d1
Landscape Form with Merged Cells

1. Change the page to landscape orientation. Create a 3-column, 9-row table.

2. Merge row 1 and key the main heading in 14-point bold. Increase the row height to .5" and center the heading vertically and horizontally in the row.

3. Merge row 2 and key the text.

4. Merge row 3; then split row 3 into 2 columns. Key **Payee Name:** and strike ENTER; key the remaining lincs in the same format. Change the row height to .8", and then center the text vertically in the cells.

5. Key the remainder of the form. Center vertically and horizontally. Save as **84d-d1**.

RECEIPT OF PAYMENT		
Receipt Number:	**Date:**	
Payee Name: Address: City, State ZIP:	Payer Name: Address: City, State ZIP:	
Item No.	Description	Amount
	Subtotal	
	Tax	
Total		

84d-d2
Table with Math

Fill in the form you created in **84d-d1** and use the math feature to perform the calculations.

1. Open **84d-d1**. Save as **84d-d2**.

2. Fill in the form with the information shown below.

3. Calculate the subtotal by using the SUM above feature. Calculate the Tax by keying the formula **=c7*.05**. The tax is 5%. Calculate the Total by keying the formula **=c7+c8**.

4. Use a decimal tab to align column C. Save and print.

RECEIPT OF PAYMENT		
Receipt Number: 1452	**Date: 6-15-04**	
Payee Name: Amazon Electronics Address: 8360 Ortega Highway City, State ZIP: Houston, TX 77001	Payer Name: James Smith Address: 55 Alpine Road City, State ZIP: Houston, TX 77002	
Item No.	Description	Amount
4319	CPU Stand	41.00
4890	Side Extension Shelf	35.50
	Subtotal	
	Tax	
Total		

Document Design—An Art and A Science **WordArt**

A writer expects a document to communicate a message to a specific audience. Likewise, effective document design facilitates communication—it does not simply decorate or make a document look aesthetically pleasing. The science of document design refers to matching the design elements to the message that the document seeks to communicate. The art of document design refers to making a document sensitive to the needs of the audience—giving the document a feeling of being familiar, comfortable, and pleasing to read.

Design Standards **first-level heading**

Design standards may vary depending on the formality of a document and the type of corporate identity an organization wishes to portray. Design standards for formal documents tend to follow the same standards that would be applied if the document were typeset by a professional printer. One space follows end-of-sentence punctuation. Spacing between paragraphs is controlled by the Spacing Before or Spacing After options on the Format Paragraph dialog box. Generally, six-point spacing is used to separate paragraphs. Special characters such as *en* and *em* dashes and special symbols such as copyright, trademark, and registered generally are used.

Design Objectives **first-level heading**

Effective document design accomplishes a number of objectives, such as:

- Supports document content and adds organizational structure
- Provides a consistent image
- Denotes formality
- Enhances readability and provides a road map to lead the reader through the document
- Emphasizes important points and simplifies content presentation
- Compacts copy and optimizes space requirements

Document design requires careful planning to accomplish the objectives listed. Many organizations research design carefully and specify standards for all documents prepared both professionally and internally. They direct employees to apply specific predefined styles available in their software, or they create customized templates and styles and provide them to employees. Online styles frequently replace hard-copy style manuals. To these organizations, visual design is a key element in corporate identity and image.

Design Elements **first-level heading**

Design elements consist of features used repeatedly and consistently in documents. Design elements include text, typeface, color, tables and graphic elements, white space, headings and layout, and paper.

Text **second-level heading**

The amount of text, the nature of the text, and the purpose for which it is being used influence the design of documents. Long documents require more structure than short documents. Technical, statistical, and complex textual materials require significant amounts of illustration to simplify them. On the other hand, the rigid requirements for a formal report may not be appropriate for an informal newsletter to employees.

Text itself is often a design element. For example, a company analyzing 20 countries for potential export opportunities might use textual categories as repeated design elements. The analysis of each of the countries might have these segments: political climate, economic conditions, market potential, barriers to entry, and recommendations. Serif typefaces, such as Times or Times New Roman, have small lines that extend from the main portion of the character. Sans serif typefaces, such as Helvetica or Arial, do not have these extenders. Typefaces used for large type or headings, such as script or Zapf Chaucery, are generally called display typefaces. Script is often used for personal or informal documents and for invitations.

LESSON 85

Assessment

SKILLBUILDING

85a
Warmup
Key each line twice SS.

alphabet	1	Jacqueline Katz made extra money by singing with the five groups.
figures	2	I sold 27 roses, 10 irises, 68 lilies, 54 tulips, and 39 orchids.
space bar	3	If she may go with me to a lake, I may do all of the work and go.
easy	4	The girls got the bicycle at the land of enchantment at the lake.

| 1 | 2 | 3 | 4 | 5 | 6 | 7 | 8 | 9 | 10 | 11 | 12 | 13 |

85b
Timed Writing
Key one 5' writing.

gwam 3' 5'

Employees who work together as a team are more effective 4 | 2 39
than those who work solo. This concept is known as synergy. 8 | 5 42
Synergy simply means that the joint action exceeds the sum of 12 | 7 44
individual actions. The results are not just in the quantity of 16 | 10 47
work; major gains in quality result when people work together as 21 | 12 49
a team. Teamwork is critical for success. 24 | 14 51

What characterizes an excellent team member? An excellent 28 | 17 53
team member understands the goals of the team and will place team 32 | 19 56
values above her or his individual objectives. An excellent team 36 | 22 59
member helps to determine the most effective way to reach the 40 | 24 61
goals that were set by the group and will help to make each 44 | 27 63
decision that affects the group. Above all, an excellent team 49 | 29 66
member will support a decision made by the team. Each member 53 | 32 68
must understand her or his role and respect the roles of others. 57 | 34 71
Every member of a team must share in both victory and defeat. 61 | 37 74

3' | 1 | 2 | 3 | 4
5' | 1 | 2 | 3

APPLICATIONS

85c
Assessment

Continue

Check

With CheckPro: When you complete a document, proofread it, check the spelling, and preview for placement. When you are completely satisfied, click the **Continue** button to move to the next document. You will not be able to return and edit a document once you continue to the next one. Click the **Check** button when you are ready to error-check the test. Review and/or print the document analysis results.

Without CheckPro: On the signal to begin, key the documents in sequence. When time has been called, proofread all documents again and identify errors.

95a
Warmup
Key each line twice SS.

alphabet	1	Express mail requested at zone twelve gave finish to a rocky job.
figures	2	Check the area codes 304, 593, 281, and 763 before dialing calls.
combination	3	Typing business letters using a simple format is often suggested.
direct reaches	4	My cousin Ed brought my brown mums to school to delight me again.

| 1 | 2 | 3 | 4 | 5 | 6 | 7 | 8 | 9 | 10 | 11 | 12 | 13 |

95b-d1
Document Format and Design

Continuous Break: Insert, Break, Continuous

Bullets: Format, Bullets and Numbering, Bulleted tab; choose style

Shading: Format, Borders and Shading tab

1. In a new document, set 1" margins on all sides and 6 pt. spacing after paragraphs.

2. Create the main heading as a banner using WordArt. Select the design in the first row of the first column of the WordArt Gallery. Add blue fill. DS below the banner and enter a blue line. DS and insert a continuous section break.

3. Key the text as one column. Insert the file **Document Design** at the end of the document.

4. Apply Heading 1 style to all first-level headings and Heading 2 style to all second-level headings. Format all headings in blue. Format bullets in blue using this style: ❖

5. Format the three sentences shown in blue shading by applying the typeface indicated in the sentence. Then select all three sentences and apply blue shading to the paragraph. Change the font color of the sentences to white.

6. Format the body of the document as two equal columns with .5" spacing between. Add a blue page border. Save as **95b-d1**, preview, and print.

7. Read the document for content.

Document Design—An Art and a Science

A writer expects a document to communicate a message to a specific audience. Likewise, effective document design facilitates communication it does not simply decorate or make a document look aesthetically pleasing. The science of document design refers to matching the design elements to the message that the document seeks to communicate. The art of document design refers to making a document sensitive to the needs of the audience giving the docum ent a feeling of being familiar, comfortable, and pleasing to read.

Design Standards

Design standards may vary depending on the formality of a document and the type of corporate identity an organization wishes to portray. Design standards for formal documents tend to follow the same standards that would be applied if the document were typeset by a professional printer. One space follows end-of-sentence punctuation. Spacing between paragraphs is controlled by the Spacing Before or Spacing After options on the Format Paragraph dialog box. Generally, six-point spacing is used to separate paragraphs. Special characters such as *en* and *em* dashes and special symbols such as copyright, trademark, and registered generally are used.

❖ Denotes formality
❖ Enhances readability and provides a road map to lead the reader through the document
❖ Emphasizes important points and simplifies content presentation
❖ Compacts copy and optimizes space requirements

Document design requires careful planning to accomplish the objectives listed. Many organizations research design carefully and specify standards for all documents prepared both professionally and internally. They direct employees to apply specific predefined styles available in their software, or they create customized templates and styles and provide them to employees. Online styles frequently replace hard-copy style manuals. To these organizations, visual design is a key element in corporate identity and image.

Design Elements

Design elements consist of features used repeatedly and consistently in documents. Design elements include text, typeface, color, tables and graphic elements, white space, headings and layout, and paper.

Text

The amount of text, the nature of the text, and the purpose for which it is being used

formal report may not be appropriate for an informal newsletter to employees.

Text itself is often a design element. For example, a company analyzing 20 countries for potential export opportunities might use textual categories as repeated design elements. The analysis of each of the countries might have these segments: political climate, economic conditions, market potential, barriers to entry, and recommendations. Serif typefaces, such as Times or Times New Roman, have small lines that extend from the main portion of the character. Sans serif typefaces, such as Helvetica or Arial, do not have these extenders. Typefaces used for large type or headings, such as script or Zapf Chaucery, are generally called display typefaces. Script is often used for personal or informal documents and for invitations.

This typeface, Times, is a serif typeface.
This typeface, Arial, is a sans serif typeface.
This typeface, Old English Text MT, is a display typeface.

The units of measure for type size are picas and points. An inch is roughly 6 picas, and a pica contains 12 points or 72 points per inch. A good rule of thumb in creating styles is to use 10- to 12-point type for the body and 14- to 18-point type for headings. Larger type sizes may be used for banners.

Vertical distance between lines of type (the height of a line) is called *leading*. Leading is set automatically, but it can be adjusted. A rule of thumb is to use 2 points more th

quickly. Color helps to link elements of a document. Special care needs to be used in selecting colors. The color that displays on a computer screen may look quite different when printed or projected. Often color is a part of a logo, and an exact match is critical.

The color scheme of a document should be simple. A good rule of thumb is to use a maximum of four colors in a document. Graphs with multiple bars or pie segments may require more than four colors and would be an exception. Consistency in the use of color is extremely important.

Tables and Graphic Elements

Tables and graphic elements should be used when they simplify and clarify information. Limit the use of graphics to those that contribute to the content of a document. A picture often gets the message across quickly and effectively. Too many graphic elements can be distracting and confusing, however. Another important consideration is matching the graphic elements with the tone of a document. A formal document must be matched with a sophisticated but simple graphic. Limited use of WordArt can be effective for informal documents such as employee newsletters. Effective design of all graphic elements is important.

White Space

The natural tendency in designing documents is to try to save space. White space is not the area to economize, however. A key way to emphasize ideas is to isolate them from other ideas. White space provides the isolation needed to make things stand out... image. A ... frequently used...

wider than the text column they can extend into the blank space of the scanning column.

Documents packed with copy look cluttered and are difficult to read. White space provides an open, uncluttered look that is restful and that leads the reader to important copy that needs emphasis.

Headings and layout

Headings follow the same structure as an outline. They are hierarchical and should be ranked from high to low. Headings with the most important content should be positioned above and in more prominent typestyle than headings with content of lesser importance. Heading styles follow this hierarchical style. Brief headings tend to be more effective than long headings. The key design consideration is consistency. Grammatical structure, as well as typeface and spacing elements, must be consistent for headings of the same level.

Layout refers to the careful positioning and spacing of the design elements on a page to

create the best visual effect. The number and width of columns influence layout significantly. Column layouts may vary on the same page. Some organizations provide templates and define layout rules for published documents is purely a science. However, in most organizations, layout rules are not always hard and fast layout is an art. It is the product of careful experimentation to create the best way to communicate the information contained in a document.

Many trade-offs exist in designing the layout of a document. For example, consistency and flexibility often conflict. Certain graphic elements may not fit in the space that a consistent layout pattern provides. However, the importance of the content dictates that the consistent layout pattern be modified to accommodate the content. Page size, weight, texture, and finish affect the design of a document.

85c-d1
Rotate Text

1. Create the table below. Center the table vertically and horizontally on the page.
2. Key the main heading, **EMPLOYEE DATA**, in 14-point bold type vertically at the left of the table. Shade the cell 15%.
3. Center all text vertically in the cells.
4. Increase row 1 height to 1.3". Text in column B should fit on one line.
5. Save as **85c-d1**. Print.

	Item	Fair Labor Standards Act	Social Security	Income Tax Withholding	Unemployment Tax
EMPLOYEE DATA	Name	Yes	Yes	Yes	Yes
	Address	Yes	Yes	Yes	Yes
	Sex	Yes	—	—	—
	Social Security Number	Yes	Yes	Yes	Yes
	Withholding allowances claimed	—	—	Yes	—
	Occupation	Yes	Yes	Yes	Yes

85c-d2
Merge and Split Cells

1. Change the orientation to landscape.
2. Key the table below and format it using merged and split cells. Use decimal tabs to align the *Rate* columns. Center the *Hours* columns.
3. Save as **85c-d2**. Print.

PAYROLL REGISTER							
For Week Ending January 19, 200-							
Name	Regular Earnings			Overtime Earnings			Total Earnings
	Hours	Rate	Amount	Hours	Rate	Amount	
Oldfield, Carry	40	8.75					
Weingard, Susan T.	40	9.25		2	13.50		
Thompson, William	40	14.50		4	22.00		
Morrison, Carl	40	16.50		6	25.00		
Pham, Vo	38	12.00					

94d-d3
Announcement

1. Format the announcement using landscape and 1" margins on all sides.
2. Insert clip art appropriate for Valentine's Day at the top left side of the document. Format it with **Square** wrapping style, **left** alignment, and size it about 1.5" wide.
3. Add **Parents' Night Out** in WordArt; use a fill color that is compatible with the clip art.
4. Key the announcement text below using 18-point type. Bold the heading below the WordArt.
5. Save as **94d-d3**, preview, and print.

Saturday, February 14, is Valentine's Day. Make it special!

The Student Chapter of the Early Childhood Education Association (ECEA) invites you to enjoy an evening out without worrying about your children and to support the ECEA Scholarship Fund at the same time. The ECEA in cooperation with the University Child Development and Research Center is offering a fun night out for your children while you have a Valentine celebration without them. Your children will enjoy games, movies, crafts, snacks, and a variety of adventures.

The University Child Development Center accommodates up to 100 children in age ranges from infant to 12 years old. Students preparing to be early childhood educators will provide the babysitting services for the evening. Drop your children off at seven o'clock and pick them up at eleven. The rate for the evening is $25 for the first child and $10 for each additional child.

94d-d4
Announcement

1. Prepare the following announcement to be posted for the Fourth of July celebration.
2. Use .75" margins on all sides and landscape orientation.
3. Select clip art appropriate for the announcement.
4. Format the clip art so that it is approximately 2" wide; center it horizontally relative to the page and .75" below the top of the page.
5. Use WordArt for the title. Select appropriate colors.
6. Key the following text using Arial and as large a font size as you can and still fit the announcement on one page.

Fourth of July Celebration

Pack your lawn chairs or blankets and bring the entire family to join your friends and neighbors for the annual Fourth of July celebration at City Park. Music and festivities begin at 7:30 and end with a spectacular fireworks display at 10:30.

7. Save the document as **94d-d4** and print.

85c-d3
Calculate and Format

1. Open **85c-d2**.
2. Write a formula that will calculate the amount of both regular and overtime earnings. Display the answer in the Amount columns with a dollar sign and two decimal places.
3. Decimal-align the Amount columns.
4. Add the Amount columns and place the answer in dollar format with two decimal places in the Total Earnings column.
5. Decimal-align the Total Earnings column.
6. Save as **85c-d3**.

85c-d4
SUM Function

1. Open **85c-d3**. Insert a row at the bottom of the table.
2. Key **Total** in cell A8. Use **SUM(ABOVE)** to place the total for the Amount columns and Total Earnings in row 8.
3. Save as **85c-d4**. Print.

85c-d5
Memo with Calculations in Table

1. Change the left and right margin to 1". Key the memo with the table.
2. Insert a column to the right of the table that will average the leads for each source. Label the column **Average**.
3. Insert a row at the bottom of the table that will total the leads for each day. Key **Total** in cell A6.
4. Apply **Tables Column 4** format to the table.

TO: Cynthia Reed, Marketing Coordinator
FROM: Ryan Ng
DATE: Current Date
SUBJECT: Lead Analysis

Please review the following statistics that were gathered the week of October 10–16. Let's meet next Monday at 9:00 a.m. in my office to do a cost analysis for the leads. Please bring a copy of the contracts with each source.

DAILY LEAD LOG

Source	Monday	Tuesday	Wednesday	Thursday	Friday
Daily Times	15	30	20	10	12
County Register	22	17	12	19	14
Internet	21	32	41	44	47
Yellow Pages	6	5	6	3	4

94d-d1
Letterhead

1. Create letterhead for Global Travel Services, Inc. Use .7" top margin.

2. Search clip art and find a clip representative of a globe. Use **Square** wrapping and **left** alignment. Size the clip to approximately 1.5" width.

3. Center the address shown below to the right of the clip art.

4. Save as **94d-d1** and print.

Global Travel Services, Inc.

3975 Buckingham Road

Annapolis, MD 21403-6820

Telephone: 301 555-0146 FAX: 301 555-0183

94d-d2
Personal Letterhead

1. Use WordArt to create a letterhead for yourself. Use .7" top margin.

2. Use the design in the second row of the last column and key your initials. Change text color to match initials.

3. Center your address information:

Your full name
Street Address
City, State, ZIP Code
Telephone Number
E-mail Address

4. Save as **94d-d2** and print.

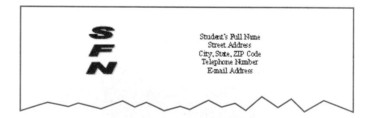

Module 13: Checkpoint

1. To increase the row height, click _____ on the Table menu.

2. The Table _____ feature enables you to apply preformatted styles to tables.

3. The _____ feature is used to align numbers at the decimal point.

4. To split one column into two columns, select the column and then click _____ on the Table menu.

5. A formula entered in the Formula text box must begin with _____.

6. Press the _____ key to recalculate an answer.

7. Access a complete list of available functions by clicking the _____ drop list arrow.

8. The _____ button allows you to rotate text from horizontal to vertical position.

9. _____ orientation positions the document horizontally on the paper.

10. Cells can be joined horizontally or vertically by selecting the cells and then choosing _____ from the Table menu.

Performance Assessment

Document
Draw Table and Calculate

1. Change the page to landscape orientation and key the table at the right.

2. Increase the height of row 1 to 1". Center headings in 14 point vertically and horizontally.

3. Calculate the total for columns C–F in row 8 (*Total Sales*). Calculate the total for rows 3–7 in column F (*Total per Person*).

4. Center the numbers in columns C–F.

5. Rotate the text in column A; center and bold the text in 20-point font.

6. Center the table vertically and horizontally on the page, save as **Checkpoint13-d**, and print.

First Quarter Sales	A-1 ELECTRONICS Eastern Division				
	Salesperson	**January**	**February**	**March**	**Total per Person**
	Cheryl Ignasio	17,000	11,000	15,000	
	Patrick Manning	21,500	19,000	23,000	
	Hillary Salinas	19,5000	18,000	21,000	
	Alex Trombley	25,000	22,100	27,600	
	Van Pham	26,000	24,300	28,900	
	Total Sales				

LESSON 94 — Announcements and Letterheads with Graphics

SKILLBUILDING

94a
Warmup
Key each line twice SS.

alphabet 1 Who enjoyed traveling to Mexico after buying a quick dozen picks?
figures 2 Send mail to ZIP Code 48279 in January and 56031 before November.
1st/2nd fingers 3 Assessment is a term used by educators when they are testing you.
adjacent reaches 4 Sara stopped here, where her ruined art was stored for the month.
| 1 | 2 | 3 | 4 | 5 | 6 | 7 | 8 | 9 | 10 | 11 | 12 | 13 |

94b
Skillbuilding
Key each set of drills (one-hand lines and balanced-hand lines) twice.

one-hand lines

5 my wax jump dress pink fast limp crease hunk brace pool extra bat
6 link grace plump trace junk zebra you zest yolk vested opinion ax
7 tax only race join target union regret puppy graze hulk fewer him
8 Holly, a stewardess saw my test grade; Holly gave my Mom a treat.
9 In my opinion, Rebecca deserves a few extra rewards; Phil agrees.
10 Jimmy gave Phillip a great red sweater at a bazaar in West Texas.

balanced-hand lines

11 duck quake lake rigor prism proxy fix usual turkey right quake of
12 skeptic quantity problem mangy dogs handle ivory elbow cubicle six
13 augment burlap formal dismay kept mentor rigor social visit world
14 Claudia and Henry may work to fix a big problem with the bicycle.
15 Jane and Kent may want to go with a neighbor to the lake to fish.
16 The city auditor, Jake Hand, may fix the problems with the audit.
| 1 | 2 | 3 | 4 | 5 | 6 | 7 | 8 | 9 | 10 | 11 | 12 | 13 |

DOCUMENT DESIGN

94c

Design Letterhead and Announcements

Attractive letterhead can be designed using clip art, pictures, WordArt, and text formatting. Generally the letterhead should fit into 1.5" or 1.75" of space so that the letter can begin no lower than 2". The default top margin can be decreased to provide additional space for the letterhead.

The design of an announcement can vary depending on whether the announcement is being posted so that it can be read as people walk by or whether it is sent directly to individuals. If the announcement is posted, landscape print and large font sizes are normally used to make it more readable from a distance. Graphics may be used to enhance announcements.

Forms and Financial Documents

- Create forms.
- Protect forms.
- Use forms.
- Format financial documents.

LESSON 86 — Skillbuilding and Forms

SKILLBUILDING

86a
Warmup
Key each line twice SS.

alphabet	1	Benji Vazquez was prepared for the very difficult marketing exam.
fig/sym	2	About 25% of my team (1,460) earned an average salary of $39,627.
adjacent reaches	3	Ty was the guy people wanted in government; he responded quickly.
fluency	4	My neighbor may tutor the eight girls on the theory and problems.

| 1 | 2 | 3 | 4 | 5 | 6 | 7 | 8 | 9 | 10 | 11 | 12 | 13 |

86b
Timed Writings
1. Key two 1' writings; work for speed.
2. Key one 3' writing; work for speed.

gwam   1'   3'

Many people who attend a concert, sporting event, or another 12 | 4
function that attracts a large number of people rarely consider 25 | 8
the consequences of those people panicking if something unexpected 38 | 13
should happen. Just taking several minutes to locate one or more 52 | 17
nearby exits could result in your life and the lives of others 64 | 21
being saved if a fire alarm buzzer should go off. The location 77 | 26
at which you entered the facility might not be the most desirable 90 | 30
place to leave it in an emergency. The way you entered may not 103 | 34
even be a possible way to leave if it is blocked by individuals 116 | 39
who are rushing to leave the building. 123 | 41

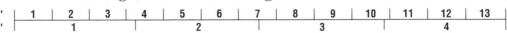

| 1' | 1 | 2 | 3 | 4 | 5 | 6 | 7 | 8 | 9 | 10 | 11 | 12 | 13 |
| 3' | | 1 | | | 2 | | | 3 | | | 4 | | |

Crown Lake News and Views

Current date

Newsletter Staff

Eric Burge
   Editor

Nancy Suggs
Christopher Hess
Anne Reynolds
   Associate Editors

Wayne Martin
   Editorial Assistant

Crown Lake News and Views is a weekly newsletter compiled by the staff of the Human Resources Department, and it is sent to all employees.

New Development Project

Crown Lake won the bid to develop and construct the new multimillion-dollar Business Center adjacent to Metro Airport. Connie McClure, one of the three senior project managers, has been named as the Business Center project manager. The project is expected to take more than two years to complete. Approximately fifty new permanent employees will be hired to work on this project. All jobs will be posted within the next two weeks. The recruiting referral program is in effect for all jobs. You can earn a $100 bonus for each individual you recommend who is hired and remains with Crown Lake for at least six months. You may pick up your recruiting referral forms in the Personnel Office.

Blood Drive Reminder

The Crown Lake quarterly blood drive is set for Friday, April 4, in the Wellness Center. The Community Blood Bank needs all types of blood to replace the supplies sent to the islands during the recent disaster caused by Hurricane Lana. Employees in all divisions are being asked to participate this quarter because of the current supply crisis. All three donation sites will be used. Several volunteers will be needed to staff the two additional sites. The regular division rotation will resume next quarter.

Lee Daye Honored

The Community Foundation honored Lee Daye of the Marketing Department with the Eagle Award for outstanding service this year.

The Eagle Award is presented each year to three citizens who have made a significant impact on the lives of others. The Community Foundation recognized Lee for his work with underprivileged children, the Community Relations Task Force, the Abolish Domestic Violence Center, and the Community Transitional Housing Project. Congratulations, Lee. You made a difference in the lives of many citizens in our community. Your award was richly deserved.

New Training Program

The pilot test of the new Team Effectiveness training program was completed last month, and the results were excellent. Thanks to all of you who participated in the development and testing of the program. Your input is vital to its success.

Underline Tabs

An option for leader tabs is an underline tab (Leader style 4), which produces a solid line. This type of leader is often used to create forms that will be filled in by hand.

FORM WITH UNDERLINE TABS

1. Format this document, setting a right underline tab at 6". Set DS; key the first two lines of the document.

2. On the third line of the document, set a right underline tab at 3" and a left tab at 3.5". (The right underline tab at 6" is still set.) Complete the document. Save it as **86c-drill1**.

Right underline tab 6" ⟶

Employee Name _____

Title _____

Reports to _____ Date _____

Review Period from _____ to _____

Right tab 3" ⟶   ⟵ Left tab 3.5"

Paragraph Borders and Shading

Borders and shading can be added to paragraphs, pages, or selected text. Various line styles, weights, and colors can be applied to borders. Shading can be applied in a variety of colors and patterns.

> This paragraph illustrates a block border with a 1-pt. black line. The shading for the paragraph is 10% gray fill.

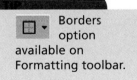

Borders option available on Formatting toolbar.

To apply a paragraph border:

1. Click in the paragraph or select the text to be formatted with a border.
2. Click **Borders and Shading** on the Format menu, and then click the **Borders** tab.
3. Select the type of border, line style, color, and width; then click **Apply to Paragraph** and **OK**.

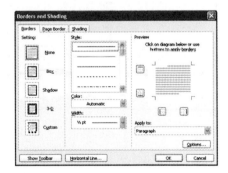

To apply shading:

1. Click in the paragraph or select the text to be shaded.
2. Click **Borders and Shading** on the Format menu, and then click the **Shading** tab.
3. Select the fill and pattern, and then apply them to the paragraph.

93d-d1
Newsletter with Clip Art

1. Open **93b-drill1** and save as **93d-d1**.
2. Open **litter clip art** from the data files.
3. Select the first clip and format it using **Square** text wrapping and **left** alignment. Size the clip to approximately 2.5" width.
4. Copy the first clip and paste it between the first and second paragraphs of the first column of the newsletter.
5. Select the second clip in the **litter clip art** file and format it using **Square** text wrapping and **right** alignment. Size the clip to approximately 2.5" width.
6. Copy the second clip and paste it before the last paragraph of the second column of the newsletter.
7. Save again, preview, and print.

93d-d2
Newsletter with Clip Art

1. Key the newsletter shown on the next page as a 1-column document.
2. Set left and right margins of .75".
3. Use WordArt for the banner heading, and adjust the size so that the banner spans all columns. Leave 2 or 3 blank lines after the heading; then insert a continuous section break (**Insert**, **Break**, **Continuous**).
4. Use 14-point Times New Roman for headings within the document and 12-point Times New Roman for body text.
5. Format the document after the banner as a 3-column document with lines between the columns. Use the following settings in the Columns dialog box.

   First column: 1.5"

   Space between columns: .025"

   Second and third columns: 2.5"

6. Use the first column for editorial information as shown; then insert a column break.
7. Insert an Eagle from the Clip Art Gallery. Use **Square** text wrapping, size it appropriately to fit in the column, and center it after the Eagle Award is mentioned.
8. Save as **93d-d2**, preview, and print.

Key the paragraph at the right. Then apply a ½-point red, double-line box border and pale blue shading to the paragraph. Save as **86c-drill2**.

> This paragraph is formatted with a ½-point red, double-line box border and pale blue shading.

Forms

Microsoft Word's **Forms** function is used to create forms that have places set aside called **fields** for the user to

- enter text (Text Form field)
- toggle a checkbox on or off (Check Box Form field)
- pick from a list of choices (Drop-Down Form field)

help keywords
Create forms, templates

The person who creates the form is called the **designer**. The person who fills in the form is the **user**.

Forms are created by inserting form fields into a document from the Forms toolbar. Shown below on the Forms toolbar are the three form fields that may be included in a document.

Text Form Field ——

Check Box Form Field ——   —— Drop-Down Form Field

You as the designer of a form need to save it as a template.

To save a form as a template:

1. Choose **Save As** from the File menu.
2. Select **Document Template** in the Save as type field.
3. Name the file and save it in a location as you would any other file.

Note: You can define the area of a Text Form field by selecting the field and adding a border around it. This creates a box in which the user keys the information.

When you want to open a particular template from the folder in the location where you save your working files, be sure that the Files of type field is set to show either All Files or Document Templates in the Open dialog box.

Text Form Field

Clicking the Text Form Field button inserts a box where the user can key information. For example, you can insert this field in a form and the user can key a name, address, or whatever information is requested. Text Form Field boxes will expand as the user keys the information.

1. Open **litter** from the data files. Save it as **93b-drill1**.

2. Click **Columns** and format the document in 3 even columns. Preview to see how it looks.

3. Format the same document in 2 columns. Preview to check the appearance.

4. Select the heading **Are You a Litter Bug?**; click **Columns** and select 1 column. Apply 36-point type. Center-align the heading. Add a hard return before column 1 to align the columns. Save again and close.

NEW FUNCTIONS

93c

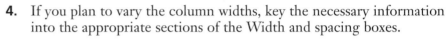

To create columns of unequal width:

1. Select **Columns** from the Format menu to display the Columns dialog box.

2. Choose one of the Preset options, or click in the **Number of columns** box and key the number of columns.

3. *Word's* default is columns of equal width. To vary the column widths, click the box to remove the check mark.

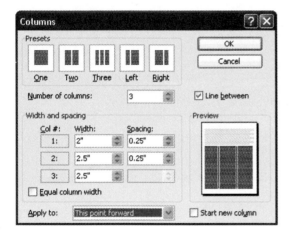

4. If you plan to vary the column widths, key the necessary information into the appropriate sections of the Width and spacing boxes.

5. If you want a vertical line between columns, click the **Line between** checkbox.

6. Click the down arrow beside the Apply to box, and choose one of the options. You can apply columns to the whole document, to one section, to selected sections, or from a particular point forward.

7. Use the Preview box to see what your layout will look like. In the dialog box shown here, the top portion of the document was formatted as a single column. At the end of that section, 3 unequal-width columns separated by lines were created. Note that in the Apply to box, **This point forward** has been selected.

To balance columns:

To balance columns so that all columns end at the same point on the page, position the insertion point at the end of the text to be balanced and insert a **Continuous section break (Insert, Break, Continuous, OK)**.

1. Open **litter** from the data files. Save it as **93c-drill2**.

2. Use the Columns dialog box to create 3 columns of equal width. Preview the document.

3. Select the heading and format it as a banner heading using 24-point bold type. Add a line between columns. Double-space below the heading. Save again and print.

4. Click in the body of the document. Display the Columns dialog box. Remove the check from the Equal Column Width checkbox and format the document in 2 columns. Decrease the size of the first column to 2". Preview the document, but do not save it.

To add a Text Form field:

1. Open the **Forms** toolbar if it is not already displayed (**View**, **Toolbars**, **Forms**).
2. Place the insertion point where you want the Text Form Field to appear.
3. Click the **Text Form Field** button.

DRILL 3   **INSERT A TEXT FORM FIELD**

1. Start a new blank document.

2. Save it in your designated work folder as a document template named **86c-drill3**.

3. Open the Forms toolbar if it is not already displayed.

4. Key the text **NAME:** followed by two spaces.

5. Click the **Text Form Field** button and then press ENTER twice to double-space.

6. Save **86c-drill3** without closing.

Check Box Form Field

Clicking the Check Box Form Field button creates a box for the user to click so that the box is filled with an X. For example, the user could place an X in a box to indicate an air-travel seating choice. If the user checks a box incorrectly, clicking on the box a second time will turn off the X.

Check your seating choice:

☐ 1st Class

☐ Business Class

☐ Coach

To add a Check Box Form field:

1. Open the Forms toolbar if it is not already displayed (**View**, **Toolbars**, **Forms**).
2. Place the insertion point where you want the checkbox to appear.
3. Click the **Check Box Form Field** button.

DRILL 4   **INSERT A CHECK BOX FORM FIELD**

1. Open the document template named **86c-drill3** if it is not displayed on your screen.

2. Display the Forms toolbar if it is not displayed.

3. Press CTRL + END to move the insertion point to the end of the document if it is not already there (a double space below the Text Form Field line).

4. Key **Check the method of contact you prefer:** and press ENTER.

5. Click the **Check Box Form Field** button; then enter two spaces.

6. Key **E-mail** and press ENTER.

7. Insert a **Check Box Form Field**; enter two spaces; key **Parcel Post**; press ENTER.

8. Insert a **Check Box Form Field**; enter two spaces; key **Telephone**; press ENTER twice.

9. Save as **86c-drill4** without closing. (*Note:* At this time the checkboxes are not active.)

LESSON 93 Columns and Newsletters

93a
Warmup
Key each line twice SS.

alphabet	1	Judging each issue will quickly prove the magazine's flexibility.
figures	2	Check the inventory for items #782, #936, #351, and #405 at noon.
double letters	3	The little bookkeeper from Mississippi keeps all books for Tammy.
easy	4	Jo goes to town each day to open her mail box at the post office.

| 1 | 2 | 3 | 4 | 5 | 6 | 7 | 8 | 9 | 10 | 11 | 12 | 13 |

FUNCTION REVIEW

93b

Columns

Most text is formatted using one column; that is, the text extends from the left margin to the right margin. However, documents may also be formatted in two or more columns. Newsletters are usually formatted in columns similar to newspapers. These documents are normally designed with headings spanning the columns (called *banners* or *mastheads*) and are usually written in an interesting, conversational style and formatted with graphics and illustrations. Text flows down one column to the top of the next column. Columns may be of equal or unequal width.

Banner

Are You a Litter Bug?

Does the appearance of your campus, your neighborhood, your city, or your state make a difference? Appearance often creates the first impression a person has of a place he or she visits—and first impressions are usually lasting. When some people think of beautiful places, they think of lakes, rivers, oceans, mountains, countryside, farms, and forests. Others may think of suburban neighborhoods or of urban settings with modern, efficient buildings. The range of options is unlimited because beauty is in the eye of the beholder.

The beauty of many areas is marred by litter left by individuals who did not care about others who would follow them. One thing is certain—no matter how beautiful a place may be—if it is littered with trash or buildings are deteriorated, it will not make a good impression.

Litter creates two different types of costs for your campus, your city, and your state. One type of cost is *lost business*. Prospective students who visit campus with littered parking lots and vending

areas are often "turned off" by the appearance of the campus and search for a more appealing environment. Tourism is a major industry for most cities and states. Tourists are not likely to want to return to places that are littered and trashy.

The second type of cost is the clean-up cost. Picking up litter along highways, parks, waterways, and forests costs thousands of dollars every year. In addition, thousand of volunteers contribute huge amounts time to clean up public areas. Picking up litter improves the appearance for a short time, but it does not solve the problem because very soon after an area is cleared someone will come along and litter it again.

The real solution comes from not littering in the first place. Littering is not only expensive; it is wrong and against the law. Public awareness programs help. Teaching young people at home and in educational institutions to dispose of their trash properly may be our best solution for the future.

To create columns of equal width:

1. Click the **Columns** button on the Standard toolbar.

2. Drag to select the number of columns.

3. Using this method to create columns will format the entire document with columns of equal widths.

Column format may be applied before or after keying text. If columns are set before text is keyed, use Print Layout View to check the appearance of the text. Generally, column formats are easier to apply after text has been keyed.

Columns

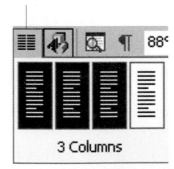

3 Columns

Occasionally, you may want certain text (such as a banner or headline) to span more than one column.

To format a banner:

1. Select the text to be included in the banner.

2. Click the **Columns** button, and drag the number of columns to 1.

Drop-Down Form Field

This field allows the user to choose from a list created by the designer. Clicking the Drop-Down Form Field button creates a box that can be expanded (dropped down) to

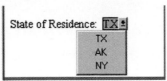

reveal a list of items from which the user can choose. For example, a drop-down box with state names included can be added to a form. The user clicks on the drop-down box, clicks on the appropriate state, and then that state appears in the box.

To add a Drop-Down Form field:

1. Open the Forms toolbar if it is not already displayed (**View**, **Toolbars**, **Forms**).

2. Place the insertion point where you want the drop-down box to appear.

3. Click the **Drop-Down Form Field** button.

Each time a Form field is placed in a document, the Form Field Options button is activated. This button allows the form's designer to make certain changes to the field. Specifically, the Form Field Options button allows the designer to add the list of choices to the Drop-Down Form Field box.

> The Drop-Down Form Field Options dialog box can also be displayed by double-clicking the Drop-Down Form field placed in the document.

> To change the order of the entries in a drop-down list field, use the up and down arrows above and below the word *Move* that is found beside the Items in the drop-down list box.

To add a list of drop-down choices:

1. Click the **Form Field Options** button to display the Drop-Down Form Field Options dialog box.

2. Key the user's first choice in the Drop-down item field. (For example, if the user is choosing from a list of state names, the first item listed might be Alabama.)

3. Click the **Add** button to move the text to the Items in the drop-down list box. Continue keying choices and clicking **Add** until all of the choices are entered.

4. Press ENTER one last time or click **OK** once you have entered all of the choices for the drop-down box.

DRILL 5   DROP-DOWN FORM FIELD

1. Open **86c-drill4** if it is not displayed on your screen.

2. Move the insertion point to the end of the document.

3. Key the text **State of Residence**: followed by two spaces.

4. Click the **Drop-Down Form Field** button.

5. Click the **Form Field Options** button.

6. Key **OH** in the Drop-down item field. Click **Add**. (The text will move to the Items in the drop-down list box.)

7. Key **KY** in the Drop-down item field. Click **Add**.

8. Key **WV** in the Drop-down item field. Click **Add**.

9. Click **OK**.

10. Save as **86c-drill5** and close the document. (*Note*: At this time the drop-down field choices are not active.)

---

1. Open a new document and display the Drawing toolbar. Click the **Insert WordArt** button.

2. Select the first style from the second row of the WordArt Gallery.

3. Key the text **Happy Birthday to you!**

4. Select the text and click the **Format WordArt** button on the WordArt toolbar. Choose **Pale Blue** *Fill color*.

5. Save the document as **92d-drill5**.

APPLICATIONS

92e-d1
WordArt and Clip Art

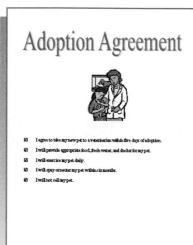

1. Open a new document. Insert WordArt; use the second WordArt style on the second row.

2. Key **Adoption Agreement.** Select *WordArt* and expand the size so that it spans the line of writing from the left margin to the right margin.

3. Use *animals* as the keyword and search for clip art. Insert a clip of an animal of your choice. Center the clip art.

4. Insert a checkbox from the symbol dialog box using a wingding font. Key the following statements DS. Save as **92e-d1** and print.

> ✔ I agree to take my new pet to a veterinarian within five days of adoption.
>
> ✔ I will provide appropriate food, fresh water, and shelter for my pet.
>
> ✔ I will exercise my pet daily.
>
> ✔ I will spay or neuter my pet within six months.
>
> ✔ I will not sell my pet.

92e-d2
Memo with AutoShapes

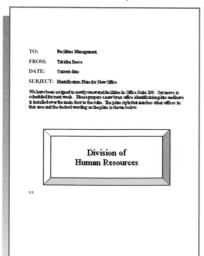

1. Open a new document and key the following memo:

> TO: Facilities Management | FROM: Takisha Reece | DATE: Current date | SUBJECT: Identification Plate for New Office
> We have been assigned to newly renovated facilities in Office Suite 208. Our move is scheduled for next week. Please prepare a new brass office identification plate and have it installed over the main door to the suite. The plate style that matches other offices in this area and the desired wording on the plate are shown below.

2. Insert a Bevel rectangle from the Basic Shapes category of AutoShapes.

3. Size the Bevel rectangle so that it is about 2" high and 5" wide.

4. Add the following text as shown at left: **Division of Human Resources**.

5. Center the text and use Bookman Old Style 24-point font.

6. Save as **92e-d2** and print.

Testing the Form

During the design stage of a form, you cannot add text to text boxes or make choices from drop-down lists. As the designer of the form, you need to *protect the form* in order to activate the various field boxes that you want to test. When you protect the form, you change it so that the fields you have inserted and the text you have keyed cannot be changed while testing the fields.

To test the form:

help keywords
Protect forms, unprotect forms, reset forms

1. Click the **Protect Form** button on the Forms toolbar.

2. Enter text in text boxes, select or deselect checkboxes, and reveal drop-down boxes.

3. Click the **Protect Form** button again to deactivate the protection.

4. Click the **Reset Forms Field** button to remove any text that remains in the forms fields.

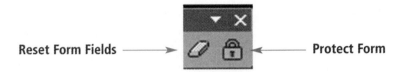

Reset Form Fields ⟶ ⟵ Protect Form

DRILL 6   FORM TEST

1. Open **86c-drill5**.

2. Click the **Protect Forms** button to enable testing.

3. Make changes to the form to test its functionality.

4. Click the **Protect Form** button to deactivate the protection.

5. Reset the form to clear any test changes.

6. Save as **86c-drill6**.

Protecting the Document

help keywords
Remove password

With *Word 2002*, even if you protect the form by clicking the Forms Protect button, the user can open the Forms toolbar and unprotect it. You need to prevent users from making changes to the form. Therefore, securely protect the form before distributing it by assigning a password with which to lock and unlock the form document. Without the password, the user cannot change the text and form fields that you have inserted.

Word 2002

Word 2003

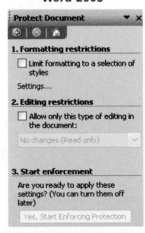

1. Click the **Rectangle** button; draw a rectangle about 2" wide. Key your name; use red color for text and lines.

2. Click the **Oval** button and draw an oval about 1" wide below the rectangle. Add blue fill.

3. Click the down arrow beside **AutoShapes**, select **Basic Shapes**, and draw a .75" smiley face below the rectangle; add yellow fill to the smiley face.

4. Save as **92d-drill4** and print.

WordArt

WordArt can also be accessed from the Insert menu (**Insert, Picture, WordArt**) or from the WordArt toolbar.

The WordArt Gallery provides a number of shapes and styles for WordArt. The first example shown below was created using the first design in the WordArt Gallery. The second example was created by adding a textured fill color and a 3-D effect to the first banner.

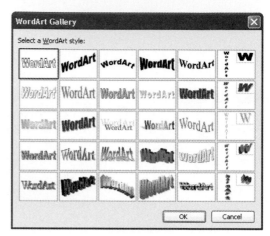

To use WordArt:

1. Display the Drawing toolbar, and click the **WordArt** button. The WordArt Gallery displays.

2. Select the desired style and click **OK** to display the Edit WordArt Text dialog box as shown at the right.

3. Key the text; change the font size or style in this textbox if desired. Click **OK**. Your text is now displayed as WordArt.

4. Select the text to display the WordArt toolbar. Format the WordArt text using the buttons on the WordArt toolbar. You may also use the buttons on the Drawing toolbar.

To protect a form:

1. Click **Protect Document** on the Tools menu to protect (lock) the document so that the user cannot alter the text or fields.

2. Select the **Forms** radio button in the Protect Document dialog box if not selected.

3. For *Word 2002*, key a password in the Password (optional) field. You will be asked to key the password a second time. If you do not add a password, the user will be able to change the document.

4. For *Word 2002*, to unprotect the form document later, choose **Tools**, **Unprotect Document**, and key the password.

> The password is case-sensitive and must be keyed exactly as it was entered when the form was locked.

DRILL 7   PROTECTING THE DOCUMENT

1. Open **86c-drill6**.

2. Protect the document (**Tools**, **Protect Document**).

3. Click the **Forms** radio button if necessary and key the password **locked**.

4. Save as **86c-drill7**.

Distributing and Using Forms

When you make your form available for others to use, it is called **distributing the form**. The forms that you create in *Word* are designed to be filled in onscreen and can be used by anyone who has *Word* available. Send the form using any method that you normally use to send someone a file. You may physically send the file saved on a disk, save the file in a shared workplace, or e-mail it as an attachment. When the receiver opens the file in *Word*, information can be filled in and printed or returned to you.

In most cases, to use a form template, open it from the General tab in the Templates dialog box that is accessible from the Task Pane.

Word 2002

New from template

85c Form

VanHuss Fax

General Templates...

Word 2003

Since you may have saved your templates in your working folder location, the template will not appear in the Templates dialog box.

To use a form that you receive:

1. Check to be sure that the Files of type field shows either All Files or Document Templates in the Open dialog box.

2. Open the form's template file from the list of files.

3. Fill in the form; use the TAB key to move from field to field.

> IMPORTANT: Scan all files you receive for viruses before opening them.

DRILL 8   OPEN AND FILL IN A FORM

1. Open **86c-drill7**.

2. Use the following information to fill in the form: **Heather Malcolm, E-mail preferred, WV**.

3. Save as **86c-drill8a**. Do not close.

4. Use the following information to fill in the form: **Franklin Howard, Telephone preferred, KY**.

5. Save as **86c-drill8b**.

6. Close the document.

INSERT PICTURE FROM FILE

1. Open a new document.

2. Key the heading **My New Pet**, at about 2"; center and bold; use 36 point.

3. Click below the heading; insert **Pet** from the data files.

4. Select the picture; use **Square** wrapping and **Center** alignment.

5. Select the **Picture** tab; crop the picture .8" from the bottom.

6. Save as **92d-drill3** and print.

My New Pet

help keywords
draw

Drawing Tools

A variety of drawing tools are available in *Word*. These tools can be accessed from the Drawing toolbar (**View, Toolbars, Drawing**). An easy way to become familiar with all of the tools is to display the Drawing toolbar and hold the mouse pointer over each object on the toolbar to display its function. Click the down arrow on each object that has one to display the available options for the tool. A canvas will display when you click a drawing tool to help with the formatting of the object.

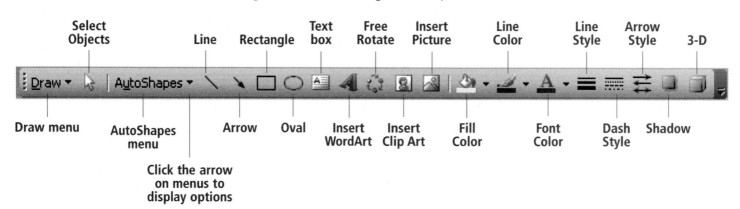

To insert a drawing tool object:

1. With the Drawing toolbar displayed, click on the desired object such as **Rectangle** or **AutoShapes**. If you choose AutoShapes, a list of various shapes displays. If a triangular arrow appears beside an object, click on it to display the available options.

2. When you choose the desired object, a "canvas" displays with the message "Create your drawing here." The mouse pointer turns into a crosshairs. Drag the mouse to create the object on the canvas.

3. Select the object and format it using the effects such as fill, lines, and 3-D that are available on the Drawing toolbar.

4. To add text to an object such as a rectangle or an oval, right-click the object and select **Add Text** from the drop-down menu. Then key your text.

86d-d1
Create and Protect
a Sales Form

1. Key **Weekly Flower Sales** in bold, 14 point at the top of the page. Press ENTER twice.

2. Create a table with three columns and 15 rows.

3. Key the following column headings in bold.

Flowers   Number Ordered   Delivery Complete

4. Insert a **Drop-Down Form Field** box in cell A2 below the *Flowers* heading.

5. Key the following six choices in the Drop-down box: **Aster**, **Daisy**, **Gladiola**, **Iris**, **Orchid**, **Rose**. Copy this field to the 13 other cells in the first column.

6. Insert a **Text Form Field** in cell B2 below the *Number Ordered* heading. Copy this field to the 13 other cells in the second column.

7. Insert a **Check Box Form Field** in cell B3 below the *Delivery Complete* heading.

8. Copy this field to the 13 other cells in the third column.

9. Protect the form and save it as **86d-d1**.

86d-d2
Fill in Sales Form

1. Open **86d-d1**. Protect the form document using the password *flowers*.

2. Fill in the form using the following information. If the delivery is complete, place an *X* in the form. Save as **86d-d2**.

Iris	112	delivered
Rose	204	delivered
Orchid	97	not delivered

86d-d3
E-Mail Form

1. Open **86d-d2**. Unprotect the form.

2. Reset, reprotect, and save the form as **86d-d3**.

3. Distribute an online copy of **86d-d3** to your instructor.

86d-d4
Handwritten Fill-In Form

1. Prepare the following form that will be handed out to students attending a basketball game. Set underline tab at 6" right, 3" right, and 4" left; 2" top margin; 14-point bold heading; DS.

2. Save the document as **86d-d4**.

Drawing for $1,000 Scholarship Given by Athletics Department

Name _____

Telephone_____

Address _____

City _____State_____ZIP Code _____

To move clip art:

1. Select the clip art.

2. Click the **Text Wrapping** button on the Picture toolbar. Then choose **Tight** (or one of the text-wrapping options) from the drop-down list. The sizing handles change to white squares.

3. Position the arrow pointer on the clip art until a four-headed arrow displays. Click and drag the clip art to the desired location.

To wrap text around graphics:

1. Insert the graphic; then place the insertion point over the graphic and right-click.

2. Select **Format Picture** to display the Format Picture dialog box.

3. Click the **Layout** tab and select the desired wrapping style (**Square**).

4. Click the desired alignment (**Left**) and then click **OK**.

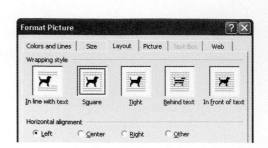

DRILL 2 **WRAP TEXT**

1. Key the paragraph at the right DS.

2. Insert clip art picturing a floppy disk.

3. Format the clip art using **Tight** *Wrapping style* and **Center** *Horizontal alignment* so the clip art will be centered and the text will wrap around it.

4. Print and save as **92c-drill2**.

> Most of us have grown accustomed to saving files on 3.5" disks. Today, however, 3.5" disks are rarely used to transport data. Technological advances make it possible to transport information over the Web, through the use of ftp sites, with zip disks, with CD-ROMs, with USB devices, and in a host of other ways, which explains why many leading computer manufacturers no longer supply 3.5" disk drives.

NEW FUNCTIONS

92d

To insert a picture from a file:

1. Click **Picture** on the Insert menu; then click **From File**.

2. Select the file, double-click or key the filename, and click **Insert**.

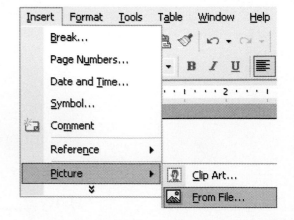

SKILLBUILDING

87a
Warmup
Key each line twice SS.

alphabet	1	Jack Meyer analyzed the data by answering five complex questions.
fig/sym	2	On May 15, my ZIP Code will change from 23989-4016 to 23643-8705.
1st/2nd fingers	3	June Hunter may try to give Trudy a new multicolored kite to fly.
fluency	4	Pamela may risk half of the profit they make to bid on an island.

| 1 | 2 | 3 | 4 | 5 | 6 | 7 | 8 | 9 | 10 | 11 | 12 | 13 |

DOCUMENT DESIGN

87b

Online and Fill-In Forms

Both online forms and handwritten fill-in forms are used for a variety of purposes. Common uses of forms include registration and reservations for various events. A form may be distributed online, in printed materials, or it may be filled in by hand at the site of the event.

APPLICATIONS

87c-d1
Fill-In Form

1. Prepare the fill-in form illustrated on p. 343.
2. Set margins: Top: 1"; Right, Left, and Bottom: .75".
3. DS the fill-in portion of the form to allow room for handwriting.
4. *Tip:* After keying the fields for the first team member, copy them for the second and third team members.
5. Check to ensure that the form fits on one page; add a page border.
6. Save the form as **87c-d1**.

87c-d2
Online Form

1. Prepare the same form as an online form; see illustration on p. 344.
2. Use default margins for the online form.
3. *Tip:* After keying the fields for the first team member, copy them for the second and third team members.
4. Note that the option to pay by check or purchase order has been deleted.
5. After you prepare the form, select and add borders to each text box; then add a page border.
6. Protect the form and save it as **87c-d2**. (For *Word 2002*, use the password *pcem*.)

Clip Art

Clip art, pictures, AutoShapes, WordArt, and other images are graphic elements that enhance documents such as announcements and newsletters. This lesson reviews inserting and formatting clip art and introduces inserting pictures from files, WordArt, and Drawing tools.

To insert clip art:

1. Click **Insert** on the menu bar, click **Picture**, and then click **Clip Art**.

2. In the Task Pane Search text box, key the type of clip art to search for such as *bicycle* and then click **Search**.

3. When the results display, select the desired clip, click the down arrow at the right of the image, and then click **Insert**.

To size clip art:

1. Select the clip art.

2. Position the insertion point over one of the handles. When the pointer turns to a double-headed arrow, drag the lower-right handle down and to the right to increase the size. Drag it up and to the left to decrease the size. Drag a corner handle to maintain the same proportion.

handle

DRILL 1 **CLIP ART**

1. Open a new document.

2. Search for a bicycle in the clip art gallery and insert it.

3. Increase the size of the clip art to approximately double the size.

4. Create the folder **Module 15 Keys**, and save the document as **92c-drill1** in this folder. Save all exercises for Module 15 in this folder.

Professional Development Seminars, Inc.
Planning and Conducting Effective Meetings

April 28-30, 200-
The Inn at Central University
Columbia, SC 29201-7459

6.75" right
underline tab

Company/Organization Name:_____

Mailing Address: _____

_____

First Team Member

Name:_____

Telephone: _____ E-Mail _____

3.5" left underline tab

Second Team Member

Name:_____

Telephone: _____ E-Mail _____

Third Team Member

Name:_____

Telephone: _____E-Mail _____

Seminar Registration Fees:

5" left tab

Individual: $350; Team of Two: $600; Team of Three: $850 $ _____

☐ Check or purchase order payable to PDS, Inc. is enclosed.   PO# _____

Charge my ☐ MasterCard ☐ Visa ☐ American Express

Card Number: _____Expiration Date_____

Print name as it appears on card _____

Mail or fax to: Ms. Jennifer Jameson   Fax: (803) 555-0178
                         Professional Development Seminars, Inc.
                         P.O. Box 3947
                         Columbia, SC 29201-3947

                         1.5" left tab

Graphic Enhancements

- Build keyboarding skill.
- Use clip art, drawing tools, and WordArt.
- Format announcements and newsletters with graphics.
- Format newsletters in columns.
- Format news releases.

LESSON 92 Skillbuilding and Graphics

SKILLBUILDING

92a
Warmup
Key each line twice SS.

alphabet 1 Viewing jungle dance experts from big cities quickly amazed them.

fig/sym 2 The yield of 18.469% on the 25-year, $730 million note was given.

3rd/4th fingers 3 Last spring was our good opportunity to zap poor display samples.

adjacent reaches 4 Where we build other stores in the west is a quiet concern of Jo.

| 1 | 2 | 3 | 4 | 5 | 6 | 7 | 8 | 9 | 10 | 11 | 12 | 13 |

92b
Timed Writings
1. Key a 1' writing.
2. Add 8 words to your base. Take three 1' writings; try to increase your rate by 8 words. Work for speed, not accuracy.

gwam 3'

Many people find that creative thinking can be nurtured 4 | 42
with effort. One way to do this is to find multiple solutions to 8 | 46
a problem. Alternatives to a problem should be sought out when 12 | 50
there seems to be only one possible solution as well as when a 17 | 54
solution has already been found. The more ideas generated, the 21 | 59
more options there may be. If a person can identify the options 25 | 63
that are available and experiment with them, then possibly he or 30 | 67
she can come up with several other options. This approach 33 | 71
fosters new ideas and stimulates the creative thinking process. 38 | 75

3' | 1 | 2 | 3 | 4 |

Professional Development Seminars, Inc.
Planning and Conducting Effective Meetings

April 28-30, 200-
The Inn at Central University
Columbia, SC 29201-7459

Company/Organization Name:

Mailing Address:

City: ZIP Code:

First Team Member

Name:

Telephone: E-Mail:

Second Team Member

Name:

Telephone: E-Mail:

Third Team Member

Name:

Telephone: E-Mail:

Seminar Registration Fees: Team of Three: $850

☐ Charge my: MasterCard

Card Number:

Expiration Date:

Name as it appears on card:

Individual: $350
Team of Two: $600
Team of Three: $850

MasterCard
Visa
American Express

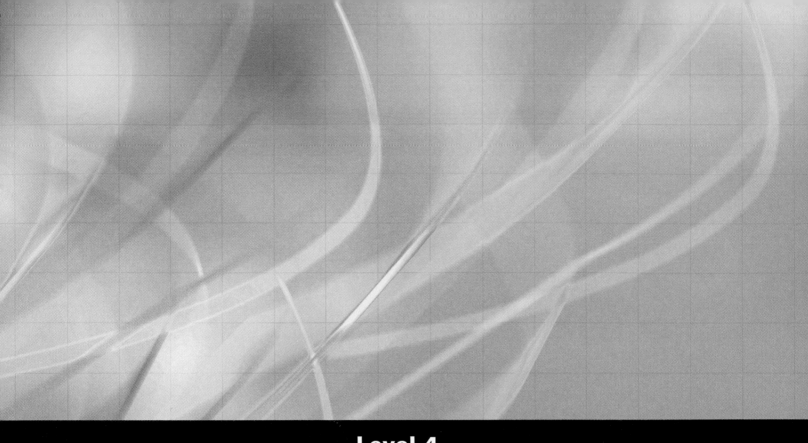

Level 4

Designing Specialized Documents

OBJECTIVES

DOCUMENT DESIGN SKILLS

To display graphics attractively in newsletters, letterheads, and announcements.

To produce mass mailings effectively using mail merge.

To format agendas, minutes, badges, and itineraries attractively.
To format legal, medical, and employment documents appropriately.

WORD PROCESSING SKILLS

To apply graphics, merge, and other commonly used word processing functions.

COMMUNICATION SKILLS

To produce error-free documents.

KEYBOARDING

To improve keyboarding speed and accuracy.

87c-d3
Online Form

1. Open **87c-d2** and save it as **87c-d3**.

2. Fill in the form using your last name + *Associates* as the company name. Use your address, telephone, and e-mail address.

3. Register as an individual using American Express, card number: 0000-000000-00000; Expiration: 10/07; and your name.

4. Resave the document.

87c-d4
Fill-In Form

Prepare a hotel reservation form that Professional Development Seminars, Inc. can use to mail to seminar participants in all seminars or group meetings held at The Inn at Central University.

1. Use the following heading information:

   The Inn at Central University

   1483 Pickens Street

   Columbia, SC 29201-7459

   Telephone: (803) 555-0193 Fax: (803) 555-0148

2. DS; set tabs to position information appropriately; add lines to fill in information:

   Group/Seminar:

   Name:

   Mailing Address:

   City: State: ZIP Code:

   Telephone: E-Mail:

   Arrival Date: Time:

   Departure Date: Time:

   Occupancy: ☐ $145 Double Room   ☐ $125 Single Room

   Room Type: ☐ Double beds   ☐ Queen bed   ☐ King bed

   Options: ☐ Nonsmoking   ☐ Smoking

   Share with:

3. Add same credit card information as used in **87c-d1**.

4. Save the form as **87c-d4**.

87c-d5
Online Form

1. Use the information in **87c-d4** to create an online hotel reservation form.

2. DS; use drop-down boxes for room information and credit card choice; add borders to text fields; move single rooms first in drop-down list.

3. Protect the form and save it as **87c-d5**.

Module 14: Checkpoint

Self-Assessment

Answer the questions below to see if you have mastered the content of this module.

1. To create blank lines for a fill-in form, set an underline tab by using one of the _____ options.

2. To place a line around the perimeter of a page, select Box on the _____ tab of the Borders and Shading dialog box.

3. To enter text fields, checkbox, or drop-down fields, first display the _____ toolbar.

4. To create a list of alternatives in a Drop-Down form field, click the _____ button.

5. To activate a form and test it, you must first _____ the form.

6. A/an _____ form can be completed electronically and transmitted to the designer.

7. The excess of assets over liabilities on a personal financial statement is known as a person's _____.

8. On a balance sheet, liabilities and _____ must equal total assets.

9. A/an _____ statement shows the net profit or earnings of an organization.

10. A/an _____ is used to ensure that expenditures do not exceed the money available for operations or a project.

Performance Assessment

Document 1
Fill-In Form

1. Create a fill-in form for the Business Club to use for its members.

   - Position heading at about 2"; center it; and use 14-point bold font.

   - Provide lines for name, address, city, state, and ZIP Code, telephone number, e-mail, major, class, and committee. Put city, state, and ZIP Code on one line with a blank line for each item.

2. Save the document as **Checkpoint14-d1a**.

3. Put the same information on an online form. Use text boxes for everything except class and committee. Use drop-down boxes with **Freshman, Sophomore, Junior,** and **Senior** for Class options and **Membership, Finance,** and **Program** for Committee options. Move the committee options so that they are in alphabetical order.

4. Protect the form and save it as **Checkpoint14-d1b**.

Document 2
Budget

1. Prepare a budget for the Business Club Banquet.

2. Your estimated sources of revenue are ticket sales at $25 per person. You expect 40 people to attend. Business Club support will add $150 to help cover costs.

3. Your projected expenses are: Fixed costs: Decorations, $100; Entertainment, $125; and Gift for speaker, $25; Variable costs: Food, $20 per person; Program printing, $.50 per person. Any excess revenues over expenditures will be used for contingencies.

4. Save as **Checkpoint14-d2**.

LESSON 88 — Custom Forms

SKILLBUILDING

88a
Warmup
Key each line twice SS.

alphabet   1   Mickey bought six lavender azaleas and quite a few nice junipers.
figures   2   We gave a 15% discount on 3 invoices (#28574, #6973, and #12095).
shift key   3   Li, Jan, Al, and Carl went with Rod, Kay, and Oki to see Big Sky.
fluency   4   Jan and six girls may go to the lake to sit on the dock and fish.

| 1 | 2 | 3 | 4 | 5 | 6 | 7 | 8 | 9 | 10 | 11 | 12 | 13 |

88b
Timed Writings
1. Key two 3' writings.

2. Work for speed.

	gwam	1'	3'
Forms provide both a productive and an effective way to col-		12	4
lect data. Designing an effective form often is not accomplished		25	8
quickly, but the time spent can be justified easily. Creating a		38	13
form is productive because once the form is finished, it can be		51	17
used multiple times. Forms provide an effective way of collecting		64	21
data because they add structure. A form can be set up so that		77	26
the data is organized in exactly the way the designer wants to		89	30
collect it. Analyzing data can be simplified by the way the form		103	34
is structured. Online forms can even be designed to tabulate the		116	39
answers as they are entered.		121	40

1' | 1 | 2 | 3 | 4 | 5 | 6 | 7 | 8 | 9 | 10 | 11 | 12 | 13 |
3' | 1 | 2 | 3 | 4 |

APPLICATIONS

88c-d1
Breakeven Analysis Form

Custom forms are forms that are tailored to the specific needs of a business or an individual. Prepare the form illustrated on the next page that can be used to determine how many seminar participants must be enrolled in a program for it to break even. Note that fixed costs are expenditures that must be made regardless of the number of participants. Variable costs are dependent on the number of people enrolled in the program. Use a table to simplify the design of this form. Note that the blank lines in the form are available for special costs that might apply to some programs but not others.

1. Key the form on p. 347 as shown. Do not key the handwritten data shown filled in on the form.

2. Use Save As to save the form as a template named *Breakeven Analysis Form*. Click **Document Template** in the Save as type box.

File name:	Breakeven Analysis Form.dot	∨	Save
Save as type:	Document Template (*.dot)	∨	Cancel

91c-d2
Personal Financial Statement

Use the following information to prepare a personal financial statement for Tonisha C. Marcus, 3947 Keatley Ave., Huntington, WV 25755-9603. Set tabs: .5" left; 3.5" left with leader 2; 4.5" right; and 6" right tab. Use a 2" top margin.

1. Include the following assets: cash, $1,025; savings, $2,486; and automobile, $14,675. Show the total assets of $18,186.

2. Include the following liabilities: credit cards, $1,000; automobile loan, $4,279. Show the total liabilities of $5,279.

3. Show the net worth of $12,907. Double-underline the net worth.

4. Add a page border.

5. Save as **91c-d2** and print.

91c-d3
Balance Sheet

Use the following information to prepare a balance sheet. Position the following heading at about 2", centered, and 14-point bold font: **Saluda Gift Shop; Balance Sheet; As of December 31, 200-**. Set tabs: .5" left tab; 4.5" right tab; and 5.75" right tab. Add a page border; save as **91c-d3** and print.

Assets

Current Assets
 Cash and equivalents $104,268
 Receivables 26,493
 Inventory 12,730
 Total Current Assets $143,491

Long-Term Assets
 Furniture and fixtures $14,862
 Equipment 12,793
 Total Long-Term Assets $27,619

Total Assets $171,110

Liabilities and Equity

Liabilities
 Accounts payable $14,378
 Accrued expenses 1,604
 Total Liabilities $15,982

Equity
 Owner's equity $155,128

Total Liabilities and Equity $171,110

Professional Development Seminars, Inc.
Seminar Breakeven Analysis

Program: Effective Presentations
Number of Days: 2

Fixed Costs:	Amount	Total Costs
Instructor fees	$1,600	
Instructor expenses	150	
Training room/equipment rental	650	
Program marketing material	450	
Advertising and promotional costs	800	
Overhead allocation	400	
Coaches/mentors	400	
Total Fixed Costs:		$ 4,450
Variable Costs:	Per Participant	
Seminar training manual	15	
Meals/breaks	30	
Parking/other fees	5	
Total Variable Costs:	$50 X 10	500
Total Costs		$4,950
Revenue Per Participant:	$495 X 10	$4,950
Breakeven Level:		10

91c
Assessment

On the signal to begin, key the documents in sequence. When time has been called, proofread all documents again and correct any errors you may have overlooked. Reprint if necessary.

91c-d1
Online Form

1. Prepare an online registration form with the heading **Central University Soccer Camp** formatted in bold, 14-point type.

2. Use the heading **Camper Information**, followed by text boxes for the following information:

   Full Name

   Date of Birth

   Name of Parent

   Street Address

   City, State, and ZIP Code

   Telephone Number

   E-Mail

3. Add borders to each text box.

4. Use a checkbox for ☐ **Boy** ☐ **Girl**.

5. Use a drop-down list for t-shirt size with the following options:

   Small

   Medium

   Large

   X-Large

6. Use the heading **Camp Options**, followed by the two subheadings for camp selection and a drop-down list with the following options:

   Regular camp for boys and girls 6–15

   Options: Half-day; June 23–27; $99 or Full-day; July 11–15; $199

   Premier residential camps for ages 10–18

   Options: Boys; June 12–16; $400 or Girls; June 18–22; $400

7. Add the following notation at the bottom of the form: ***Note:*** **Checks must be received within 5 days to hold your reservation.**

8. Protect the form, save it as **91c-d1**, and print. (For *Word 2002*, use password *soccamp*.)

88c-d2
Fill-In Form

1. Open the Breakeven Analysis Form you prepared in **88c-d1**. Save it as a *Word* document named **88c-d2**.

2. Complete the form, keying the handwritten data on the form illustrated on p. 347.

3. Resave the document.

88c-d3
Online Form

1. Create the online form shown on p. 349. Use .75" side margins and 1.5 spacing.

2. Use text boxes for all responses except the following:

   a. Ownership status: use three drop-down options—Own home, Rent home, Rent apartment

   b. Length of time: use three drop-down options—Less than 1 year, 1-3 years, More than 3 years

   c. Coapplicant: use checkboxes with Yes and No

3. Add a page border.

4. Protect the form and save it as **88c-d3**.

88c-d4
Fill in Online Form

1. Open **88c-d3** and save it as **88c-d4**.

2. Complete the form using your own information. Do not use your actual social security number; use 000-00-0000. If you do not know the current monthly payment of your residence, use $650 per month.

3. If you are not employed part-time or full-time, use your institution as the employer and an hourly wage of $10 per hour.

4. Resave the completed form.

88c-d5
Fill in Online Form

1. Open **88c-d3** and save it as **88c-d5**.

2. Complete the form for a coapplicant. As coapplicant, select a spouse, a parent, or any other relative. Do not use an actual social security number; use 000-00-0000. If you do not know the current monthly payment of your coapplicant's residence, use $800 per month.

3. If your coapplicant is not employed, use the name of a local bank and a salary of $35,000.

4. Resave the completed form.

91a
Warmup
Key each line twice SS.

alphabet	1	Gwen and Jackie both analyzed our five complex physics questions.
fig/sym	2	Room #1507 is 42'6" long and 38'9" wide; it can accommodate them.
home row	3	Jake said Sally and Klaus gladly did all I asked the staff to do.
fluency	4	Claudia and Clement may go with their neighbor to fish for smelt.

| 1 | 2 | 3 | 4 | 5 | 6 | 7 | 8 | 9 | 10 | 11 | 12 | 13 |

91b
Timed Writings
Take two 5' timed writings.

  all letters

gwam 3' | 5'

Most people find it amazing that mobile telephones can create a number of etiquette and safety problems. The use of hand-held, mobile telephones has increased dramatically in the past few years. Just because a mobile telephone can be taken almost anywhere does not mean that it is appropriate to use it in any place it can be carried. Common sense and good manners seem to have been forgotten when it comes to using a mobile telephone.

4	3
9	5
13	8
18	11
22	13
26	16
29	18

The major safety hazard of using a hand-held telephone results from its use in moving automobiles. A significant percentage of all accidents is the result of drivers being distracted. Of all the distractions reported, the most frequent are those that occur while a driver is holding a telephone in one hand and trying to drive at the same time. A hands-free telephone is not as dangerous, but it can still cause a driver to be distracted.

33	20
38	23
42	25
47	28
51	31
56	33
59	35

The etiquette problem is the result of a person speaking on a telephone in a place that disturbs another person. Either the individual doing this just does not care or does not realize how rude he or she is being to another person. It is not unusual to see signs that prohibit the use of a mobile telephone in meeting rooms, restaurants, movie theaters, concert halls, and a number of other places. What is most shocking is that these signs are necessary. Except in rare cases, a telephone should not be used in these places. What has happened to basic courtesy?

63	38
67	40
71	43
76	45
80	48
84	51
88	53
93	56
96	58

3' | 1 | 2 | 3 | 4 |
5' | 1 | 2 | 3 |

Pat's Catering Service
1947 First Ave.
Olympia, WA 99504-2863
Telephone: (360) 555-0103 Fax: (360) 555-0182

Credit Application

Applicant Information

Full Name: [   ]

Date of Birth: [   ]   Social Security No.: [   ]

Current Residence

Street Address: [   ]

City, State, and ZIP Code: [   ]

Telephone Number: [   ]   E-Mail: [   ]

Ownership Status: Own home   Length of time: Less than 1 year

Monthly Payment/Rent: [   ]

```
Own home
Rent home
Rent apartment
```

Previous Residence

Street Address: [   ]

City, State, and ZIP Code: [   ]

Telephone Number: [   ]

Ownership Status: Own home   Length of time: Less than 1 year

Monthly Payment/Rent: [   ]

```
Less than 1 year
1-3 years
More than 3 years
```

Employment Information

Current Employer: [   ]

Employer Street Address: [   ]

City, State, and ZIP Code: [   ]

Telephone Number: [   ]

Position Held: [   ]   Length of Employment: [   ]

Compensation Status: Hourly

Hourly Rate: [   ]   Annual Salary: [   ]

Coapplicant: ☐ Yes ☐ No   If yes, complete a credit application form for coapplicant.

Prepare a budget for a seminar that Professional Development Seminars has scheduled. Use the following information to prepare the budget.

1. Use the heading **Professional Development Seminars, Inc./Effective Presentations Seminar/** and the current date. Position the heading at about 2"; center it and use 14-point bold font.

2. Set a left tab at .5" and right tabs at 4.5" and 5.75".

3. Key the data shown below.

4. Use capitalization, underlining, and bold as illustrated.

5. Add a page border to the document.

6. Save as **90c-d2** and print.

Projected Revenues

Number of participants projected	18	
Revenue per participant	$495	
Total Revenue Projected		$8,910

Projected Expenses
    Fixed Costs

Instructor fees	$1,600	
Instructor expenses	150	
Training room/equipment rental	650	
Program marketing material	450	
Advertising and promotional costs	800	
Overhead allocation	400	
Coaches/mentors	400	
Total Fixed Costs		$4,450

    Variable Costs

Seminar training manual ($15 each)	$270	
Meals/breaks ($30 each)	540	
Parking/other fees ($5 each)	90	
Total Variable Costs		$900
Total Projected Expenses		$5,350
Profit		$3,560

The same seminar whose budget you prepared in **90c-d2** above is being offered again one month from today. The projected number of participants is 30. The fixed costs are the same. The variable costs must be adjusted based on the number of participants. Prepare the budget for the seminar. Save as **90c-d3**.

LESSON 89

Financial Documents

SKILLBUILDING

89a
Warmup
Key each line twice SS.

alphabet	1	Zack and Jimmy explored a quaint town and bought five neat gifts.
fig/sym	2	They got discounts (25% and 10%) on gifts priced $1,389 and $476.
adjacent reaches	3	We were going to walk to a new polo field with three junior guys.
fluency	4	Pamela and Jakken may go to town with a neighbor and eight girls.

| 1 | 2 | 3 | 4 | 5 | 6 | 7 | 8 | 9 | 10 | 11 | 12 | 13 |

APPLICATIONS

89b-d1
Personal Financial Statement

A personal financial statement often is used when individuals apply for loans or other types of credit. Financial documents are usually formatted in tabular form with leaders so that the data is easily readable. If the information contained in a financial document is complicated and contains multiple columns, the document may be formatted as a table or a spreadsheet. The financial documents in this lesson are relatively simple and formatted using tabs and leaders.

1. Key the document shown on p. 351 using the format illustrated.
2. Position the main heading at about 2"; center the heading using 16-point bold font; bold the names and address.
3. Set the following tabs: .5" left tab; 3.5" left tab with Leader 2; 4.5" right tab; and a 6" right tab.
4. Use all caps for the three main headings; double-underline the final net worth.
5. Add a page border to the document.
6. Print and save as **89b-d1**.

89b-d2
Personal Financial Statement

Use the following information to prepare a personal financial statement for Hayden S. Robinson, 3549 Woodview Dr., Las Cruces, NM 88012-9367.

1. Include the following assets: checking account, $1,975; savings account, $40,639; automobile, $28,910; apartment furnishings, $7,190; and art collection, $8,240. Show the total amount of assets.
2. Include the following liabilities: credit cards, $1,290; automobile loan, $2,073; college tuition loan, $6,539; and a personal loan, $1,496. Show the total amount of liabilities.
3. Determine the net worth by subtracting the total liabilities from the total assets; double-underline the net worth.
4. Add a page border to the document.
5. Save as **89b-d2** and print.

Central University Foundation
Operational Budget for Unrestricted Funds
For Fiscal Year 200-

Estimated Revenues

Investment income	$1,025,000	
Annual fund—unrestricted portion	485,000	
Unrestricted gifts	1,275,500	
Unrestricted endowment income	487,300	
Endowment assessment income	1,720,000	
Total Revenues		$4,992,800

Projected Expenditures

Academic Expenditures

Scholarships	$1,075,325	
Graduate fellowships	448,950	
Distinguished professor supplements	484,975	
Administrative officer supplements	135,000	
Faculty research awards	25,000	
Faculty teaching awards	25,000	
Graduate and undergraduate student awards	25,000	
Faculty recruitment and retention	1,050,000	
Total Academic Expenditures		$3,269,250

Fundraising and Marketing Expenditures

Marketing	$145,000	
Gift acquisition and announcement costs	85,000	
Fundraising support	260,725	
Total Fundraising and Marketing Expenditures		$490,725

Operational Expenditures

Foundation operations	$775,250	
Board expenditures	35,000	
Total Operational Expenditures		$810,250
Total Projected Expenditures		$4,570,225
Excess Revenues over Expenditures[1]		$422,575

[1] Excess revenues are available as contingencies for this budget year. If they are not needed, excess revenues are added to the reserves for future use.

Personal Financial Statement

Luiz C. and Sara R. Cortez
4935 Fifth St.
Dallas, TX 75221-8601

ASSETS

.5" left tab

Cortez financial statement annotations: 3.5" left leader tab, 4.5" right tab

Cash	$ 24,375	
Investments	273,287	
Home and furnishings	330,500	
Other real estate	196,250	
Automobiles	62,920	
Total Assets		$887,332

6" right tab

LIABILITIES

Credit cards	$ 13,869	
Home mortgage	186,374	
Other real estate	106,985	
Automobile loans	36,425	
Total Liabilities		$343,653
NET WORTH		$543,679

90a
Warmup

Key each line twice SS.

alphabet	1	A huge crowd went from Jackson Square to the lively Plaza by six.
fig/sym	2	Our meal was very expensive—$137.95 + 18% tip ($24.85) = $162.80.
direct reaches	3	Celia and June are great friends who swam long hours for my team.
fluency	4	Jamale may own the bicycle, but a neighbor owns the antique auto.

| 1 | 2 | 3 | 4 | 5 | 6 | 7 | 8 | 9 | 10 | 11 | 12 | 13 |

90b
Technique Builder

Key each set of lines 3 times;
DS between 9-line groups;
work at a controlled rate.

direct reaches

5 red much brief hunt bred zany check jump decrease music many brat
6 polo excel munch brake junk swim wreck lunch curve kick dazed bed
7 Cec and Kim enjoy a great hunting trip in June after school ends.

adjacent reaches

8 were guy sad junior tree trio fast point rest joint walk gas join
9 opt crew going port backlog poster web suit few folder buy porter
10 Porter saw two important guys after we walked past Union Station.

double letters

11 bell look deed glass upper inn odd committee cabbage effect inner
12 add spell pool happy jazz mass scurry connect office fall setting
13 Debbie Desselle called a committee meeting at noon at the office.

| 1 | 2 | 3 | 4 | 5 | 6 | 7 | 8 | 9 | 10 | 11 | 12 | 13 |

90c-d1
Operational Budget

Budgets are financial documents used to ensure that expenditures do not exceed the money available for a company or organization's operations. Budgets may be for the whole organization, for a department, or for a specific project or event. The budget illustrated for this activity is the budget for the year for the operation of a university foundation. Unrestricted money refers to money that the foundation can spend as its board of directors determines. Restricted money is spent according to the gift agreement of a donor.

1. Key the document shown on p. 355 using the format illustrated.
2. Center the heading at about 1" and use 14-point bold font.
3. Set the following tabs: .25" left tab, 4.5" right tab, and 6" right tab.
4. Use capitalization, underlining, and bold as illustrated.
5. Add a page border to the document.
6. Save as **90c-d1** and print.

89b-d3
Balance Sheet

Financial documents are used to show the financial condition of a business. Common financial documents include the balance sheet, income statement, and statement of cash flows. Financial statements can be formatted as a document using tabs to position columns of numbers, as a table, or as a spreadsheet. In this lesson, a balance sheet and an income statement are illustrated. Both of these documents are formatted by setting tabs. Different businesses vary the entries that are capitalized and the use of bold. Within a business, the format used for financial documents should be consistent.

1. Key the document shown on p. 353 using the format illustrated.
2. Center the heading using 14-point bold font.
3. Set the following tabs: .25" left tab, 4" right tab, and a 5.75" right tab.
4. Use capitalization, underlining, and bold as illustrated.
5. Add a page border to the document.
6. Save as **89b-d3** and print.

89b-d4
Balance Sheet

1. Use the same format and all headings as in **89b-d3** to prepare a balance sheet for The Pet Place as of December 31, 200-.
2. Substitute the following numbers for the various categories; total the amounts to determine the figures to be shown in the second column of the balance sheet.

Cash and equivalents	$125,000
Receivables	102,450
Inventory	150,975
Prepaid expenses	58,932
Building and equipment (depreciated)	183,206
Furniture and fixtures	98,065
Accounts payable	92,351
Short-term debt	23,074
Accrued expenses	18,649
Long-term debt	46,824
Other liabilities	12,706
Owner's equity	285,014
Retained earnings	240,010

3. Proofread all numbers carefully, print, and save as **89b-d4**.

Pat's Promotions, Inc.
Balance Sheet
As of December 31, 200-

Assets

Current Assets

.25"— left tab

4" right tab

5.75" right tab

Cash and equivalents	$326,175	
Receivables	198,403	
Inventory	283,476	
Prepaid expenses	102,964	
Total Current Assets		$911,018

Long-Term Assets

Building and equipment (depreciated)	$209,685	
Furniture and fixtures	117,482	
Total Long-Term Assets		$327,167

Total Assets		$1,238,185

Liabilities and Equity

Current Liabilities

Accounts payable	$158,964	
Short-term debt	84,623	
Accrued expenses	42,701	
Total Current Liabilities		$286,288

Long-Term Liabilities

Long-term debt	$103,728	
Other liabilities	98,605	
Total Long-Term Liabilities		$202,333

Total Liabilities		$488,621

Equity

Owner's equity	$390,476	
Retained earnings	359,088	
Total Equity		$749,564

Total Liabilities and Equity		$1,238,185

Capitalize

1. First word of a sentence and of a direct quotation.

   We were tolerating instead of managing diversity. The speaker said, "We must value diversity, not merely recognize it."

2. Names of proper nouns—specific persons, places, or things.

   Common nouns: continent, river, car, street
   Proper nouns: Asia, Mississippi, Buick, State St.

3. Derivatives of proper nouns and geographical names.

American history	English accent
German food	Ohio Valley
Tampa, Florida	Mount Rushmore

4. A personal or professional title when it precedes the name or a title of high distinction without a name.

Lieutenant Kahn	Mayor Walsh
Doctor Welby	Mr. Ty Brooks
Dr. Frank Collins	Miss Tate
the President of the United States	

5. Days of the week, months of the year, holidays, periods of history, and historic events.

   Monday, June 8   Labor Day   Renaissance

6. Specific parts of the country but not compass points that show direction.

   Midwest   the South   northwest of town

7. Family relationships when used with a person's name.

   Aunt Helen   my dad   Uncle John

8. Noun preceding a figure except for common nouns such as *line, page,* and *sentence.*

   Unit 1   Section 2   page 2   verse 7   line 2

9. First and main words of side headings, titles of books, and works of art. Do not capitalize words of four or fewer letters that are conjunctions, prepositions, or articles.

   Computers in the News   Raiders of the Lost Ark

10. Names of organizations and specific departments within the writer's organization.

    Girl Scouts   our Sales Department

Number Expression

General guidelines

1. Use **words** for numbers *one* through *ten* unless the numbers are in a category with related larger numbers that are expressed as figures.

   He bought three acres of land. She took two acres. She wrote 12 stories and 2 plays in the last 13 years.

2. Use **words** for approximate numbers or large round numbers that can be expressed as one or two words. Use **numbers** for round numbers in millions or higher with their word modifier.

   We sent out about three hundred invitations. She contributed $3 million dollars.

3. Use **words** for numbers that begin a sentence.

   Six players were cut from the ten-member team.

4. Use **figures** for the larger of two adjacent numbers.

   We shipped six 24-ton engines.

Times and dates

5. Use **words** for numbers that precede o'clock (stated or implied).

   We shall meet from two until five o'clock.

6. Use **figures** for times with *a.m.* or *p.m.* and days when they follow the month.

   Her appointment is for 2:15 p.m. on July 26, 2000.

7. Use **ordinals** for the day when it precedes the month.

   The 10th of October is my anniversary.

Money, percentages, and fractions

8. Use **figures** for money amounts and percentages. Spell out *cents* and *percent* except in statistical copy.

   The 16% discount saved me $145; Bill, 95 cents.

9. Use **words** for fractions unless the fractions appear in combination with whole numbers.

   one-half of her lesson   5 1/2   18 3/4

Addresses

10. Use **words** for street names First through Tenth and **figures** or ordinals for streets above Tenth. Use **figures** for house numbers other than number **one**. (If street name is a number, separate it from house number with a dash.)

    One Lytle Place   Second Ave.   142—53d St.

Punctuation

Use an apostrophe

1. To make most singular nouns and indefinite pronouns possessive (add **apostrophe** and **s**).

   computer + 's = computer's   Jess + 's = Jess's
   anyone's   one's   somebody's

2. To make a plural noun that does not end in s possessive (add **apostrophe** and **s**).

   women + 's = women's   men + 's = men's
   deer + 's = deer's   children + 's = children's

3. To make a plural noun that ends in s possessive. Add only the **apostrophe**.

   boys + ' = boys'   managers + ' = managers'

4. To make a compound noun possessive or to show joint possession. Add **apostrophe** and **s** to the last part of the hyphenated noun.

   son-in-law's   Rob and Gen's game

5. To form the plural of numbers and letters, add **apostrophe** and **s**. To show omission of letters or figures, add an **apostrophe** in place of the missing items.

   7's   A's   It's   add'l

Use a colon

1. To introduce a listing.

   The candidate's strengths were obvious: experience, community involvement, and forthrightness.

2. To introduce an explanatory statement.

   Then I knew we were in trouble: The item had not been scheduled.

Use a comma

1. After an introductory phrase or dependent clause.

   After much deliberation, the jury reached its decision.
   If you have good skills, you will find a job.

2. After words or phrases in a series.

   Mike is taking Greek, Latin III, and Chemistry II.

3. To set off nonessential or interrupting elements.

   Troy, the new man in MIS, will install the hard drive.
   He cannot get to the job, however, until next Friday.

4. To set off the date from the year and the city from the state.

   John, will you please reserve the center in Billings, Montana, for January 10, 2000.

5. To separate two or more parallel adjectives (adjectives could be separated by and instead of a comma).

   The loud, whining guitar could be heard above the rest.

6. Before the conjunction in a compound sentence. The comma may be omitted in a very short sentence.

   You must leave immediately, or you will miss your flight.
   We tested the software and they loved it.

7. Set off appositives and words of direct address.

   Karen, our team leader, represented us at the conference.
   Paul, have you ordered the CD-ROM drive?

Use a hyphen

1. To show end-of-line word division.

2. In many compound words—check a dictionary if unsure.
   - Two-word adjectives before a noun:
     two-car family
   - Compound numbers between twenty-one and ninety-nine.
   - Fractions and some proper nouns with prefixes/suffixes.
     two-thirds   ex-Governor   all-American

Use italic or underline

1. With titles of complete literary works.
   College Keyboarding   *Hunt for Red October*

2. To emphasize special words or phrases.
   What does *professional* mean?

Use a semicolon

1. To separate independent clauses in a compound sentence when the conjunction is omitted.

   Please review the information; give me a report by Tuesday.

2. To separate independent clauses when they are joined by conjunctive adverbs (*however*, *nevertheless*, *consequently*, etc.).

   The traffic was heavy; consequently, I was late.

3. To separate a series of elements that contain commas.

   The new officers are: Fran Pena, president; Harry Wong, treasurer; and Muriel Williams, secretary.

Use a dash

1. To show an abrupt change of thought.

   Invoice 76A—which is 10 days overdue—is for $670.

2. After a series to indicate a summarizing statement.

   Noisy fuel pump, worn rods, and failing brakes—for all these reasons I'm trading the car.

Use an exclamation point

After emphatic interjections or exclamatory sentences.

Terrific!   Hold it!   You bet!   What a great surprise!

Proofreading procedures

Proofread documents so that they are free of errors. Error-free documents send the message that you are detail-oriented and a person capable of doing business. Apply these procedures after you key a document.

1. Use Spelling.
2. Proofread the document on screen to be sure that it makes sense. Check for these types of errors:
   • Words, headings, and/or amounts omitted.
   • Extra words or lines not deleted during the editing stage.
   • Incorrect sequence of numbers in a list.
3. Preview the document on screen using the Print Preview feature. Check the vertical placement, presence of headers or footers, page numbers, and overall appearance.
4. Save the document again and print.
5. Check the printed document by comparing it to the source copy (textbook). Check all figures, names, and addresses against the source copy. Check that the document style has been applied consistently throughout.
6. If errors exist on the printed copy, revise the document, save, and print.
7. Verify the corrections and placement of the second printed copy.

Proofreaders' marks

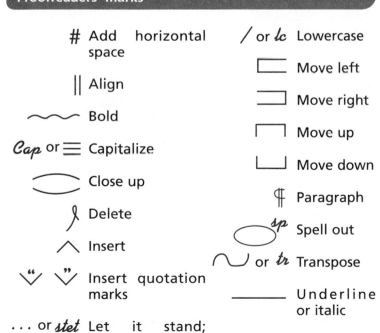

Add horizontal space

|| Align

~~~ Bold

Cap or ≡ Capitalize

⌣ Close up

ℓ Delete

∧ Insert

˘˘ ˘˘ Insert quotation marks

... or stet Let it stand; ignore correction

/ or lc Lowercase

⌐ Move left

¬ Move right

⊓ Move up

⊔ Move down

¶ Paragraph

sp Spell out

⌣ or tr Transpose

___ Underline or italic

Word division

With the use of proportional fonts found in current word processing packages, word division is less of an issue. Occasionally, however, you will need to make decisions on dividing words, such as when using the Columns function.

The following list contains generally accepted guidelines for dividing words.

1. Divide words between syllables only; therefore, do not divide one-syllable words.

2. **Short words:** Avoid dividing short words (five letters or fewer).

   area   bonus   since   ideal

3. **Double consonants:** Divide words with double consonants between the double letters unless the root word ends with the double letters. In this case, divide after the second consonant.

   mis- sion   trim- ming   dress- ing   call- ing

4. **One-letter syllables:** Do not divide after a *one-letter* syllable at the *beginning* of a word or before a *one-* or *two-letter* syllable at the end of a word; divide after a *one-letter* syllable within a word.

   enough   abroad   starter   friendly
   ani- mal   sepa- rate   regu- late

5. **Two single-letter syllables:** Divide between two single-letter syllables within a word.

   gradu- ation   evalu- ation

6. **Hyphenated words:** Compound words with a hyphen may be divided only after the hyphen.

   top- secret   soft- spoken   self- respect

7. **Figures:** Avoid dividing figures presented as a unit.

   #870331   190,886   1/22/02

8. **Proper nouns:** Avoid dividing proper nouns. If necessary, include as much of the proper noun as possible before dividing it.

   Thomas R./Lewiston   *not* Thomas R. Lewis/ton
   November 15,/ 2002   *not* November/ 15, 2002

Addressing procedures

The envelope feature inserts the delivery address automatically if a letter is displayed. Title case, used in the letter address, is acceptable in the envelope address. An alternative style for envelopes is uppercase with no punctuation.

Business letters are usually mailed in envelopes that have the return address preprinted; return addresses are printed only for personal letters or when letterhead is not available. The default size of *Word* is a size 10 envelope (4 1/8" by 9 1/2"); other sizes are available using the Options feature.

When preparing an envelope using an electronic typewriter, follow the spacing guidelines below:

Small envelope. On a No. 6 3/4 envelope, place the address near the center—about 2 inches from the top and left edges. Place a return address in the upper left corner.

Large envelope. On a No. 10 envelope, place the address near the center—about line 14 and .5" left of center. A return address, if not preprinted, should be keyed in the upper left corner (see small envelope).

An address must contain at least three lines; addresses of more than six lines should be avoided. The last line of an address must contain three items of information: (1) the city, (2) the state, and (3) the ZIP Code, preferably a 9-digit code.

Place mailing notations that affect postage (e.g., REGISTERED, CERTIFIED) below the stamp position (line 8); place other special notations (e.g., CONFIDENTIAL, PERSONAL) a DS below the return address.

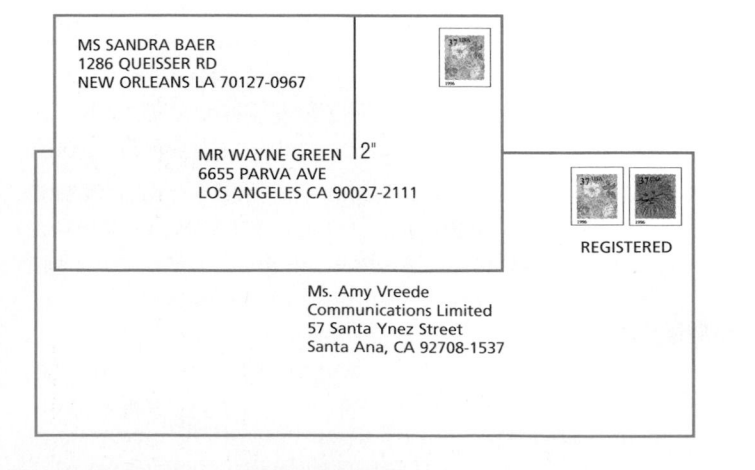

Folding and inserting procedures

Large envelopes (No. 10, 9, 7 3/4)

Step 1	Step 2	Step 3

Step 1: With document face up, fold slightly less than 1/3 of sheet up toward top.

Step 2: Fold down top of sheet to within 1/2" of bottom fold.

Step 3: Insert document into envelope with last crease toward bottom of envelope.

Small envelopes (No. 6 3/4, 6 1/4)

Step 1	Step 2	Step 3

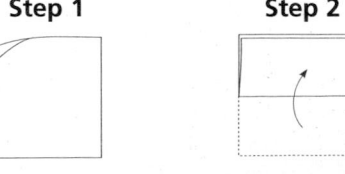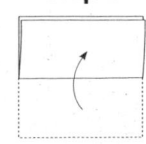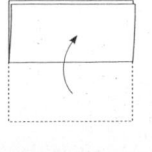

Step 1: With document face up, fold bottom up to 1/2" from top.

Step 2: Fold right third to left.

Step 3: Fold left third to 1/2" from last crease and insert last creased edge first.

Window envelopes (full sheet)

Step 1	Step 2	Step 3

Step 1: With sheet face down, top toward you, fold upper third down.

Step 2: Fold lower third up so address is showing.

Step 3: Insert document into envelope with last crease toward bottom of envelope.

Two-letter state abbreviations

Alabama, AL	Florida, FL	Kentucky, KY	Montana, MT	Ohio, OH	Texas, TX
Alaska, AK	Georgia, GA	Louisiana, LA	Nebraska, NE	Oklahoma, OK	Utah, UT
Arizona, AZ	Guam, GU	Maine, ME	Nevada, NV	Oregon, OR	Vermont, VT
Arkansas, AR	Hawaii, HI	Maryland, MD	New Hampshire, NH	Pennsylvania, PA	Virgin Islands, VI
California, CA	Idaho, ID	Massachusetts, MA	New Jersey, NJ	Puerto Rico, PR	Virginia, VA
Colorado, CO	Illinois, IL	Michigan, MI	New Mexico, NM	Rhode Island, RI	Washington, WA
Connecticut, CT	Indiana, IN	Minnesota, MN	New York, NY	South Carolina, SC	West Virginia, WV
Delaware, DE	Iowa, IA	Mississippi, MS	North Carolina, NC	South Dakota, SD	Wisconsin, WI
District of Columbia, DC	Kansas, KS	Missouri, MO	North Dakota, ND	Tennessee, TN	Wyoming, WY

Letter parts

Letterhead. Company name and address. May include other data.

Date. Date letter is mailed. Usually in month, day, year order. Military style is an option (day/month/year: 17/1/02).

Letter address. Address of the person who will receive the letter. Include personal title (*Mr.*, *Ms.*, *Dr.*), name, professional title, company, and address.

Salutation. Greeting. Corresponds to the first line of the letter address. Usually includes name and courtesy title; use *Ladies and Gentlemen* if letter is addressed to a company name.

Body. Message. SS; DS between paragraphs.

Complimentary close. Farewell, such as *Sincerely*.

Writer. Name and professional title. Women may include a personal title.

Initials. Identifies person who keyed the document (for example, *tr*). May include identification of writer (*ARB:tri*).

Enclosure. Copy is enclosed with the document. May specify contents.

Copy notation. Indicates that a copy of the letter is being sent to person named.

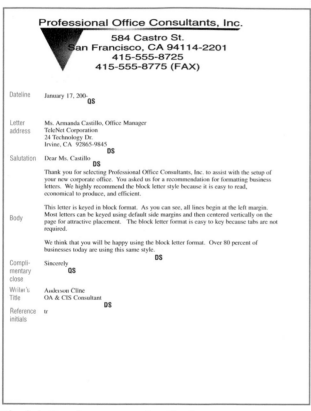

Block letter (open punctuation)

Modified block letter (mixed punctuation)

Envelope

Letter placement table

Length	Dateline position	Margins
Short: 1-2 ¶s	Center page	Default
Average: 3-4 ¶s	Center page or 2.1"	Default
Long: 4+ ¶s	2.1" (default + 6 hard returns)	Default

Default margins or a minimum of 1".

Personal business letter

Scott T. Fischer
1001 Hogan Street, Apt. 216A • Mobile, AL 36617-1001 • (334) 555-0103 • sfischer@cu.edu

August 13, 200- **QS**

Mr. Coleman Stanberry
Financial News
706 Kentwood Street
Honolulu, HI 96822 **DS**

Dear Mr. Stanberry **DS**

My bachelor's degree with double majors in graphic design and information technology and my graphic design work experience in the United States and Japan qualify me as a junior graphic designer for your international newspaper. **DS**

As a result of my comprehensive four-year program, I am skilled in the latest office suite as well as the current versions of desktop publishing and graphics programs. In addition, my excellent research and writing skills played a very important role in the Cother University Design Award I received last month. Being able to locate the right resources and synthesize that data into useful information for your readers is a priority I understand well and have practiced in my positions at the Cother University College Alumni Office and the Cother University Library. **DS**

My technical and communication skills were applied as well as I worked as the assistant director and producer of the *Cother University Alumni News*. I understand well the importance of meeting deadlines and also producing a quality product that will increase newspaper sales. Additionally, my intern experience in Japan provides me with a global view of international business and communication. **DS**

After you have reviewed the enclosed résumé as well as my graphic design samples located on my Web page at http://www.netdoor.com/~sfischer, I would look forward to discussing my qualifications and career opportunities with you at *Financial News*. **DS**

Sincerely **QS**

Scott T. Fischer **DS**

Enclosure

Personal business letter

Special letter parts/features

Attention line. Directs the letter to a specific title or person within the company. Positioned as the first line of letter address; the salutation is *Ladies and Gentlemen.*

Company name. Company name of the sender is keyed in ALL CAPS a DS below complimentary close.

Enumerations. Hanging indent format; block format may be used if paragraphs are not indented.

Mailing notation. Provides record of how the letter was sent (FACSIMILE, CERTIFIED, REGISTERED) or how the letter should be treated by the receiver (CONFIDENTIAL). DS below date.

Postscript. Used to emphasize information; DS below last line of copy.

Reference line. Directs the reader to a source document such as an invoice. DS below letter address.

Return address. Sender's address in a personal business letter. The return address may be keyed immediately above the date or personal letterhead stationery may be used as shown at the left.

Second-page heading. Addressee's name, page number, date arranged in block format about 1" from the top edge. Second sheet is plain paper of the same quality as letterhead.

Subject line. Indicates topic of the letter; DS below salutation at left margin. It may be keyed in ALL CAPS or cap-and-lowercase.

Samantha's Fashions
422 Main St.
Wichita, KS 67202-1304 • (316) 125-3342

March 15, 200-

Attention Fashion Buyer
Amason Fashion Mart
4385 Felten Dr.
Hays, KS 67601-2863 **DS**
Ladies and Gentlemen **DS**
FALL FASHION CAMPAIGN **DS**
The demand for two of the items that were sent last week was

Attention line/Subject line

Your order should be shipped via Pony Express within the next two weeks.

Thank you for your order; we appreciate your business.

Sincerely **DS**
STYLES BY REX **QS**

Ms. Ellen Turnquist
General Manager

rt

Company name

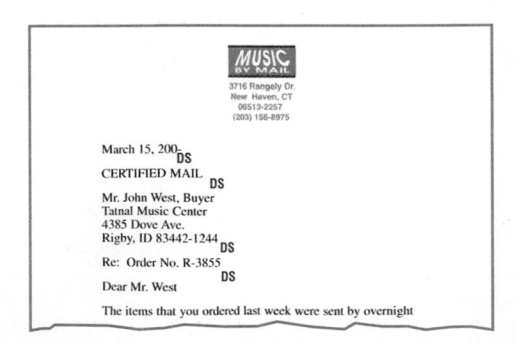

MUSIC BY MAIL
3716 Rangely Dr.
New Haven, CT
06513-2257
(203) 196-8975

March 15, 200- **DS**
CERTIFIED MAIL **DS**
Mr. John West, Buyer
Tatnal Music Center
4385 Dove Ave.
Rigby, ID 83442-1244 **DS**
Re: Order No. R-3855 **DS**
Dear Mr. West

The items that you ordered last week were sent by overnight

Mailing notation/Reference line

.5"
Mr. Jason Artis
Page 2
April 9, 200- **DS**
You will need to perform the following steps:

1.   Review the sample projects and proposed guidelines.
2.   Determine the specific responsibilities of the project manager and put these in writing.

Thank you, Mr. Artis, for your cooperation. It is always a pleasure working with you.

Very truly yours

Second-page heading
Enumerated items (hanging indent format)

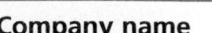

Turner Roofing Co.
10318 Rearview Ave.
Dayton, OH 45029-1927

CERTIFIED MAIL

Mr. Jack Brown
Quality Training Associates
28 Revina Drive
Atlanta, GA 30346-9105

Envelope with mailing notation

Sincerely **QS**

Ms. Rae Mathias, President **DS**

pr **DS**
The cashmere sweaters will be shipped by air to you just as soon as our stock is replenished. You will find them well worth the wait.

Postscript

Personal business letter

Janna M. Howard
587 Birch Cir.
Clinton, MS 39056-0587
(601) 555-4977

Current date

The return address may be keyed immediately above the date, or you may create a personal letterhead as shown here.

Mrs. Linda Chandler
Financial News
32 North Critz St.
Hot Springs, AR 71913-0032

Dear Mrs. Chandler

My college degree in office systems technology and my graphics design job experience in the United States and Taiwan qualify me to function well as a junior graphic designer for your newspaper.

As a result of my comprehensive four-year program, I am skilled in the most up-to-date office suite packages as well as the latest version of desktop publishing and graphics programs. In addition, I am very skilled at locating needed resources on the information highway. In fact, this skill played a very important role in the design award that I received last month.

My technical and communication skills were applied as I worked as the assistant editor and producer of the *Cother Alumni News*. I understand well the importance of meeting deadlines and also in producing a quality product that will increase newspaper sales.

After you have reviewed the enclosed resume, I would look forward to discussing my qualifications and career opportunities with you at *Financial News*.

Sincerely

Janna M. Howard

Enclosure

Resume

JANNA M. HOWARD

Temporary Address (May 30, 2000)	Permanent Address
587 Birch Cir.	328 Fondren St.
Clinton, MS 39056-0587	Orlando, FL 32801-0328
(601) 555-4977	(407) 555-3834

CAREER OBJECTIVE — To obtain a graphic design position with an opportunity to advance to a management position.

EDUCATION — *B.S. Office Systems Technology*, Cother University, Mobile, Alabama. May 1998. Grade-point average: 3.8/4.0. Serve as president of Graphic Designers' Society.

SPECIAL SKILLS
Environments: *Microsoft Windows®* and *Macintosh®*
Application software: *Microsoft Office Professional®/ Windows 95®, PageMaker®, CorelDraw®, Harvard Graphics®*
Internet: *Netscape®, Mosaic®*
Keyboarding skill: 70 words per minute
Foreign language: Chinese
Travel: Taiwan (two summers working as graphic design intern)

EXPERIENCE — *Cother University Alumni Office*, Mobile, Alabama. Assistant editor and producer of the *Cother Alumni News*, 1997 to present.
• Work 25 hours per week.
• Design layout and production of six editions.
• Meet every publishing deadline.
• Received the "Cother Design Award."

Cother Library, Mobile, Alabama. Student Assistant in Audiovisual Library, 1996-1997.
• Worked 20 hours per week.
• Created *Audiovisual Catalog* on computerized database.
• Processed orders via computer.
• Prepared monthly and yearly reports using database.
• Edited and proofed various publications.

REFERENCES — Request portfolio from Cother University Placement Office.

Standard memo

Tab (1" from left margin)   1.5"

TO: Executive Committee
                                   DS
FROM: Colleen Marshall

DATE: November 8, 200-

SUBJECT: Site Selection
                                   DS
Please be prepared to make a final decision on the site for next year's Leadership Training Conference. Our staff reviewed the students' suggestions and have added a few of their own. The following information may be helpful as you make your decision:
                                   DS
1. New York and San Francisco have been eliminated from consideration because of cost factors.
                                   DS
2. New Orleans is still open for consideration even though we met there three years ago. New Orleans has tremendous appeal to students.

3. Charleston, San Antonio, and Tampa were suggested by students as very desirable locations for the conference.

Site selection will be the first item of business at our meeting next Wednesday. I'm attaching various hotel brochures for each site.
                                   DS
xx
   DS
Attachments

Standard memo with distribution list

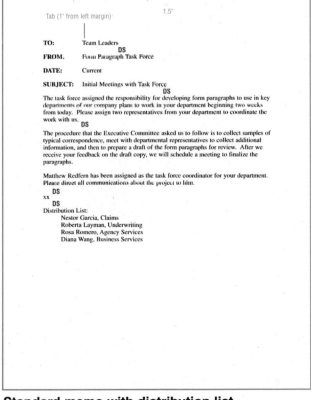

Tab (1" from left margin)   1.5"

TO: Team Leaders
                                   DS
FROM: Form Paragraph Task Force

DATE: Current

SUBJECT: Initial Meetings with Task Force
                                   DS
The task force assigned the responsibility for developing form paragraphs to use in key departments of our company plans to work in your department beginning two weeks from today. Please assign two representatives from your department to coordinate the work with us.
                                   DS
The procedure that the Executive Committee asked us to follow is to collect samples of typical correspondence, meet with departmental representatives to collect additional information, and then to prepare a draft of the form paragraphs for review. After we receive your feedback on the draft copy, we will schedule a meeting to finalize the paragraphs.

Matthew Redfern has been assigned as the task force coordinator for your department. Please direct all communications about the project to him.
                                   DS
xx
   DS
Distribution List:
   Nestor Garcia, Claims
   Roberta Layman, Underwriting
   Rosa Romero, Agency Services
   Diana Wang, Business Services

Standard unbound report

Margins: *Top* 2" for first page and reference page; 1" for succeeding pages; *Side* 1" or default; *bottom* 1".

Spacing: *Educational reports*: DS, paragraphs indented .5". *Business reports:* SS, paragraphs blocked with a DS between.

Page numbers: Second and subsequent pages are numbered at top right of the page. DS follows the page number.

Main headings: Centered; ALL CAPS; 14 pts.

Side headings: Bold; main words capitalized; DS above and below.

Paragraph headings: Bold; capitalize first word, followed by a period.

NOTE: Styles may also be used for headings.

Report documentation

Internal citations: Provides source of information within report. Includes the author's surname, publication date, and page number (Bruce, 2002, 129).

Footnotes: References cited in a report are often indicated within the text by a superscript number (. . . story.[1]) and a corresponding footnote with full information at the bottom of the same page where the reference was cited.

Bibliography or references: Lists all references, whether quoted or not, in alphabetical order by authors' names. References may be formatted on the last page of the report if they all fit on the page; if not, list on a separate, numbered page.

0.5"
3

2.1"

REFERENCES ←—— 14 pt.

Gilreath, Erica. "Dressing Casually with Power." < http://www.dresscasual.com > (23 March 2001).

Monaghan, Susan. "Business Dress Codes May Be Shifting." *Business Executive*, April 2000, pp 34-35.

Sutphin, Rachel. "Your Business Wardrobe Decisions are Important Decisions." *Business Management Journal*, January 2000, pp. 10-12.

Tartt, Kelsey. "Companies Support Business Casual Dress." *Management Success*, June 1995, pp. 23-25.

Reference page

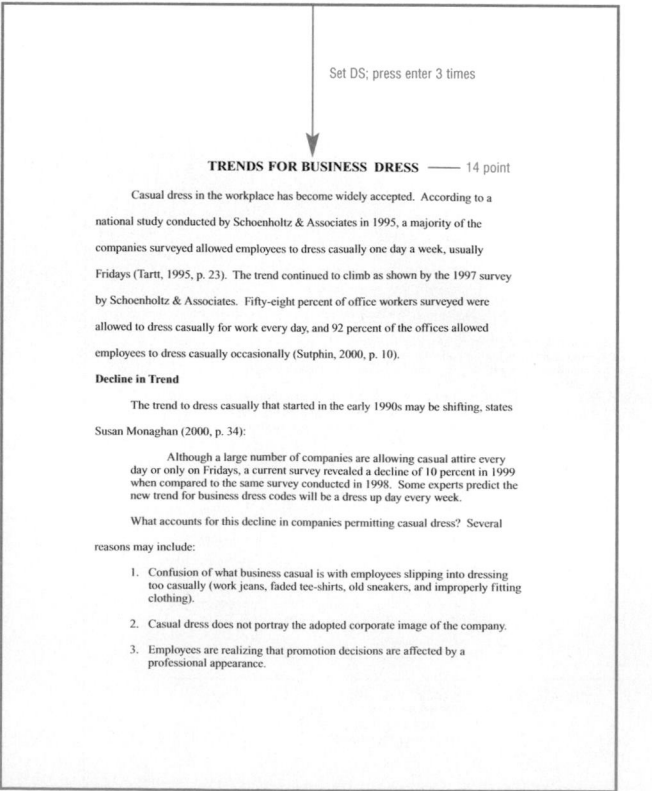

First page of unbound report

0.5"
2

Guidelines for Business Dress

Companies are employing image consultants to teach employees what is appropriate business casual and to plan the best business attire to project the corporate image. Erica Gilreath (2000), the author of *Casual Dress*, a guidebook on business casual, provides excellent advice on how to dress casually and still command the power needed for business success. She presents the following advice to professionals:

- Do not wear any clothing that is designed for recreational or sports activities, e.g., cargo pants or pants with elastic waist.
- Invest the time in pressing khakis and shirts or pay the price for professional dry cleaning. Wrinkled clothing does not enhance one's credibility.
- Do not wear sneakers.
- Be sure clothing fits properly. Avoid baggy clothes or clothes that are too tight.

In summary, energetic employees working to climb the corporate ladder will need to plan their dress carefully. If business casual is appropriate, it's best to consult the experts on business casual to ensure a professional image.

Second page of unbound report

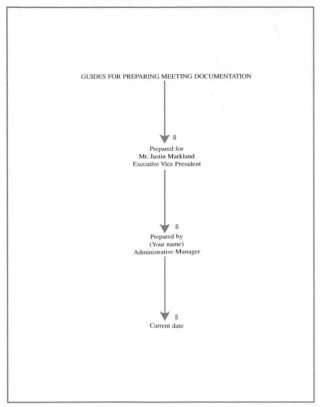

Title page—leftbound

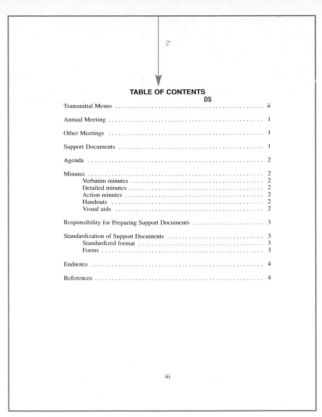

Table of contents—leftbound

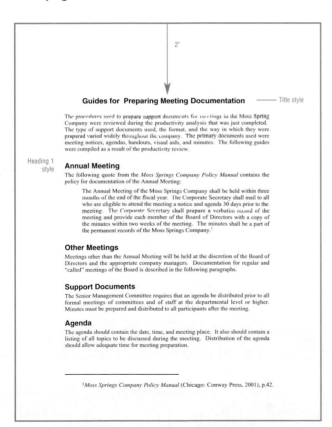

First page of leftbound report (with styles)

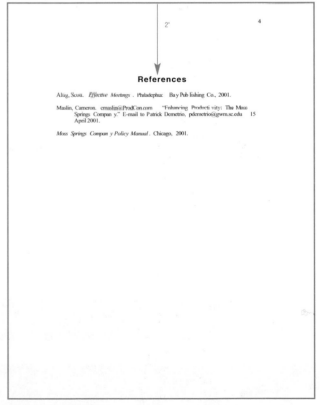

Reference Page

FUNCTION SUMMARY

Function	Menu Command	Keyboard Shortcut	Toolbar Button
Alignment: Left, Center, Right, Justify	Format, Paragraph, Indents and Spacing tab		
AutoCorrect	Tools, AutoCorrect Options		
AutoFormat	Table, AutoFormat		
Autoshapes	Drawing toolbar		AutoShapes ▾
Borders: Page	Format, Borders and Shading		
Borders: Paragraph	Format, Borders and Shading, Border tab, Apply to Paragraph		
Bullets	Format, Bullets and Numbering		
Clip Art and Images	Insert, Picture, Clip Art		
Columns: Create	Click Columns button or Format, Columns		
Copy	Edit, Copy	Shift + F2	
Date and Time	Insert, Date and Time		
Double-underline	Format, Font, Underline style		
Envelopes and Labels	Tools, Letters and Mailings, Envelopes and Labels		
Font: Color	Format, Font		
Footnotes/Endnotes	Insert, Reference, Footnote, Insert. Move the insertion point before the reference and use Tab to indent it.		
Footnotes: Edit	Double-click on the reference number; select reference number to delete footnote.		
Forms: Text Form Field	Forms toolbar		
Forms: Check Box Form Field	Forms toolbar		
Forms: Drop-Down Form Field	Forms toolbar		
Graphic: Wrap Text	Select graphic, Format, Format Picture; Layout tab select wrapping style.		
Graphic: Size	Select graphic; drag resize handle. Double-click graphic; Format picture dialog box, choose Size tab; enter dimensions.		
Hanging Indent	Format, Paragraph, Indents and Spacing tab	Ctrl + T	
Headers and Footers	View, Headers and Footers		
Hyperlink: Remove	Right-click hyperlink; then click Remove Hyperlink		
Indent	Format, Paragraph, Indents and Spacing tab		Increase Indent / Decrease Indent
Insert File	Insert, File, locate file		

Function	Menu Command	Keyboard Shortcut	Toolbar Button
Keep with Next	Format, Paragraph, Line and Page Breaks tab		
Landscape	File, Page Setup, Margins tab		
Merge	Tools, Letters and Mailings, Mail Merge Wizard		
Merge: Labels	Tools, Letters and Mailings, Mail Merge Wizard, Labels		
Numbering	Format		▣
Nonbreaking Space	Insert, Symbol, Special Characters		
Page Numbers	Insert, Page Numbers		
Page Number: Change Format	Page Number dialog box, choose position; click Format to change number format		
Paste Function	Table, Formula		
Protect Document	Tools, Protect Document, Forms		🔒
Section Breaks	Insert, Break		
Save As Web Page	File, Save as Web Page		
Shading	Format, Borders and Shading, Shading tab		▣
Spelling and Grammar	Tools, Spelling and Grammar	F7	▣
Styles: Apply	Click down arrow on Style button and make selection.		Normal ▾
Symbols	Insert, Symbols		
Tables: Create	Insert, Table		▣
Tables: Merge or split	Select cells, click the Merge Cells or Split Cells button on the Tables and Borders toolbar.		▣ ▣
Tables: Total Column	Click in cell; then click the AutoSum button on the Tables and Border toolbar.		Σ
Tab: Decimal	Format, Tabs		
Tab: Leader	Format, Tabs, Option 2		
Tab: Underline	Format, Tabs, Option 4		
Tabs: Set	Format, Tabs or Horizontal Ruler; set Tab Alignment, click Ruler.		
Template	File, New, General Templates		
Template: Save as	File, Save as, click drop list and choose Document Template as the type of file.		
Text Orientation	Click in table cell, Format, Text Direction		
Undo	Edit, Undo	CTRL + Z	↶ ▾
Widow/Orphan Control	Format, Paragraph, Line and Page Breaks tab		
Wizard	File, New, Templates		
WordArt	Drawing Toolbar, Insert WordArt button; choose style; type text; select font, size, and style; click OK.		📃

INDEX

A

addresses, ref1
addressing procedure, ref4
adjacent keys, 466
agendas, 412–413, 425, 428, 458
alignment, TM9
alphabetic sentences, 466
announcements, 372–374, 387, 394
apostrophe ('), ref2
articles of incorporation, 433; fill in, 434
attachments to e-mail, 272, 273
attention line, 252; block letter format with, 254
AutoFormat, 317, 318, 320
AutoShapes, 365; interoffice memo with, 367
AutoSum, 322
average calculation, 325

B

balance sheet, 352–353, 359
billing form, 460
block letter format, 248, 277; with attention line, 254; with blind copy notation, 253; center page in, 250; with copy notation, 253, 254; dateline in, 249; margins in, 249; reference initials, 249; with special features, 262; with special letter parts, 251–254; with subject line, 253, 254; two-page, 275
borders: paragraph, 335; toolbar, 317
budgets, 354–356, 360; operational, 354–355; project, 356
bullets, 242, TM11
business plans, 449–456

C

calculations, 333; average, 325; in tables, 322–326, 332
capitalization, ref1; in endnotes, 303
cells: merging, 319, 321, 331; split, 321, 331
center page, 250, TM12
character styles, 282
check box form field, 337
clip art, 363–364; newsletters with, 370
Clipboard, TM11
Close command, TM5
colon (:), ref2
columns, 368–369; inserting, 320, 323; newsletters with, 375–377; simple, 369
comma (,), ref2
commands, TM3
consent for release of information form, 438–439; completing, 441
Copy command, TM10

copy notation, 252; blind, 252, 253; block letter format with, 253, 254
Cut command, TM10

D

dash (–), ref2
data sources, 389; editing, 397–398, 400, 404, 406, 409; filters, 400
Date and Time command, TM13
dateline, 249
dates, ref1
DELETE key, TM6
disclosure statement, 438, 440; completing, 441
distribution list, interoffice memo, 268
document(s): edit, 240; financial, 350–353; new, TM6; open, TM6; protecting, 339–340; saving, 239; with tabs, 240
drawing tools, 365–366
Drill Practice, 239
drop-down form field, 338

E

e-mail, 272–273, 276; attachments, 272, 273; formatting, 272; forms, 341; message, 273
editing: data sources, 397–398, 400, 404, 406, 409; documents, 240; reports, 293; reports with styles, 298; review, 238–245, 244; tables, 319–321
Endnote Separator, 300
endnotes, 299–300; capitalization in, 303; leftbound reports with, 302–304
envelopes, 256, 404; mailing, 409; merging, 401–402; notation, 261
exclamation point (!), ref2

F

fax cover sheets, 450
fields: drop-down form, 338; form, 336–338; mail merge, 389
financial documents, 350–353
Find function, TM16
fingers, specific, 467
folding and inserting procedures, ref4
footnotes, 296; deleting, 296; inserting, 295; reports with, 297, 459; unbound reports with, 294–298
formatting: announcements, 372–374, 387, 394; application letters, 445; balance sheet, 352–353; block letter format, 248; columns, 368–369; e-mail, 341; fill-in forms, 342; forms, 336–339; interoffice memo, 267; itineraries, 417–418; letterhead, 372–373; modified block letter for-

mat, 255–256; news releases, 381; newsletters with columns, 375; newsletters with graphics, 378; numbers, 324; online forms, 342; operational budgets, 354–355; page numbers, 280; paragraphs, 280, TM9; personal financial statement, 350–351; pleading forms, 429; project budgets, 356; resumes, 442; with styles, 282; tables, 317–318, 319–321; toolbar, TM8; unbound reports, 285
form(s), 334–341; billing, 460; breakeven analysis, 346–347; consent for release of information, 438–439, 441; custom, 346–349; designer, 336; distributing, 340–341; e-mail, 341; fields, 336–338; fill-in, 342–345, 348, 360; formatting, 336–339; handwritten fill-in, 341; lease, 448; legal, 432–434; letters, 389; medical, 438–441; online, 342–345, 348, 358; pleading, 429–431, 447; protecting, 339, 341; sales, 341; SOAP note, 436; templates, 336; testing, 339; with underline tabs, 335; user, 336; using, 340–341
formulas, 322–325; pasting, 324–325; tables with, 453; writing, 323
fractions, ref1
function summary, ref10–ref11

G

grammar, TM16
Grid 8 style tables, 318

H

headings, unbound report, 285
HTML, 411
hyperlinks, removing, 297, 298
hyphen (-), ref2

I

Indent feature, TM14–TM15
inserting: columns, 320, 323; footnotes, 295; pictures, 364–365; rows, 320; text, TM6
interoffice memo, 266–269, 276, 277, ref7; with AutoShapes, 367; with calculations in tables, 332; distribution list, 268; formatting, 267; from template, 270–271, 276; two-page, 267, 269
italics, ref2
itineraries, 427; formatting, 417–419; revising, 419

K

Keep with next, 297

L

labels, 420; address, 422; file folder, 422, 423; mailing, 407; merging, 402–403, 420–421; name badge, 422, 423; portfolio, 423
landscape orientation, 328; with merged cells, 329
leader tabs, 281, 289
leftbound report(s), ref9; with endnotes, 302–304; references, 304, 312–314; table of contents for, 304, 314; title page for, 304, 314
legal forms, 432–434
letterhead, 372–374; creating, 450; medical, 435–437; personal, 373
letter(s): application, 444–445; business, 247; follow-up, 445; form, 389; page numbers in, 264; parts, ref5; personal business, ref7; reference, 445; with special features, 259–262; special parts of, 251–254, ref6; standard business, ref7; thank-you, 445; two-page, 264–265
line breaks, 280
logos, 450

M

mail merge, 388–394, 396, 403, 406, 408–409, 458; data source, 389, 397–398, 400; with envelopes, 401–402; fields, 389; filtering, 399–400, 407; with labels, 402–403; letterhead, 451; main document, 389; records, 389; sorting, 398–399, 407; toolbar, 397
Mail Merge Wizard, 390–393; toolbar, 397
mailing notation, 260
margins, TM13; in block letter format, 249; of unbound reports, 285
math, tables with, 329
MAX function, 326
medical forms, 438–441
medical letterhead, 435–437
memo. See interoffice memo
menu bar commands, TM2
merging cells, 331; landscape form with, 329; in tables, 319, 321
Microsoft Word: saving to Web pages in, 411; starting, TM1
minutes, 414–416, 426, 461; action, 428
modified block letter format, 255–258, 275, 277; with notations, 261
money, ref1

N

name badges, 404, 459; labels, 422, 423
Net Profits, 326
news releases, 380–382, 386; formatting, 381; one-page, 381; two-page, 382
newsletters, 370–371, 394–395; with clip art, 370; with columns, 375–377; with graphics, 378–379; logos in, 451; two-column, 387; with WordArt, 370
nonbreaking space, 295

Notes page, 301
number expression, ref1
number format, 280, 324
Numbering, TM11

O

Open command, TM6
opposite-hand combinations, 245
orphan control, 280
outside reaches, 466

P

page breaks, 280
page numbers, 279; changing, 300; formatting, 280; in letters, 264; in sections, 307–309; of unbound reports, 285
page orientation, 327–329
paragraph: borders, 335; formats, 280, TM9; shading, 335; styles, 282
passwords, 339–340
Paste, TM10; formulas, 324–325; MAX function, 326
percentages, ref1
personal financial statement, 350–351, 359
pictures, 364–365
pleading forms, 429–431, 447; table on, 434
postscript, 252
Print command, TM4
Print Preview, TM5
Progressive Writings, 462–465
proofreaders' marks, 240, ref3
proofreading, 263; procedures, 239, ref3
protecting: documents, 339–340; forms, 339, 341
punctuation, ref2; mixed, 249; open, 248, 249

R

recalculate, 324
records: filtering, 399–400; mail merge, 389; sorting, 398–399
Redo command, TM9
reference initials, 249
reference line, 260
references, 296, ref9; leftbound report, 304, 312–314; unbound report, 286; updating, 296
Remove Hyperlink, 297, 298
repeat last action, 322
Replace function, TM16
report(s), 315. See also leftbound report(s); unbound report(s); business plan, 454; documentation, ref8; editing, 293; with footnotes, 297, 459; with sections, 305–310; with side headings, 309–310; with styles, 283–284, 298, 459
resumes, 442–443, ref7
rotating text, 331
row(s): deleting, 320; height, 319; height adjustment, 321; inserting, 320; specific, 468

S

Save/Save As command, TM4
saving document, 239
section breaks, 306–307; for leftbound reports, 314
sections, 306–308; page numbers in, 307–309
semicolon (;), ref2
shading, 317; paragraphs, 335; tables, 318
Show/Hide button, TM7
side headings, reports with, 309–310
Skillbuilding, 251, 372
SOAP notes, 435–437, 447; forms, 436; key, 437
spacing, TM10
spelling, TM16
split cells, 321, 331
styles: formatting, 282; paragraph, 282; reports with, 283–284, 298, 459; unbound reports with, 292–293
subject line, 252; block letter format with, 253, 254
Sum Above, 453
SUM function, 322, 332; tables with, 323

T

table of contents, 291, 298, 315; automatic, 310; for business plans, 454; leftbound, ref9; for leftbound reports, 304, 314; for reports with side headings, 310; for unbound reports, 289–291, 293
tables, 316–318, 333, TM15–TM16; AutoFormat, 317, 318, 320; calculations in, 322–326, 332; decimal tab in, 320; editing, 319–321; formatting, 317 318, 319–321; with formulas, 453; Grid 8 style, 318; in interoffice memos, 332; with math, 329; merging cells in, 319, 321; on pleading forms, 434; recalculate in, 324; row height in, 319; with shading, 318; with SUM function, 323; toolbar, 317
tabs, TM14; decimal, 319, 320, 453; document with, 240; leader, 281, 289; right, 321; underline, 335
Task Pane, TM1
Technique Builder, 241, 243, 266, 272, 278, 292, 305, 354, 388
templates: forms, 336; interoffice memo, 270–271, 276
text: alignment, TM9; deleting, TM6; entering, TM2; form field, 337; inserting, TM6; orientation, 327–329; rotating, 331; selecting, TM7; wrapping, 364
Timed Writings, 238, 241, 243, 245, 246, 255, 259, 274, 279, 294, 305, 311, 316, 327, 330, 334, 346, 357, 362, 378, 383, 395, 405, 410, 424, 446, 449, 457
times, ref1
title page, 291, 298, 315; for business plans, 454; leftbound, ref9; for leftbound reports, 304, 314; for reports with side headings, 310; for unbound reports, 286, 293

toolbar: borders, 317; commands, TM3; Drawing, 365; formatting, TM8; mail merge, 397; tables, 317

U

unbound report(s), 285–288; with footnotes, 294–298; formatting, 285; headings, 285; margins, 285; multipage, 286–288, 290–291; page numbers, 285; references, 286; spacing, 285; with

styles, 292–293; with table of contents, 289–291, 293; title page, 283, 286; title reports, 293
underline, ref2
Undo command, TM9

W

Web pages: saving agendas as, 412; saving as, 425; saving *Word* documents as, 411

widow control, 280
word division, ref3
WordArt, 366–367; newsletters, 370
wrap text, 364